ChinAmerica

ChinAmerica

THE UNEASY
PARTNERSHIP
THAT WILL CHANGE
THE WORLD

HANDEL JONES

New York   Chicago   San Francisco
Lisbon   London   Madrid   Mexico City   Milan
New Delhi   San Juan   Seoul   Singapore
Sydney   Toronto

The *McGraw·Hill* Companies

To my parents, David and Ruth Jones, who gave me life

CONTENTS

FOREWORD
BY JOHN DICKSON

THE GROWTH OF CHINA is clear, imposing, and seemingly inevitable. Meanwhile, the United States is operating with large deficits and a perceived and real loss of its global leadership role. What does this mean for the future of America and China and the generations of citizens of both as yet unborn?

ChinAmerica provides great clarity of the characteristics of the Chinese people and their ambitions for themselves and their nation. If any sense is to be made of the future relationship between the two countries an understanding of the evolving trade and competitive dynamics between them is essential and this *ChinAmerica* delivers.

ChinAmerica is essential for government and business-people who want to understand China as well as to anyone who has an interest in geopolitics and global markets.

The consequences, which even great nations suffer, because of internal inefficiencies and the pressure from outside competitors, need to be understood in detail. It is clear from the book that unless the United States makes radical changes in investment and competitive strategies, a dramatic weakening in global competitiveness and wealth is inevitable.

Pleas from the United States for level playing fields and the protection of yesterday's industries will not save the day. It is no good asking or expecting China to change its trajectory. China is on a growth path with a confidence and ebullience that has not been seen in the world of economics since the

United States in the early post–war years. It is the United States that needs to change and to change dramatically and soon.

This book is relevant and timely for readers in each of the megapowers. Predicting the future is more often than not a fools' game, but grasping what is actually happening today and how that will shape the future is not. Thanks to Handel Jones' experience over many years this book provides an excellent basis for at least determining the risks and opportunities facing both nations. It is a very valuable and timely contribution.

ACKNOWLEDGMENTS

THE IDEAS IN THIS BOOK came together after decades of my being involved with international businesses and meeting thousands of very smart and knowledgeable people. Ideas and concepts need to be substantiated by recent and verified data, and I would like to thank the large number of acquaintances who provided the input that enabled me to validate or discard these concepts.

To understand China, there is the need to spend time there and feel the pulse of the people who live there. My many visits to China, especially those in late 2009 and early 2010, have been invaluable in enabling me to meet a wide variety of people who have contributed input to my understanding of the strengths and weaknesses of China. I would like to thank the people in China who have shown me the factors driving the industrialization of China.

A significant amount of the coordination of the research in China has been done by Zhou Min, who also provided valuable feedback on the data.

A book is more than just a gathering of insights and facts. I would like to thank the members of the International Business Strategies (IBS) team who assisted me in the development of this book. Research and editing of the information have been admirably done by Sarah Nocé and Joanne Kim. Sarah has also managed the production process efficiently. Robin Soe contributed in the verification of information, and Jay Marcorelle provided invaluable guidance and support. Lastly, IB Kim has provided strong suppport and has been instrumental in making sure all the pieces fit together.

A number of industry experts in academia and in the electronics and venture capital industries provided valuable ideas and were vital sounding boards for providing feedback on my views. I would like to thank Richard Kulle, John Dickson, Don Lucas, and Dr. Henry Kressel for their input on early concepts.

Other industry officials who provided guidance included Michael Jones and Megan Jones. They provided feedback on the banking perspectives with respect to China. By being in Hong Kong and traveling extensively in Asia, Michael has developed a deep understanding of the role of China.

I am especially appreciative of the support and guidance from my publisher, McGraw-Hill. Mary Glenn has been an enthusiastic supporter who understood my intent from the beginning and provided vital guidance and direction. Her colleague Tania Loghmani was a very efficient editor, making the book more readable. A special thanks to Tania. Thanks also to Karen Schopp of McGraw-Hill for her strong encouragement and distribution ideas.

Another key person in the process has been Larry Marion of Triangle Publishing, who, in addition to being an active agent, has been very thorough in editing and reformatting the book. Thank you, Larry.

A complex project requires strong support and effective implementation. Thank you all very much.

INTRODUCTION

CHINA IS THREATENING TO USURP the position of the United States as the global leader in wealth. Will the United States remain wealthy and strong, or will the United States be financially weakened by China?

This book analyzes why the United States is in a downward financial spiral while China is in an upward financial spiral, one that will decimate the U.S. economy and lifestyle if changes aren't made. At the end of the book, I offer a restructuring plan to help Americans redirect our country back on the road to an equilibrium with China, so that the two countries can continue to work together rather than separately and in a state of economic tension.

My first real exposure to China and Chinese leaders was in Dallas, Texas, in the early 1980s. At that time, I was a vice president of strategic planning and engineering of a large multinational electronics company, and I was invited to give a speech about the future of data communications technologies. After the presentation, I had lunch with the former president of the People's Republic of China, Jiang Zemin, who at that time was the minister of electronic industries. We had a detailed conversation about the outlook for new electronics technologies.

A few months later, I was invited to give a talk in Beijing on the future of the communications industry. I accepted, but I could not attend because the U.S. government requested that I not visit China for security reasons. Naturally, I was disappointed, but I started to develop a deep curiosity regarding China.

In the late 1980s, I launched a market research and consulting company called International Business Strategies (IBS). We provide in-depth market and technology analyses of many electronics industry sectors, for a wide variety of American, European, and Asian clients. As our firm's interest in China grew, I read extensively on China. However, my reading produced only a limited knowledge of the country. To gain a deeper understanding, I would have to have face-to-face interactions with people in China and Asia.

So beginning in the early 1990s, I began to visit China and Taiwan and other countries in Asia. Over the next 15 years, I would make at least 8 trips a year to Asia—in 2008, I made 10 trips to China —learning firsthand as much as I could about Chinese companies and their relationships with Japanese, South Korean, Singaporean, and other Asian companies.

The original idea for this book came from driving through the Pudong industrial zone in Shanghai in late 2008. I wondered how it was possible to take a marsh and build on it within a short time the tall office complexes and hotels and the hundreds of factories that I was seeing.

I could also see as I drove through the area that, while the new development was extensive, behind the new buildings there were run-down structures and squalor. I wanted to understand which was the real China: the glowing new buildings or the drab old ones? Was the country like a Hollywood studio lot where there was nothing behind the façades of the new buildings? Was industrialized China just a big Potemkin village?

Or was China, as its people have been proud to describe it, really a phoenix rising from the ashes? Indeed, a year later, many of the old buildings I had seen in Pudong were gone, replaced by new buildings. It was, and still is, a tidal wave of progress.

I quickly learned that there was energy there and that the business leaders were confident of the future. But was their energy and confidence an illusion, or was it real? And what did was it mean for the global industrial environment?

Over time I was able to find answers to many of those questions.

Inside Chinese Factories

While there is a human and entrepreneurial side to China, the industrial side of China is a big machine that runs 24 hours a day, seven days a week, and 50 weeks a year. The factories close only during the Chinese New Year and the National Day holidays. The machine takes in large amounts of people, materials, and components, and it turns out a wide array of finished products.

The factories can be the size of multiple football fields, and entire communities have been razed to provide the space needed to build them. Since the government owns the land, it can be easy for the government to decide that an industrial zone should be established where there were once homes or farms.

I have seen many factories in the United States, Japan, Germany, South Korea, Taiwan, India, and other countries. The factories of China are extremely impressive, especially since most have been established only in the past 10 years.

Deeper in the Country

Beijing is different from Shanghai because of a deeper history. Visiting the Forbidden City, there is a feeling that one is very small. The capital city exudes power. (In contrast, Shanghai, in the south, projects the image of urban sophistication.) As one goes deeper and deeper into the Forbidden City, one can only wonder what drove this kind of architecture. Was it that the Chinese liked to build walls within walls so that it would take a big effort to get to the core? Was it a defensive strategy to erect gate after gate?

The gates and walls of the Forbidden City seem to express the feeling one gets in China: an outside that has to be penetrated, and when one gets inside, there is another gate to be crossed. And as one gets deeper inside, the steps leading up to the gates become higher.

The more I traveled in China, the more I learned and the more I wanted to understand what was driving the people to achieve their spectacular growth. I wanted to understand more of China than one gets from visiting modern urban shops and eating meals in hotels.

Clearly, I had to research the history of China, but this was not easy. China has a history that goes back 5,000 years, and what has been written is conditioned by what "should" be written. Only what was politically correct was included in many of the history books written by the Chinese.

Indeed, the Chinese in many cases say only what they think should be said. The Chinese are very proud of China, and they do not want foreigners to think badly of it. The Chinese also have a deep initial distrust of foreigners, a distrust that usually goes away gradually after many "gates" are traversed.

During the past 10 years, I have become involved with a number of Chinese businesses as a strategic consultant and market analyst. While the senior-level managers of the Chinese companies have been willing to work hard and have been highly committed to succeed, their level of management sophistication has been low. However, their energy and commitment have been strong, and they are willing to endure a lot of pain to achieve gain.

Understanding business in China was an intriguing challenge for me after three decades of doing business in Japan, Taiwan, South Korea, France, Germany, Sweden, India, and Russia. I wanted to understand where the industrialization activities would take China and what its growth meant for the United States. Was the Chinese market a big opportunity for the U.S. companies that were my clients? How could companies do business in China?

The rise of China reminded me of the rise of Japan three decades ago. I began traveling to Japan in 1979 and experienced at close proximity the rise of Japan, as well as its subsequent decline. My analysis indicates that China will not experience the same steep downward trajectory as Japan. The growth of China will continue for decades.

What Are They Really Thinking?

In the many meetings I have had with top leaders of Chinese companies and government officials, it was clear that they were not being transparent in what they were saying or what they were deciding. Leaders were strongly committed to establishing businesses that would provide employment, but getting to the Chinese consumers would not be easy. Gate after gate would have to be opened, and there was no assurance that the next gate would lead to any significant business.

Under the friendly façade, there is an element of steel. As I have worked with them, it has become clear that the leaders in China are determined not to repeat past mistakes and allow foreigners to dictate their future.

With deeper exposure into the country and greater familiarity with its middle class and its leaders, it became clear to me that China is on a mission. There is strong top-level leadership to guide the economy. It is clear that senior leaders view their people as assets to be used or discarded. The people of China are viewed by their leaders as a river that flows into the sea. If the water is not used as it passes by, its value will be lost.

During my research, I realized that, as China strengthens, it can have a big negative impact on the United States. While one branch of my research was to learn more about China as representing a very large potential market for U.S. products, when I have been in China, I have not seen or bought any products that were made in the United States. But when I have returned to the United States, almost everything from clothes to electronics has been made in China.

Chinese companies are very skilled at making copies of products. A simple product can be copied overnight and can be in the market the next day with the same name as the original product. It is survival of the lowest cost and most nimble. There is no respect for the original inventor, only the one who can make it the cheapest.

Over time I started to become concerned. The United States was importing oil from many countries, automobiles from Japan and Germany, and thousands of different products from China. What was the

United States exporting? Movies? Boeing aircraft? Beef? Would these cover the costs of the imports?

As my research progressed, the picture regarding the United States and China became very bleak. Projecting future trends showed a clear dichotomy: China was ascending, and the United States was descending. While this was not an original idea, I still wanted to understand what this meant for the future of the United States.

I also know that the devil is in the details, and I wanted to understand more. It has taken many journeys to understand what is going on in China. This book details many of the conclusions of my scores of trips to China over the past 20 years.

Some Personal Notes

I have been shown generosity and kindness in China in situations that have been completely unexpected. I have been given free food from people I hardly know and have been told that they would be insulted if I paid.

And I have been cheated and continue to be cheated when I visit China. In China there is an attitude that it is a sign of strength to get the upper hand in a negotiation with foreigners. This attitude is not only about making profits; it is also about being morally good. The prevailing thinking now is that if foreigners are so stupid that they do not know the prices of goods, they deserve to be cheated.

The attitude of urban citizens in the markets in China is remarkable for a country that was tightly in the embrace of communism only 40 years ago. The sellers of copied goods on Nanjing Road in Shanghai told me once that if they paid 10 renminbi (the new name for Chinese currency, replacing the yuan) for an item, their goal was to get 100 renminbi. In many cases, they were able to get 150 to 200 renminbi. No wonder they are persistent in trying to get foreigners to look at their goods in the backstreet stores.

During my visits to China, while meeting with many of its industrial leaders and political figures, I showed curiosity, but I did not give any indication that I was planning a book on China. I wanted their unguarded input, at least at the level that is possible in China, to gain some visibility into their inner thoughts.

What I saw is a growing strength as the country emerges as a modern industrial superpower. In the past, China was like a single bamboo stick that could be bent but not easily broken. Today, China is like a number of bamboo sticks tied together—difficult to bend and almost impossible to break.

Whether China stays together as the bound bamboo sticks will determine how well China competes for global wealth. While the individual sticks are strong, there is also extensive corruption in China, which weakens the bonding of the bamboo sticks.

Why I Wrote This Book

The United States is my home, and I have deep gratitude for what the United States has given me. My children were born here, as were my grandchildren. And I am very worried about the future for my grandchildren.

The United States has become too complacent and conditioned to enjoying wealth without creating wealth. The internal efficiency of the United States is declining, which reduces its ability to compete for global wealth.

The ideal situation is that wealth can be shared, but the reality is that people and nations compete for wealth. China and the United States are in direct competition for the generation of wealth.

I wrote this book because I want to share my understanding of China and also because I want to give the United States a wake-up call. Although we are starting to become more concerned than we have been in the past with the government's deficits and our increased dependence on imports, we are in serious trouble, and we are clearly not ready to take the hard actions required to reverse the downward spiral. Societies, such as Rome, have weakened because of their internal inefficiencies, which ultimately allowed an external force or enemy to inflict a fatal blow.

China is not likely to threaten the United States militarily, but China is in direct competition with the United States for global wealth. China is a friend to a strong United States, but China is a threat to a weak United States. It is up to us in the United States to control our destiny. Time is, however, the enemy because the longer we wait, the deeper is the hole that we are digging for ourselves.

I hope this book allows us to understand China and see where we need to take actions to become a long-term partner to China rather than being the victim of our own overconsumption. We need to become *ChinAmerica*, a collaboration for sharing our wealth in an equitable way.

ChinAmerica

PART I

BEATING
AMERICA

THE DEVASTATION OF EUROPE AND JAPAN during World War II gave the United States a unique opportunity to dominate international commerce and, later, to dominate the world political stage as the biggest superpower. Before the war, Britain, France, and Germany were viewed as the world's superpowers, but that ended in the ashes of fires and bomb fragments in Dresden, Coventry, and throughout the rest of the Continent. During the decades in which Europe, Russia, and Japan recovered from the war's devastation, the United States was able to exploit its own unchallenged economic and political power. The result was a new world order.

Another momentous economic shift is happening now. The rise of China as the second most economically powerful country is occurring in a historically short amount of time. The Middle Kingdom passed Germany, France, and the United Kingdom in 2008, and it raced ahead of Japan in 2009 to become the second largest economy on Earth.

Furthermore, the Great Recession of 2008 to 2009, and the slow economic progress thereafter by the United States and the West, accelerated China's pace. China is closing the gap with America in terms of gross domestic product (a key measure of economic output). While forecasters such as PricewaterhouseCoopers and others differ on exactly when China will overtake the United States, they agree that it will occur and that it is only a matter of a few decades.[1]

It is painful and bewildering for the American Colossus, which almost single-handedly rebuilt Western society after the devastation of World War II, to face the reality that it will lose economic supremacy. Essentially, the United States is in the same position that Europe was in after World War II—watching another car roar past it on the economic highway.

In the following chapters, I review the situation at the crucial inflection point: in 2009 China's economy grew 8.7 percent while the rest of the world's economies declined. I describe how China and the United States are locked in a battle over national wealth. In addition, I explain how military strategies and tactics are being used by some countries and companies to successfully conquer new territories. Other countries, unfortunately, have ignored or misapplied these strategies and are now vulnerable to economic invasion.

Indeed, CEOs have replaced generals as the leaders of conquering armies. It doesn't matter if one views this as a good thing or a bad thing—it is a fact of life in the twenty-first century. Global competitiveness at the corporate level is the way to win the international battle for wealth.

1

THE FRONT LINES OF THE CHINAMERICA WEALTH BATTLE

As THE SUN GOES DOWN in the United States, the day starts in China.

Figuratively speaking, the financial sun has been rising in China for several years, and it is starting to set on the United States. How long the sun shines on China, and how long the United States will remain in twilight, depends not only on China but also on the actions of the United States.

The industrialization of China since the 1980s has been nothing short of astounding. In a historically short amount of time, China has built a huge base of educated employees working in a vast network of factories producing a broad array of consumer and industrial products, primarily for export. In addition, the surge in production has provided hundreds of millions of Chinese with televisions, cell phones, and other touchstones of a thriving middle class.

The frenetic growth of Chinese manufacturing and the rise of the middle class are leading to a conflict with other nations, especially the United States. The pollution pouring from Chinese factory smokestacks and effluent pipes is a source of tension worldwide. But it is also the visible symbol of a more profound confrontation: the demand for increasingly scarce and strategic natural resources.

China is absorbing large quantities of increasingly expensive copper, oil, iron ore, wood, and other commodities from around the world. The huge surge in demand for raw materials has inflated the prices of these commodities for the entire developed world. So not only has the cost of wire and cable jumped but so too has the price of steel, cement, and other materials. Housing and school construction costs in Boston, Birmingham, and Boise as well as in Beijing skyrocketed during the economic boom times before the economic crash of September 2008.

Since most developed countries have been importing copper wire, steel, wood furniture, and other finished goods from Chinese factories that were absorbing all of these raw materials, trade imbalances have become more skewed. The flood of clothes, televisions, laptop computers, cell phones, automobiles, and other manufactured goods from China to the rest of the world has triggered a massive flow of dollars, pounds, francs, lira, yen, rubles, and other currencies in the opposite direction. While the United States has been importing an increasingly large amount of finished goods from China and other parts of Asia for decades, the surge in commodities prices has led to an even larger trade deficit. This massive deficit is the source of another long-term conflict with China.

In fact, a substantial amount of the world's wealth has moved to China. As of September 2009, the Chinese government held foreign exchange reserves of almost $2.3 trillion,[1] roughly a quarter of the foreign currency reserves of the entire world. How much is $2.3 trillion? According to the reserve rankings by the International Monetary Fund, it is more than the combined foreign exchange holdings of Japan, Russia, and the entire European community. Here's another way of understanding the financial power in China's treasury: $2.3 trillion is more than five times the amount of foreign exchange reserves that Saudi Arabia has accumulated from exporting oil as of May 2009. Or consider this comparison: The United States had $83 billion in foreign exchange reserves in September 2009.

Published estimates have indicated that roughly 70 percent of the foreign currency reserves held by China are in U.S. dollars or their equivalents.[2] No wonder several U.S. late-night talk show hosts chortled in November 2009 that President Barack Obama's visit to China was arranged so that he could "visit our money." The tension over the shift of American wealth to China is growing quickly.

In fact, while all nations compete to increase the wealth of their population, China and the United States appear to be headed toward a particularly contentious conflict. The Chinese realize that wealth is created by the amount of goods produced and sold to others, not by the amount of goods consumed. The Chinese understand that the growth of the wealth of nations is based on having a positive trade balance, along with an efficient infrastructure and the fair distribution of the resulting wealth among the population. A positive trade balance occurs when the value of exports exceeds imports. A positive trade balance also is a measure of competitiveness against other countries, and wealth is built by having superior competitiveness.

Beginning in the late 1970s, the Chinese people were forced to sacrifice in the short term to accumulate wealth in the long term. They focused most of their efforts on manufacturing goods for export. That attitude continues to this day.

Contrast that approach to building wealth with the behavior of the majority of the U.S. population in the twenty-first century. An entitlement mentality prevails among most of the middle- and upper-class populations. If people have been wealthy for a long time, they develop an attitude of entitlement—they indulge in a high standard of living without worrying about the consequences of living beyond their means. Instead of building personal and national wealth, many Americans are focused only on consuming, and they are hampering the rest of the country's population's quest for a better life.

The conflicting motivations between China and the United States are leading to a war over wealth. Indeed, some would say that a war has already begun: there have been several trade sanctions enacted by the U.S. Congress, and there is a growing number of complaints that Chinese companies have been selling goods in the United States at prices that are less than their cost of manufacture. This technique to capture foreign markets is called *dumping*.[3] The Chinese retaliated against the sanctions in October 2009 with new registration requirements for companies that want to sell products to the Chinese government.[4] These trade restraints must not be allowed to escalate into provocative actions—neither side will survive armed conflict or the economic equivalent, trade protectionism in the form of tariffs or other barriers.

The tariff warnings and dumping complaints reflect what happens when a nation loses economic power—it feels threatened. A nation that perceives itself to be losing wealth will feel insecure in its relationships with other nations. Meanwhile, a nation that perceives itself to be gaining wealth and therefore economic power will want to exercise that power in its relationships with other nations. Strong economic power usually leads a country to want to expand its power by controlling additional resources, or manipulating weaker competitors so that its own economic and political supremacy continues. The declining fortunes of the United States and the continued increases in the wealth of China could ultimately destabilize the current political structure of the planet.

There has to be another path to defuse the tensions and avoid conflict that would damage both sides. This book is about how China and America can develop a mutually beneficial relationship, a *modus vivendi*. A partnership I call ChinAmerica would benefit both countries, helping them "unwind their mutual suicide pact," as highly respected international expert Fareed Zakaria described the situation in the 2009 preface to his book *The Post-American World*. The ChinAmerica partnership will help the Chinese and American governments and populations achieve their goals without gravely damaging each other.

The crucial foundation of a successful partnership between China and America is a better understanding of what led to the current dichotomy in the fortunes of China and the United States. *ChinAmerica* explores the behaviors and decisions made by American leaders and the population over the past few decades that led to the decline of America as the unchallenged leading industrial giant, and to the current economic crossroads. In addition, *ChinAmerica* explains how 2,000 years of wars and political change strongly influenced China's economic behavior.

ChinAmerica is more than a summary of the past though. In Chapter 5, I describe the behavioral and governmental policy changes that must be effected for the ChinAmerica partnership to succeed. If executed, my "turnaround plan" will help China and America achieve equilibrium in their relationship, and that balance will be based on mutual respect and dependence. The China market would be a large opportunity for U.S. companies if China would be more open to American imports of automobiles, construction equipment, and electronics devices. In addition, an invigorated U.S. market would prove lucrative for American as well as Chinese companies to sell more goods.

If the appropriate actions are not taken, it is likely that Chinese corporations will gain increasing percentages of global markets, as well as their domestic markets, for a wide variety of manufactured goods. If that happens, U.S. citizens and the U.S. government will suffer. Indeed, the United States' economic and political strength will decline precipitously. And if the economic strength of the United States continues to decline, China will have a smaller export market.

Some would say the economic strength of the United States has already declined, due to the unprecedented levels of its buying imports from China and the government's skyrocketing deficit spending. Indeed, imports from China had been growing for decades, but as the U.S. economy recovered from the dot-com bust of 2001, those import levels were turbocharged, as Figure 1.1 shows.

In addition to the trade imbalance with China, the United States also is importing large amounts of oil and manufactured goods from other countries. All those automobiles from Japan, South Korea, and Germany, wine from France, Chile, and Australia, and designer watches from everywhere cost money too. In 2008, the U.S. trade deficit was almost $700 billion,[5] the total of more than 20 years of negative trade balances. The large trade deficits between the United States and

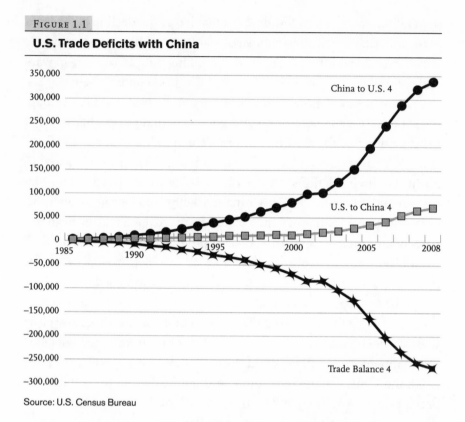

FIGURE 1.1

U.S. Trade Deficits with China

Source: U.S. Census Bureau

China are a key indicator that American trade and manufacturing policies are failures.

Although, the trade deficit is diminishing America's wealth and political power, it is not the only deficit that plagues the United States. The U.S. government has been spending more than it takes in as taxes since before 2000. The fiscal deficits of the past decade were incurred in part to support the wars in Iraq and Afghanistan and to make up for huge tax cuts.[6]

The burgeoning fiscal deficit of the U.S. government also made the trade deficit worse. This spending spree by the government, and additional cash in the pocketbooks of the wealthiest Americans, triggered a tidal wave of consumption in the early years of the twenty-first century. The middle and lower classes also joined in the fun, courtesy of overeager and underregulated mortgage brokers, credit card companies, and other providers of easy money. Access to funds from home equity loans and no-interest mortgage loan refinancings launched the flood of spending.

The economic meltdown on Wall Street in September 2008 made a bad fiscal deficit situation much worse. The administration of President George W. Bush borrowed $700 billion to prop up AIG, Bank of America, Wells Fargo, and a host of other rescued banks and other organizations holding worthless mortgages. After the stock market crash wiped out a substantial portion of the net worth of most Americans, the Obama administration organized a $585 billion stimulus program to restart the economy with jobs and rebuild America's deteriorating infrastructure, again financed by the U.S. Treasury's borrowing more money. The Obama administration announced in October 2009 that the fiscal year deficit was in excess of $1.4 trillion, up 212 percent from fiscal year 2008.[7]

The U.S. government's policies to increase consumption without stimulating domestic manufacturing increased the trade imbalance as well. For example, many foreign companies, such as Toyota and Hyundai, benefited from the Cash for Clunkers program funded by the stimulus package.[8]

Another troubling ramification of the twin deficits is their impact on the value of U.S. currency. The deficits weakened the value of the dollar, although the negative impact of the deficits on the value of the dollar and the purchasing power of the United States has been moderated by the willingness of foreign countries to hold dollar reserves. Since the dollar is the leading global currency, these dollars buy goods from other countries. This means that it is vitally important for the United States to ensure that the dollar remains the leading global currency and to avoid any dramatic weakening of the value of the dollar. Without this effort to maintain the primacy of the dollar, there will be low levels of incentive for countries such as China, Japan, and others to be willing to hold dollars.

If other countries, such as China or Japan, were to decide to dispose of their dollar reserves, the dollar could weaken rapidly, and the buying power of the United States would decline rapidly. In 2009 the Chinese appeared to be loathe to sell their dollars because they knew that the surplus of dollars on the currency markets would depress their value even more. However, the precarious position of the dollar leaves the United States vulnerable—an example of how economic weakness can lead to political weakness.

Building economic strength to maintain and extend political strength is not new. Kings, queens, emperors, and dictators throughout the history of Europe and Asia were focused on these objectives for hundreds of years before the New World was discovered and settled. To understand the why and how of ChinAmerica, it is important to grasp that corporations are now viewed by government leaders as the key tools to building the wealth of their nation. In Chapter 2, I will explain how economic power from corporations became the prerequisite for political hegemony.

2

HOW CEOS REPLACED GENERALS

IN THE PAST, THE WEALTH of nations depended mostly on military prowess. While internal threats always loomed large—usually societal unrest such as the American and French revolutions—the most common and potent threats were from external military forces. As invading armies took control of territory, they plundered the riches of their victims and enslaved the citizens.

Today's external threats are corporations that invade and obtain a substantial share of a market outside of their home country, reducing the wealth-generating potential of the defeated territory. Corporations are the armies of the late twentieth and the early twenty-first centuries, attacking vulnerable external markets while protecting their markets within their home turf as well.

Just as it was and is important for nations to have strong armies, it is critical for corporations to be strong within the present economic environment. These days it is corporations that conquer territories and markets—think about how the armies of Toyota, Honda, and Nissan conquered the U.S.

automobile market and helped bring about the bankruptcy of GM and Chrysler. Or how Sony, Toshiba, Panasonic, and Sharp essentially wiped out the U.S. television industry. They are two industries that were essentially invented in the United States but conquered by overseas corporate armies. CEOs have become the new generals, leading the troops to save the country and grow wealth.

Corporations build wealth by creating products and services that can be exported, providing employment, generating a return for the stockholders who provided the capital for the corporation, and by paying taxes to a government that provides infrastructure and security. Corporations that succeed in these roles also develop key technologies, products, and services that increase the health, well-being, and standard of living of their populations, as well as build wealth and security.

Let's examine these roles in more detail, highlighting the countries that have been supporting their corporations in their pursuit of national wealth.

Providing Employment

Don't forget that there are direct and indirect benefits of having large corporations that employ many workers. The direct benefits include the ability of workers to have salaries, buy products, and pay taxes. The indirect benefits include a stable society, in which there is the opportunity for upward mobility in terms of responsibilities, status, and standards of living.

In many industries, the supporting infrastructures can provide four to five times the employment that is needed for the core industry. An example is the network of component suppliers and professional services providers that support the automotive industry. GM, Ford, Chrysler, and other automakers do not make the seats, tires, window glass, engine control electronics, and other parts of a car but instead buy them from other companies. This overall industry ecosystem provides a large and diverse employment base.

A big and thriving corporation will need a wide variety of skill sets to maintain its operations and find growth opportunities. Corporations employ managers, engineers, technicians, and assembly workers, and they offer additional job opportunities as employees learn and improve their efficiency. Corporations also provide employment for new graduates, which creates the motivation for citizens to improve their education level. The Finnish cell phone giant Nokia exemplifies this approach, providing excellent employment opportunities for graduates in Finland as well as in other countries in Europe.[1]

Political and business leaders in China, Taiwan, Japan, Germany, and other countries have long recognized the importance of corporations in generating exports. Unfortunately, U.S. political leaders have been slow to recognize the dire need for American companies to be strong enough to increase their exports. U.S. government funding to encourage and support exports of manufactured goods woefully lags behind the efforts of European or Asian governments. In addition, many American CEOs have been slow to focus on the export opportunities because the American domestic market has been among the largest in the world. That situation has changed now because of the recent growth of the Chinese market and contraction of the U.S. market. This change has made the shift to an export mentality a business imperative.

American government officials all but ignore the following important roles of corporations: generating exports, generating wealth for shareholders and other stakeholders, generating tax revenues, and creating technologies.

Generating Exports

Globally competitive corporations successfully export products. A global marketplace helps corporations expand their production runs, spread their unit costs of production over a larger base, and stay attuned to prevailing trends and pricing patterns around the world.

A global perspective and healthy level of exports helps protect the local markets. Features, quality, and pricing lessons learned from selling in foreign markets can prevent overseas competitors from invading a local market and winning market share from the domestic company. But if the domestic companies fail to learn those lessons, trading internationally can lead to the erosion of their home market share. The state of the U.S. automotive manufacturers in the beginning of the twenty-first century is a painful example of this phenomenon. Weaknesses at domestic manufacturers General Motors, Ford, and Chrysler led to the growing level of cars being imported from Japan, Germany, Sweden, South Korea, and elsewhere or made in U.S. factories under the direction of overseas owners.

The cost of losing domestic market share to imports is difficult for a country to overcome. Consider the trade imbalance impact of the weak domestic automotive makers in the United States. If 10 million automobiles are imported at an average value of $20,000 per automobile, the total level of imports is $200 billion annually, plus the value of the replacement parts that need to be imported for 5 or 10 years thereafter. Only a small number of industries can generate exports of $200 billion annually. For example, worldwide 2008 revenues of the movie studios in Hollywood were approximately only $28 billion.[2]

It is true that globalization of procurement, assembly, distribution, and sales of products has been diminishing the true financial benefits of exports beginning in the late 1990s. An iPod from Apple, an inkjet printer from Hewlett-Packard, or a laptop PC from Dell may have an American brand on it, but device assembly may have been outsourced to a company in China, Taiwan, or Mexico. That outsourcer bought parts made in the United States, Singapore, Taiwan, and elsewhere to assemble the device according to specifications from the American company. Consequently, when those devices are sold in China, Japan, Korea, or other markets, they are not U.S. exports since only the brand, the intellectual property, and the design came from America.

The shift to globalization has warped the true value of exports for many industries and countries. Computers, printers, automobiles, cameras, and other complex products' carrying the corporate brand and nationality of one country doesn't mean that the product was assembled by the brand or in the country associated with the brand. CEOs defend this practice by saying that it is better to have some of the value of the exported product accrue to the brand name rather than none. When it comes to the U.S. trade imbalance, that means it is better if an American consumer in San Francisco buys a notebook computer from Apple rather than Sony because more of the consumer's cash stays in the United States.

Generating Wealth for Shareholders and Other Stakeholders

Since the underlying operating principle of a market economy is that risk should be rewarded, corporations need to generate profits to develop new products for revenue growth and provide a return for investors. Shareholders who are rewarded for taking risks are encouraged to invest in new businesses, which progresses to a virtuous cycle of increasing exports as well as domestic production. Successful corporate investments help create national wealth.

When many CEOs and boards of directors of major corporations focus on short-term returns from stock options and stock buyback plans instead of long-term growth, they are effectively strangling future export growth. Asian corporate leaders, who are not rewarded with the lush stock options programs common among large U.S. corporations, are much more focused on long-term strategic success, which is based on increasing exports.

Generating Tax Revenues

Corporations pay taxes, which covers the costs of government services. When U.S. companies close domestic factories and open them in Asia, America not only loses the jobs but it also loses the tax revenues. The 500 largest American companies passed a dubious milestone in 2008: they paid more in foreign taxes than in U.S. taxes due to sales of goods and services overseas that were not exported from the United States.

The data was collected from a July 2009 analysis of 2008 foreign revenues, profits, and taxes of 253 large U.S. corporations.

"It's no longer just jobs that we're exporting. It's taxes," noted Howard Silverblatt, senior index analyst at Standard & Poor's and author of a report on foreign sales and taxation: *Foreign Sales by U.S. Companies Continue to Rise* (press release dated July 14, 2009).

Many countries view corporations as strategic assets that generate revenues. To foster the health of their corporations, governments provide tax incentives in the forms of loans, tax abatements, and other forms of financial support in exchange for long-term commitments to build factories, hire employees, and otherwise contribute to the wealth of the nation through exports as well as domestic sales. In some countries, such incentives are part of a national plan while in other countries the incentives are part of a more piecemeal approach used by the local governments.

Creating Technologies

Corporations create and utilize many technologies, which results in a myriad of benefits to the developers and their customers, and their country. New technologies improve the standard of living, create new industries, and can increase life expectancy. The corporations that develop leadership technologies can have high revenue growth and high market share in global markets in the future.

Consider the pharmaceutical industry's long history of creating new medicines through making large expenditures in new technologies. Also, the electronics industry has become a diversified trillion-dollar industry thanks to the continued generation of new technologies. These industries have succeeded as export engines as well as strong domestic suppliers, despite the lack of focused government support in many cases.

In the future, the creation of new technologies, to create new industries and new jobs, needs to be a more vital part of the relationships between government and industry if the United States is going to regain its fiscal health. Government funding to identify and develop new technologies needs to be increased and focused on the most promising and lucrative opportunities. And such major funding should not be invested on the basis of the political clout of key senators and members of the U.S. House of Representatives.

Government support for new technology development is not new. In the past, overt conflict or the threat of armed conflict opened government treasuries to technological development. Traditionally, wars led to new technological developments—jet aircraft engines for fighter jets and the atomic bomb research of World War II are two examples of weapons research that led to commercial uses.

Beginning in the 1950s, many governments began to support a wide range of research and development programs unrelated to a specific military threat. Governments provided this support either through direct grants, tax credits, or other financing mechanisms. The Internet itself was the offspring of U.S. Defense Department grants in the 1960s to support the linkage of computers at military research centers, for example. Most of the developed and developing nations of the world now support R&D to one extent or another.

Currently there is a spirited race among countries to support research and development for new vehicle propulsion systems, such as improved batteries for automobiles. Other areas attracting government support are medical devices and other solutions to the burgeoning challenges of providing health care to aging populations in developed nations.

Different Tactics Needed for Different Battles

As the competition among nations and corporations intensifies, wise leaders realize they can't fight every battle with the same tactics. CEOs and government leaders have to pick their opportunities carefully these days, attacking where their strengths can overcome an opponent's weaknesses. They must analyze which markets are important to ensure that corporations are able to gain large shares of various markets. For example, because of the high cost base in the United States compared to countries such as China, India, and other emerging markets, the

United States should focus on developing advanced technologies, products, and services that represent high value.

Many countries with leaders conversant in economics, technology, and strategic thinking have directed their nations to successfully build export-based businesses. Consider these examples that have been strong since they began in the 1970s:

- Japan has had large exports due to the strengths of its automobile and electronics industries. While Japan's position in the automobile industry has weakened since 2005, due to a relatively high cost base in comparison to the new competitors from emerging markets, its companies retain leading market shares for many products in many markets. In consumer electronics, however, Japan is weakening rapidly.
- South Korea has had large exports of a wide variety of electronic and electrical products, from chips to cell phones to televisions to washing machines and refrigerators. In fact, South Korean companies Samsung and LG Electronics have become global leaders in many of these segments.
- Germany has had large exports by its chemical, automotive, and electrical industries. Many of the automobiles manufactured in Germany for export around the world are high cost, but they have had strong global success due to a perception of their technological and quality leadership.
- Taiwan has maintained a positive balance of payments because of its strong electronics industry, built up through a highly entrepreneurial environment as well as through intelligent government support. In addition to its success selling in the West, China is becoming a key market for the Taiwanese corporations.

Other countries have not supported their industrial base with the same combination of investment, zeal, and industry insight. The United Kingdom is a prominent example. It has a negative trade balance of payments due to its weakening industrial base. The government in the United Kingdom is not oriented toward building corporations and exports. Instead, it is focused on the impact of very large immigration from developing countries.

As a result, the wealth of the country will continue to decline. The average annual gross domestic product (GDP) growth has lagged that of the United States since 1971. And no wonder: At this point the United Kingdom has little or no indigenous automotive, computer, or electronics industry, even though key parts of these industries were pioneered in the United Kingdom. One example: The British military and colleges were at the forefront of cryptography during World War II, but almost all of the cryptographic products and services in use today are from U.S. companies, not British firms. The United Kingdom has become an example of what happens when government policies are not aligned to the realities of the modern high-technology industrial age.

Picking which battles to fight, where to fight them, and when to fight them are the hallmarks of successful generals and CEOs, as well as government leaders. Governments should not pick winning and losing companies—that's the role of a market economy. However, governments in the twenty-first century can and must develop and execute a strategy to support key industries. Like a company, a country must position itself in the right industry sectors and markets, where it can establish a competitive edge. There's an instructive lesson in the positioning actions taken by Taiwan's leaders beginning in the early 1970s.

Taiwan did not have any inherent competitive advantages that would have enabled its corporations to dominate in any market segments. In fact, Taiwan has limited land space, limited water supplies, and no significant natural resources. However, it has had a large and well-educated population, and it is located near major Asian markets and prospects.

In the early 1970s, the Taiwanese government identified certain sectors of the capital-intensive electronics industry as ideal markets for it to enter and ultimately dominate. The production of semiconductors and other electronics devices required massive investments (one chip plant could cost $200 to $300 million to construct and equip in those days) as well as a skilled workforce and an inventory of technology knowledge.

In 1973, three Taiwanese government research organizations were merged into the Industrial Technology Research Institute (ITRI).[3] It was charged with obtaining the necessary technologies, educating the workforce, and building the chip factories, as well as developing other industries, such as bicycles. ITRI licensed a variety of semiconductor technologies from American companies and other sources. Generous tax benefits, as well as the technology development activities of ITRI, were major catalysts of the nation's development as a center of electronics technology.

In less than four decades, Taiwan's support for capital-intensive industries created a large manufacturing base for key segments of the electronics industry, in many cases achieving worldwide market leadership. While the technology base in Taiwan in the early 1990s was weak compared to that in the United States, Japan, and Europe, by 2009 the technology base in Taiwan had become world class in a number of manufacturing areas.

Taiwan currently produces more than 80 percent of the silicon wafers manufactured in the open market each year.[4] Silicon wafers are disks that range from 5 to 12 inches in diameter that resemble large DVDs or CDs. Memory and microprocessor chips are etched onto these wafers and then cut into the tiny slivers used in personal computers, cell phones, televisions, DVD players, and other electronics devices. These disks are to the electronics industry what crude oil is to Exxon-Mobil or milk is to Ben & Jerry's ice cream.

In addition to having a dominant market share in wafers, Taiwan also produced 37 percent of the flat-panel displays for televisions in 2008, achieving second place in market share behind South Korea's 45 percent.[5] Most laptop computers built since 2005 were produced by Taiwanese companies in their factories in China.[6]

Taiwan's success in wafer and display and laptop manufacturing was due to more than just government incentives and investments. The encouragement of an entrepreneurial environment and the opportunity to trade equities in a sanctioned stock market provided investors and employees the ability to achieve large financial benefits. An ability to raise funds and easily extract profit from equity investments is a tremendous stimulant to the willingness of financial institutions to invest in new companies, especially those in new markets.

Government agencies in China are also active in promoting the building of capital-intensive industries to create an employment base and generate exports. To date, China has made substantial investments in factories to make electronic chips as well as flat-panel displays for computers and televisions. It is no accident that the strategic investment strategies in China have many similarities to those that have been successfully adopted in Taiwan. China has effectively used approaches that have been successful in other countries; however, it has been able to develop these approaches more quickly than other countries have.

Meanwhile, the U.S. government is not currently providing large-scale support for its domestic electronics companies. In fact, the U.S. government–funded Export-Import Bank supported the construction of a chip factory in Singapore with a $652 million loan guarantee.[7] It is ironic that the primary support of one of the few U.S. chip factories under construction in 2009—being built by the Globalfoundries company—was coming from Abu Dhabi, using money earned from the Middle Eastern state's crude oil exports. (The state of New York is also providing funds—roughly 33 percent of the $4.2 billion cost of the chip plant.[8])

At a time when the global competitiveness of the United States is under siege, it is painful to say that agriculture has a higher level of support in Congress than do electronics and other high-technology industries. Each midwestern farming state has the same number of senators as a high-tech state like California, even though the midwestern farming states are relatively sparsely populated in comparison to the handful of high-tech states that are more densely populated. The result is that there is a disproportionate number of farming state senators versus high-tech state senators. Thus, in May 2008, Congress passed and President Bush signed into law a farm bill that provided $288 billion over five years in support of agriculture.[9]

Some countries have long-term strategies for developing their military, but more importantly, countries should have long-term strategies for building corporations that could gain a high market share in global markets. There has been no conceptual transformation from a military-oriented approach to sustaining national security to a business-oriented approach in the United States. Yet the truth is that a nation's corporate strength is its basis for having offensive as well as defensive strategies for building wealth. In reality, while corporations are viewed as stand-alone, independent entities, they are actually the key drivers in the building of a nation's wealth.

More than 200 years ago, the founders of the United States realized that new technologies exploited by businesspeople would be vital to the growth and development of the nascent nation. The patent system included in the U.S. Constitution, along with natural resources and other factors, became the foundation for two centuries of economic development leading to political power. In Chapter 3, I review how and why the United States grew to be a superpower and economic colossus and how it is in grave danger of losing its position.

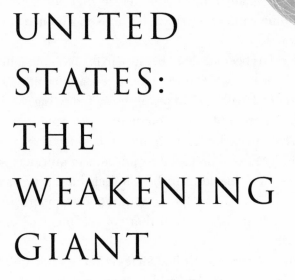

PART II

UNITED STATES: THE WEAKENING GIANT

THINK OF THE UNITED STATES as a large and mature oak tree. It is tall and has many branches, representing the political, geographical, and economic diversity of the country.

The oak tree has deep roots, and for more than 200 years, it has weathered a variety of storms, insect invasions, droughts, and other natural calamities. Branches have bent and swayed during storms, but they have eventually returned to their former position. When an extremely strong wind or ice storm has broken a branch, a new one has quickly grown.

The tree has been resilient because in the past, the rains were plentiful and the leaves were numerous, green, and healthy. The tree was well maintained, with careful pruning and fertilizing.

Beginning in the 1990s, though, the tree's environment began to change. The rains were not as frequent. Less fertilizer was applied to the ground. The tree didn't get the same level of nutrition as in the past.

As its support has diminished, insects have penetrated the tree, draining it of vital nutrients. In addition, caterpillars are eating the leaves. Struggling with less nutrition, some of the tree's branches have become brittle.

Like the oak tree, the United States is being weakened from within as well as from outside. And as the decay accelerates, the country's resistance to other threats declines even faster.

In this weakened state, adverse weather has more of an effect. Snow and ice and strong winds break more branches. As the tree weakens, new branches do not emerge as rapidly as before. The bare wounds from broken limbs provide easy access for insects and disease. Although the oak tree is strong, it is not impervious to all of these threats, and eventually it will die if not properly cared for.

Many storms have challenged the United States during the past 60 years: the rise of the Soviet Union as a military power and aggressor in

Berlin and Cuba, the Japanese electronic and manufactured and automotive export storm, then the Mexico and Taiwanese floods of goods. The biggest storm of all is coming, though. The winds will be very strong. This storm is China.

To date, the China winds have been relatively weak, compared to what they will be as China continues building its strengths. How severely the China storm will harm the United States and other countries will be determined by many factors. How the United States weathers this storm will be determined by how it is nurtured. If it is not strengthened and continues to be abused, it will fare poorly.

By far the biggest internal threat facing the United States is its mounting personal and governmental debt. Let's examine that in detail.

U.S. Drowning in Debt

The U.S. economy continues to be the largest in the world, but it has had low GDP growth over the past decade.[1] In addition, the key driver for GDP growth in the United States in the early years of the twenty-first century has been the use of fiscal deficits to stimulate consumer consumption rather than increasing productivity. The United States has become addicted to deficits as a means to generate economic growth. In fact, the new deficits pay for the old deficits. What's more, the deficits become larger at each refinancing cycle.

While there is a lot of talk about reducing the fiscal deficits, no plans are in place to reduce them. President Obama and some economists have expressed optimism that the economic recovery from the 2008 to 2009 recession will help pay off the debts. However, the modest economic recovery predicted by most economists will not be large enough to diminish the debt tsunami.

Don't forget that the U.S. economy was in a severe recession in 2008 primarily due to the excessive leverage assumed by the financial institutions, along with the excessive leverage of home buying by consumers. Not only did government officials indulge in indiscriminate borrowing but so did supposedly smart bankers and real estate developers, as well as consumers in all strata of society. The expectation was that house and office building prices would continue to increase at a faster rate than the debt load on the properties. This type of artificial growth was clearly not sustainable, though, and the result is that the government has had to absorb a big part of the losses.

Consumers in the United States thought they could buy houses with no money down, with very low monthly payments. Also, they assumed that as real estate prices increased, they would be able to refinance and get additional equity out of their houses. Others arranged for home equity loans and then didn't use the cash to increase the value of their home. They took the short-term excess liquidity and spent it on material goods, typically made overseas.

The bankers created financial instruments out of the mortgages and then borrowed money to trade those esoteric collateralized mortgage obligations, credit default swaps, and other repackagings of debt. Essentially, the banks indulged in leverage on the leverage. The 2008 to 2009 recession was inevitable in its timing and in its severity. While a modest recovery began in late 2009, it was based primarily on the bailout and stimulus packages financed by debt taken on by the U.S. government.

Some of the financial institutions that succumbed to the leverage collapsed or were forced to borrow from the government. What is worse, the government continues to fund the consumption based on debt.

The $4,500[2] that the government paid for automobile clunkers promoted the illusion that Americans can continue to consume. It's an illusion because it is based on increasing government debt. As noted, the U.S. government borrowed more than $1 trillion to fund the stimulus programs.

The People Problem

Even with the understanding of the factors that caused the economic crisis, the United States continues to be living in an illusion that consumption can continue at a high rate, without regard for the origin of the products being consumed or even more fundamental issues, such as the need to create value and maintain the strength of the country. Too few citizens are paying attention to the nutrition needs of the U.S. oak tree.

In the 1950s, U.S. consumers scoffed at products stamped Made in Japan. While the products were inexpensive and in some cases (portable transistor radios) technologically impressive, the quality was poor. Nowadays the prevalence of Made in China, Made in Taiwan, Made in Vietnam, or other identification from an overseas country doesn't faze Americans. Indeed, there are few concerns regarding who is making the products that are being consumed in the United States. All consumers care about is the fact that the products are inexpensive.

However, the real cost of an item for the U.S. consumer is not just the number of dollars needed to buy the product. The real costs also include the hidden costs of the loss of employment within the United States.

Furthermore, few seem to care about the long-term implications of the rising level of imports and the subsequent increases in the trade balance deficit. While it is important to have global competitiveness and allow consumers to buy the cheapest products, the full impact of that freedom needs to be understood.

Another lack of concern is even more troubling. There is a rapidly declining perception of the need to work and create value in the United States. The working contracts that are being negotiated by unions for government employees mean 60 years of pay for 20 years of work. A worker starts at 22 years of age and works 20 years until age 42 for the government, and he or she gets a pension at close to the average annual pay for the last 2 years of work. The worker will collect the pension and benefits for another 40 years based on living to age 82. There are also annual cost-of-living increases at 3 percent per year.

Even current tax policy has helped to perpetuate the illusion of easy money. In the United States, 47 percent[3] of the households do not pay federal taxes, and another 30 percent pays relatively little in federal taxes. The bulk of federal taxes are paid by 20 percent of the population.

Politicians have manipulated tax and spending policies to such an extent that it has affected Americans' relationship with their country. Gradually the culture has evolved from one in which everyone was expected to make a contribution to build the economy to one in which a large percentage of people are trying to extract as much as possible from the economy. In less than 50 years, we have reversed John F. Kennedy's call in 1960 to "ask not what your country can do for you—ask what you can do for your country." There are exceptions in the United States, of course. Some individuals and organizations make large contributions to the building of wealth. American inventors and entrepreneurs such as Steve Jobs and Apple's iTunes have created huge lucrative industries. Also, corporations such as Boeing that generate large exports and have large employment in the United States are key contributors to national wealth building.

The overall perspective, however, is that of entitlement, which is based on the continuation of past patterns. The following is a summary of some of the key trends showing how Americans are more focused on themselves than on their country:

- *Politicians use the approach of reallocating taxes to gain votes.* This means that the more money the politicians can appropriate out of the federal budget for their local projects, affectionately known as "pork-barrel politics," the higher the probability of their being re-elected. U.S. politicians are not the only ones to use this approach, but they have taken it to an extreme.
- *Poverty in the United States has become a way of life for 10 to 15 percent of the population.*[4] In many cases, children of welfare recipients also go on welfare when they grow up because they are not well educated and have not developed work skills.
- *Government employees receive high compensation and very generous retirement packages.* The levels of compensation in many cases are not consistent with their contributions as employees.
- *Government regulators have failed to police the banks and other financial institutions that created the 2008 to 2009 recession.* This error was

compounded by many of the financial institution leaders, who were too greedy or too foolish, or both. Indeed, the 2008 global financial crisis was caused by greed and foolishness.

- *While new regulations are being added to reign in the financial services industry, a key ingredient that created the global financial crisis was a lack of enforcement of the existing regulations.* The 2008 election was, in effect, a decision by the electorate to terminate the government officials who did not enforce the regulations. And while the Obama administration has promised tougher enforcement, it remains to be seen whether the historical pattern of inadequate regulatory oversight of the financial services industry will be reversed. No one is effectively monitoring the monitors.

- *Trade unions in a number of industries have taken short-term approaches to compensation.* They have not taken a global perspective on cost competitiveness. Equitable compensation must be balanced against cost competitiveness. While the primary responsibilities of the trade unions are to protect the jobs and welfare of their members, they must also ensure that costs and contributions are competitive on a global basis.

- *CEOs and top management of many corporations have been focused on very high, short-term compensation.* Instead, they should have been taking a longer view and using today's profits to build tomorrow's world-class corporations.

The entitlement mentality and greed have resulted in a major cultural change in the United States over the past 20 to 30 years. Employees' expectations of a long and lucrative career at one company in exchange for devoted service and occasional sacrifice have been torn apart by vicious rounds of layoffs, often conducted in a brutal fashion. The new cultural norm is for employees to focus on "What's in it for me, now?" When rank-and-file employees see the CEOs of major Wall Street corporations stripped of their jobs but retaining their stock options, pensions, and other financial benefits, it isn't a surprise that everyone has an attitude of emphasizing short-term consumption at the expense of long-term wealth.

Greedy behavior stems from the cultural decay of the United States. This started with the weakening of the image of government and government leaders as honest. The Watergate scandal of the Nixon administration and subsequent misbehaviors by other presidents diminished the respect accorded the presidency of the United States and other national leaders. Furthermore, the failure to incarcerate those responsible for the subprime mortgage scandal of 2008 convinced many people that there are no major penalties or punishment for lying and cheating.

While greed was the primary motivation for many Americans during the boom times beginning in 1995 or so, higher taxes to pay for the deficits and new health care programs may "demotivate" the entrepreneurs and wealthy investors who have provided the capital and inspiration for growth in the past.

Demotivated Investors

The increase in taxes on the wealthy will redistribute wealth and reward the low achievers at the expense of the high achievers. And higher taxes will inevitably discourage risk taking by investors.

Another form of demotivation may occur as well, due to government actions in 2009. In the past, investors were a powerful force in finance and in regulatory offices, but this is changing rapidly. The Bush and Obama government-led bailouts of GM and Chrysler automakers essentially deprived stock and bond holders of most of their investments.[5] The change in the power base from the investors to the government and the unions is evident in the change of ownership of Chrysler. Now the United Auto Workers (UAW) union owns 67.69 percent of Chrysler.[6] A similar situation exists with General Motors: the government owns 60 percent,[7] and the UAW owns 20 percent.[8] This change in the power structure will clearly demotivate investors. When the government wiped out the equity and debt holders of GM and Chrysler, it cast a pall over future investments in these companies.[9]

These major changes in cultural and ethical values are at the core of the decline in U.S. competitiveness.

In the past, it took decades or even centuries for societies to weaken to the point of collapse, but today, the competitive environment can change rapidly—in as little as 5 to 10 years.

The oak tree is weakening, and as the weakening progresses, there is less ability to counter the external threats. It is, consequently, important to react rapidly and make sure that the storms of the coming winter do not cause permanent damage. It is up to the citizens of the United States to protect and restore the oak tree to its prior health. We have to halt the damage from the inside and strengthen it to absorb the impact of future storms.

To do this, we must first burrow deeply into the cornerstones of American industrial might, to understand its real strengths, weaknesses, opportunities, and external threats.

A Perspective on U.S. Industries

A key characteristic of U.S. corporations in the 1960s and 1970s was their focus on the local market, and it was safe for them to keep that focus because the U.S. market was large. Indeed, for many products, the U.S. market was the largest in the world.

The consumers and businesses in the United States were wealthy, and they had predictable buying patterns. By having a large share of a huge market in the United States, domestic corporations were leaders in the global market as well. Their advertising activities were geared at not only increasing the market share of specific brands but also at increasing the size of the total markets, creating new markets, and taking advantage of the large and growing buying power of the U.S. consumers. American high-tech companies proved especially adept at introducing new products that would create large and vibrant domestic markets.

However, corporations that limited their horizons to domestic markets were blind to the capabilities of successful competitors in other geographic areas. For far too long, General Motors, Ford, and Chrysler remained ignorant of or oblivious to the high levels of quality control and efficiency being achieved in Japanese auto factories, as well as their success in making more fuel-efficient vehicles.

In addition to ignoring their tactical advantages in entering overseas markets, U.S. companies lost a strategic opportunity. While it is important to protect the local market against competition (by maintaining a strong internal base and having defensive strategies), it is also critical to take a global perspective on market opportunities. This is a crucial offensive strategy for corporations. Indeed, having high global market share is one of the key metrics for financial success, as demonstrated by GE during and after the Jack Welch era.

The thinking behind this type of offensive strategy is simple. In many cases, it is important to attack the enemy (competing corporations) within their home base to ensure that they do not have the strengths to compete in global markets. If it is not economically viable to take market share away from competitors in their local markets, it is critical to try to contain the enemy and not allow them to generate high market share in other geographic regions. In business as well as in war, there must be strategies to defeat and dominate competition within selected geographic areas.

A key tactic in becoming a global market share leader is for the offensive thrust to be based on feature or technology uniqueness. Using price as the primary tool to invade foreign markets generally results in low profits. The innovative technologies introduced by Apple—the iPod, the iPhone, and the Mac—are great examples of premium-priced products that successfully conquered global markets. Toyota's Prius hybrid car is another example of an innovative product that achieved profitable success outside of its home market.

Many U.S. corporations have consistently underestimated the global competitive threats. As a result, there has been a weakening of U.S. corporations in a number of market segments. This has enabled their competitors in some geographic regions to increase market share within their local markets. A key example is that of the Japanese automobile companies that built strong positions in Japan and then launched major export drives in the United States, South America, and elsewhere.

Even though the population in Japan is 127 million,[10] versus 307 million[11] in the United States, companies such as Toyota have become global market leaders because they were able to build strong domestic businesses with enough profits to launch overseas ventures. Once they had established a strong domestic market, the products they had developed for their Japanese market could be sold in high volumes in other geographic regions.

Japanese auto companies were not the only ones to follow the model of building strong positions in local markets as stepping stones to overseas conquests. Companies such as Samsung and Nokia had even smaller local markets than did Toyota and Honda in Japan. Out of necessity, they developed the skill base required to compete in global markets. Nokia became the global leader in the wireless handset market. And, according to IBS, Samsung became the global market share leader in LCD televisions and memory chips for computers and other electronic devices, as well as the world's second-largest wireless handset vendor.

Let's drill down to understand the competitiveness of U.S. corporations in a number of markets, including automobiles, steel, computers, consumer electronics, cell phones, memory, microprocessors and other integrated circuits, aircraft manufacturing, military equipment, agriculture, and pharmaceuticals.

3

THE DECLINING
U.S. AUTOMOBILE
AND STEEL
INDUSTRIES

THE U.S. AUTOMOBILE COMPANIES were world leaders in the 1950s through 1970s, though their overseas sales were minimal. Their domestic market was so large that a substantial market share in the United States automatically led to a large global market share. That was how General Motors became one of the premier companies in the world during this time. Ford also was predominantly a U.S. company, yet it too was considered a powerful global brand. Chrysler was a smaller company, but it was considered a major force in the automotive market. Niche brands such as Studebaker, Jeep, and others disappeared or were ultimately absorbed by the three major companies.

A small but strong group of domestic automobile manufacturers precluded a large number of automotive imports. With a modest global presence through subsidiaries in multiple geographic regions, the U.S. automobile corporations' overseas sales provided a positive balance of trade.

That all ended in a few decades. The biggest downfall of all the U.S. automakers occurred at General Motors in 2008 and 2009. At its peak in the 1970s, GM had 395,000 employees,[1] with a larger number in the supporting industries. It manufactured more automobiles than any other company globally, even in the early years of the twenty-first century.[2] However, the 2008 recession, a bloated cost structure, and a seriously uncompetitive product line led to bankruptcy in June 2009. To avoid adding to the already high national unemployment and political strife, a loan of more than $50 billion[3] from the U.S. government allowed General Motors to continue to operate. The company sold several small brands and overseas operations to raise sorely needed cash, but it failed to find buyers for its larger but weakest domestic and foreign brands, including the Saturn, Pontiac, and Opel divisions. It succeeded in selling the Saab brand and technology to a small European company.[4]

The number 2 domestic U.S. automaker, Ford, fared better during the recession of 2008 and 2009, but not by much. Revenues for most of fiscal year 2009 were down roughly 24 percent from the prior year, to $82.9 billion, and the company reported an operating loss of $1.3 billion.[5] The recession and a weak product lineup led Ford to a 13 percent shipment decline between 2007 and 2008.

Ford avoided GM's bankruptcy fate because it had new management. The company was led by industry outsider Alan Mulally, who in 2006 had anticipated a cash squeeze in the future. He was able to mortgage all of the company's properties and other assets to create a war chest before the credit markets dissolved in 2008.[6] Despite the subsequent strong financial pressures, Ford survived the recession without emergency government funding. Ford manufactured 5.4 million vehicles in 2008 (compared to 9.2 million for Toyota and 8.3 million for GM),[7] however, the company is not considered a global powerhouse in the automobile industry even though it is the fourth-largest manufacturer.

Ford's decline as a global player is due in part to its sales of overseas brands. Ford sold marques such as Volvo,[8] Jaguar, Land Rover, and part of its minority ownership in Mazda. Ford sold these relatively small and weak brands to companies in India and China so that it could focus all of its efforts on a few large and more important core products. Mazda has relatively strong performance, but Ford had not adopted some of Mazda's successful business strategies.

Ford and GM used to be completely integrated manufacturing powerhouses, making almost all of the components that they needed when assembling a car or truck. However, over the past 10 years, they have unloaded their loss-ridden component manufacturing arms. Ford's manufacturing spin-off Visteon and GM's automotive parts spin-off Delphi Automotive both declared bankruptcy in 2005 and 2008, respectively. In 2005, Delphi disclosed irregular accounting practices and filed for Chapter 11 bankruptcy protection to reorganize. In the 2008 and 2009 recession, Visteon filed for bankruptcy to reorganize the corporation and certain of its U.S. subsidiaries. Meanwhile, their joint ventures with Chinese auto parts suppliers are thriving. Their manufacturing base is being built up in China, and an increasing percentage of automobile components for GM and Ford are from China.

Clearly, the U.S. automobile industry has gone through a major decline. In addition to the costs of the company's pension obligations, management faces enormous product challenges. Despite the appointment of new CEOs at all three U.S. automakers since 2006, they have been completely ineffective in developing automobiles that can dominate the U.S. market as well as generate exports. Despite 30 years of competing against imports from Japan, most American autos rank lower than Toyota or Honda in quality and reliability, according to extensive surveys and research by *Consumer Reports* magazine.[9] While new data shows improved effectiveness of new management in terms of better quality, the competitiveness of the U.S. automobile industry is still in doubt.

Due to its weak automobile industry, the United States is a net importer of automobiles (automotive exports totaled $7.5 billion[10] in September 2009 whereas imports were valued at $16.4 billion[11]). While part of the trade imbalance is offset by Japanese and German automobile companies manufacturing in the United States, this is very different from having a local manufacturer with an extensive domestic supply chain support base. The most important technologies for autos—the engines, transmissions, and other drivetrain elements—are imported into the United States. This deprives many U.S. companies from fully participating in the supply chain of the Japanese and South Korean factories in the United States.

Chrysler as a Hot Potato

A further testament to the depth of the problems of the U.S. automobile industry is Chrysler's situation. Daimler-Benz acquired Chrysler for $38 billion[12] in 1998 and then sold 80.1 percent of it to the financial speculator and distressed-asset operator Cerberus Capital Management for $7.4 billion[13] in 2007. The value of the remaining 20 percent became essentially zero.

From 1998 to 2007, Daimler-Benz invested billions of dollars in Chrysler, but it was unable to make the company profitable. While Daimler-Benz is a successful company by global metrics, it was unable to overcome the poor quality, inefficiencies, incorrect product planning, and operating and pension fund costs accumulated by Chrysler. Daimler-Benz failed to change the culture of Chrysler to manufacture world-class automobiles.

Due to weakening demand for its automobiles, Cerberus experienced large losses in Chrysler as well as in its own financing arm. Cerberus is a very shrewd company that has access to large financial resources. It was, however, significant that the U.S. taxpayers were forced to rescue Chrysler—Cerberus walked away from its investment during the takeover of some Chrysler assets by Fiat in 2009 because it didn't want to continue to fund a money loser. The UAW also has significant equity in Chrysler.

The U.S. automobile companies have gone from a position of having one of the largest employment bases to being a drain on the taxpayer. The government loaned $62 billion[14] to GM and Chrysler. In return for its loan to GM, the U.S. government owns 61 percent of the equity in what was once the largest company in the world. The U.S. government also owns 10 percent of Chrysler as part of the loan bailout. In addition, the Obama administration loaned $5.9 billion[15] to Ford to help it develop fuel-efficient automobiles. And the outlook isn't promising.

More Overseas Competition for U.S. Automakers

Competition from other countries is strengthening, ratcheting up the external competitive pressures for the domestic U.S. automakers. Hyundai from South Korea is increasing the volumes of automobiles it ships to the United States and manufacturers in Alabama, with the goal of becoming a global brand. Since the market in South Korea is small, it is critical for Hyundai to be successful in the global market, which means increasing its market share in the United States.

And Chinese automakers are rapidly ramping up their production too. The number of automobiles manufactured in China was 9.3 million[16] in 2008 compared to 2.1 million[17] in 2000. In 2009, almost 14 million automobiles were manufactured in China, according to the China Association of Automobile Manufacturers.[18] Approximately 15 million automobiles are projected to be manufactured in 2010[19] and 20 million in 2020,[20] which will vastly exceed the almost 16 million vehicles produced in U.S. auto factories at their peak. While Chinese automobile manufacturers focus on the local market in the short term, they are increasingly emphasizing exports. Geely's buyout of Volvo will strengthen the competitiveness of a Chinese company in the United States as well as in Europe, as it gains a famous global brand, distribution network, and advanced assembly and engine control technologies.

The U.S. automobile industry will continue to suffer, due to the combination of noncompetitive products and high costs. As the U.S. automobile industry continues to lose domestic market share, imports will increase and employment will further decline.

The U.S. automobile industry is on track to follow in the steps of the United Kingdom—a country that lost its automobile industry due to noncompetitive products and high costs. British cars were highly prized around the world in the 1950s and 1960s, but poor quality and reliability and outmoded technologies put British car companies into a downward spiral. As more economical and reliable cars were imported from Asia and elsewhere, British auto companies lost the economies of scale required to remain competitive. So they sold out to American and German automakers, or just went bankrupt. Sound familiar? The downward spiral is painfully reminiscent of what has happened to American automakers.

This dour view of the future of U.S. automakers is in part due to their sluggish new product development programs. While Japanese, European, South Korean, and even Chinese automobile companies are advanced in developing fuel-efficient automobiles, the U.S. automobile companies continue to try to sell mostly obsolete models, and they are committing slowly to responding to the demand for fuel-efficient vehicles.

Employment by the U.S. automakers will further decline as their market shares continue to shrink. GM's bankruptcy reorganization plan predicted laying off most of its employees—it would retain only 38,000 employees in the United States, or roughly 10 percent of the head count at its peak—but head count reductions in the United States have been postponed because of the government bailout programs. By the end of 2009, the company still had over 200,000 employees.[21] GM had 32,000 employees in China,[22] and employment there could become larger than that in the United States in the next five years due to the huge boom in car purchases in China. Note that GM is able to generate profits from the China market through its joint venture activities.

The European and Japanese automobile companies have also suffered financial problems as a result of the 2008 to 2009 recession, but they are likely to emerge from the downturn in strong competitive positions. Their strong brand names, reputation for quality, and reliability, together with the decline of their U.S. competitors, provide a once-in-a-lifetime opportunity. Toyota's hold on being the leader is in jeopardy, which represents an opportunity for U.S. companies. Honda could overtake Ford by 2015, if not sooner. Their U.S. operations will continue to gain market share. Volkswagen could become the largest automobile vendor globally in the future.

One of the more compelling dramas of the beleaguered U.S. auto industry is the operational takeover of Chrysler by Fiat. The Italian automaker manufactured 2.5 million[23] vehicles in 2008, and together with Chrysler's output, it outranked Honda in terms of total production. However, losses will continue at Chrysler as its market share plummets. It will take several years before Fiat's more fuel-efficient cars appear at Chrysler dealers. It is likely that the U.S. government will be forced to provide additional funds to save jobs and maintain the pension programs.

The U.S. Automobile Industry Outlook

The U.S. automobile industry's losses are being reduced, but recovery is not assured. Lost jobs, lost profits, lost companies. It is likely that GM will sell automobiles manufactured in China into the U.S. market. It will be ironic that the future of GM—an icon of U.S. industry—will depend on manufacturing its automobiles in China. Of course, if GM manufactures automobiles in China for export to the United States, the American balance of trade will suffer as well as employment.

Don't think that the rise of U.S. auto plants operated by Asian companies will offset the employment losses of what was once known as the Big Three. The domestic factories of Honda, Toyota, and other Asian manufacturers have fewer employees and pay lower wages. Furthermore, the technology base for the automobiles of Japanese companies assembled in the United States is in Japan. A similar situation also applies to the European manufacturers, such as Mercedes-Benz.

In addition to employment losses in the automobile industry in the United States, there are also employment losses in the supporting industries. The increased outsourcing of subassemblies and components from the Far East by the U.S. automobile companies has a huge impact on U.S. employment—employment in the supporting industries is double or triple of that in automobile manufacturing. While overseas outsourcing reduces costs, the trade imbalance gets worse for the United States. The outsourcing also builds up competence in a range of technologies and manufacturing skills in countries such as China, essentially helping our competitors become stronger.

Lessons to Be Learned

Because of the combination of strong external competitive pressures and poor execution, the U.S. automobile industry has changed from a world leader to a laggard, struggling for survival. The dramatic weakening has occurred in less than a decade, which is indicative of how rapidly a market can change.

Other industries face similar problems in the United States, such as the Internet software industry. For example, the confrontation between Google and China over the amount and type of information the search engine provides Chinese citizens is really a battle over Internet control—China is developing a coordinated approach to accessing Internet content, while Google is essentially left to fend for itself with little support by the U.S. government. The weak internal capabilities and external competitive threats need to be addressed at both the micro level (company by company) and also at the macro level (industry by industry).

Understand the Breadth of Competition in the Automobile Industry

The health of the automobile industry is an indicator of the globalization of the supply base, and it is an example of the size and number of external threats that must be addressed by U.S. corporations in the twenty-first century. A crucial lesson in what not to do can be found in the low level of emphasis that U.S. automakers placed on their competitors outside of the United States. The U.S. automakers' lack of understanding of the impact of the Japanese threat in the automobile markets in the 1970s and 1980s led to their undoing. The U.S.

automotive companies did not change their strategies to counter the Japanese threat until it was too late to prevent financial disaster. As a result, the Japanese automobile corporations have eroded the market share of the U.S. automobile companies in the United States and in other geographic regions. The U.S. automotive industry has also weakened against the European automotive companies by not having automobiles that competed with those from BMW, Mercedes-Benz, and others. Until recently, and with few exceptions, luxury cars from Europe (especially Germany) were perceived to offer better quality and the cachet of wealth.

Manage Labor Costs

High pension and labor wages drive higher production costs and can make product pricing uncompetitive. The UAW ownership stakes in GM and Chrysler make it difficult to imagine that pension and labor costs will be reduced further to become more competitive with Chinese or South Korean costs.

Invest in Research and Development

Beware of the downward spiral. As corporations become weak, they lose the ability to invest in more efficient factories and develop new technologies. As their products lose competitiveness against more technically advanced rivals, market share declines accelerate. One of the reasons Ford and GM had to borrow money from the government for advanced fuel-efficient design funding was their lack of cash for research and development.

Pay Attention to Customer Preferences

One of the most important lessons to be learned by the automakers' debacle is the price of ignoring customer preferences. A key problem was that the U.S. automobile companies did not understand the change in the buying habits of U.S. consumers. For decades, Detroit automakers produced cars with notably more defects than their Japanese competitors. And while the domestic companies paid lip service to improving the quality of their vehicles, it took more than 20 years for GM and Ford to approximate quality parity with Toyota, Honda, Nissan, and the other members of their cohort.[24] Constant frustration with the products from Detroit, plus exposure to the high quality of Japanese automobiles, led to a mass exodus of customers for American car companies. The management of the U.S. automobile industry failed to respond to their own customers in their home market.

Toyota is also facing similar problems by not paying close enough attention to customer problems. The control by a family entity has clearly hurt Toyota.[25]

Too Big to Fail, Again?

Considering all of the problems facing the U.S. automakers, it is a fair question to wonder whether government support should continue. Is it a case of throwing good money after bad? Since their prospects are grim, won't additional funding just delay the inevitable? The answer is complex.

Additional financial support by the government to the automobile industry will be a drain on taxpayers. To pay for the additional subsidies, taxes will need to be increased. That means every U.S. taxpayer will be supporting the automakers, even citizens who do not buy automobiles.

The danger of letting the U.S. automakers fold was the too-big-to-fail argument we heard about the Wall Street banks during the 2008 financial meltdown. Part of that argument was that if the employment base in the automotive and support industries continued to decline, unemployment benefits would be needed for those who had lost their jobs. This would, again, require increases in taxes, and it would also cause a decline in tax receipts.

And don't forget the deleterious effect of further car imports from Asia and Europe. If the U.S. automobile industry is allowed to fail, imports will skyrocket, further sinking the already underwater trade figures. Imagine the cost of building other industries to generate comparable employment, balance of trade, and the potential profits to replace those achieved by the automobile industry. Not likely.

The key issue is whether the United States will respond and take the necessary actions. The pattern in the U.S. automobile industry is similar to that which has occurred in other industries such as clothing, shoes, and furniture. A falling domino effect across multiple industries leaves the United States with fewer factories, more unemployed workers, strengthened overseas competitors, and increased trade deficit.

It has been evident for some time that the competitiveness of the industry was weakening. If the U.S. government had acted in 2005, the costs to taxpayers would have been much lower than what they are at the present time. The government's 2009 loans to car manufacturers and others focusing on advanced automotive technologies are a start, but they are not nearly enough.

The need for more fuel-efficient and lower-pollution automobiles gives the United States the opportunity to develop technology leadership. If the U.S. government provided the same level of support for building new generations of automobiles as it has invested in new generations of military aircraft, the benefits to the U.S. economy and employment would be much greater. Unfortunately, the culture in the United States is that military strength is more important than corporate strength.

New automotive platforms, such as the Volt electric car from General Motors, are being developed, but it is not likely that these products will experience strong demand due to their limited range (the Volt has a range of only 40 miles) and high price (the Volt's initial price is close to $40,000).[26] There are, however, other new platforms, such as the sedan from Tesla, that have potential because they are priced to fit within the middle-class income range and they have the allure of being electric cars. The U.S. government's recent loan guarantee for Tesla is another important step,[27] but it is important to note that the Tesla initiative is the result of the entrepreneurship of some individuals; it is not the result of top-level visionary leadership from the government.

The Tesla situation also shows how other countries are positioning themselves for the advanced auto technology sweepstakes in the future. Daimler-Benz took an almost 10 percent equity ownership in Tesla,[28] but it subsequently sold part of its ownership (approximately 40 percent[29]) to Abu Dhabi. It is important to note that Abu Dhabi owns 10 percent of Daimler-Benz, so the German auto giant was clearly bowing to the wishes of its largest stockholder when it sold part of its Tesla stock.[30]

There is clearly a lack of corporate and government leadership in the United States regarding the country's ability to have a large share of the global market for automobiles. Even during the present crisis, the emphasis is on short-term survival (until the next election), not on the long-term actions that can enable the United States to be significantly ahead in the technology and energy efficiency of automobiles.

Because of the large size of the automobile market, it is paramount for the United States to strengthen the automobile industry. The U.S. automotive industry needs to be world class to survive the competitive marketplace, which will require many changes in management as well as low-cost business models. And those business models must include high employment in the United States while maintaining low unit costs to satisfy the majority stockholders—the government and the unions.

The two conditions are not necessarily contradictory. There has to be a change in conceptual thinking about the relationship between government and corporations and their roles as the generators of wealth.

While the United States continues to provide large funding to the military, and while military strength is important, national wealth is more likely to be built on corporation success than on military success.

Steel Production

U.S. companies were the global leaders in steel capacity and global competitiveness in the 1960s and 1970s. U.S. Steel was considered one of the global leaders during this time.

But by the late 1970s, the large, fully integrated American steel companies' not keeping up with technological developments, high labor costs, and other self-inflicted wounds led to red ink hemorrhaging from their balance sheets. First, they lost market share to upstart "mini-mills" that were using new technologies and lower-cost business models. Weakened by the intense price competition, stronger overseas firms such as ArcelorMittal were able to buy up the U.S. wrecks, further consolidating the industry.

In 2008, U.S. Steel was the tenth-largest manufacturer of steel. An upstart minimill competitor, Nucor, was ranked at 12, according to the World Steel Organization.[31] And U.S. Steel's production lead over Nucor remains slim at around 15 percent. This is what happens when an established company becomes arrogant and complacent and ignores new technologies. We saw the same thing with GM.

Fortunately, the consolidation of the steel industry has not meant that revenues, profits, and employment were entirely lost to the United States. Steel is the foundation of a wide range of industries, including construction, appliances, and automobiles. It is a baseline capability for an economy in a developed or developing country.

Since steel is extremely expensive to transport over long distances, manufacturers establish steel mills at locations close to the geographic locations of large customers. To benefit from technological advances around the world, though, the steel companies need to operate their factories in each major local market, where they can leverage knowledge from one location to reduce their costs and improve productivity at other locations.

A European and Indian company, ArcelorMittal is now the world leader in steel production.[32] It is a global operation, and it has taken over steel companies in Europe, Asia, the United States, and Africa. Japanese, Chinese, and Indian firms also are leaders of the steel industry. They and others are buying iron ore producers to control the sources of raw materials.[33] This approach builds competitive barriers that are very powerful during times when there are shortages of raw materials. When there is overcapacity or slowing of demand, however, owning a lot of raw materials that have declined in value increases the level of financial risk.

In the past, the U.S. government has established tariff barriers to protect the steel industry from bargain basement imported steel, but the barriers' effectiveness has been low to date. The reason is the declining competitiveness of the domestic steel corporations. Their costs are so high that imported steel can be less expensive, even including the shipping costs.

Another form of U.S. government support is the targeted infrastructure stimulus programs. Projects using the 2008 to 2009 infrastructure stimulus funds must use steel from U.S. manufacturers unless the total project cost would be increased by 24 percent or more. This attempt to stimulate local demand with the use of taxpayer money does not encourage the U.S. steel companies to be cost competitive. Furthermore, the 24 percent pricing umbrella may not be enough to protect domestic manufacturers from imported steel.

Domestic steel manufacturers face another challenge, though. Financial institutions in the United States are not supportive of capital-intensive investments for steel manufacturers, due to concerns over the large financial losses experienced in times of overcapacity. Consequently, competitors from Japan, South Korea, China, and India are increasing their market share of the global steel market thanks to the willingness of their bankers to invest in new technologies and new factories.

The weakening of the U.S. steel industry indicates that another domino is about to fall. When the United States increases its imports of steel, it increases the trade imbalance. Therefore, the United States needs to export another product that can compensate for the trade imbalance of steel.

4

U.S. COMPUTER INDUSTRY—A WINNER TO DATE

Computers

IBM, BURROUGHS, UNIVAC, NCR, Control Data, Honeywell, Digital Equipment, and other American companies dominated the computer industry in the 1960s through the early 1980s. Their primary competitors were from Japan and Europe.

The technologies within the computer industry have changed dramatically since the 1980s. U.S. companies, including Intel and IBM, have driven many of these technology enhancements. Faster and more powerful computers at lower cost have enabled the U.S. computer companies to maintain a high market share on a global basis. European companies abandoned the computer industry when they couldn't compete.

U.S. companies are the global leaders in servers. IBM, HP, Oracle (Sun), and Dell dominate the industry. Their weak competition includes Fujitsu, NEC, and Hitachi. Also,

Fujitsu, NEC, and Hitachi use microprocessors from Intel, AMD, and IBM.

IBM also has a strong position in supercomputers. It is important to note that IBM continues to be committed to continued technology leadership, with extensive research on chips, systems, and software. IBM is obtaining support from U.S. government agencies; $16.1 million in funding for Phase 1 of the DARPA Systems of Neuromorphic Adaptive Plastic Scalable Electronics (SyNAPSE) initiative[1] is one example. This is an investment in nanotechnology—that is, the development of extremely tiny products. These initiatives are a key part of both military and commercial environments, and while there is initial funding, the amount is very small compared to the cost of ensuring technology leadership.

HP and Dell had (Acer is now in second position) the largest shares of the desktop U.S. computer market, due to their cost-competitive products as well as their highly efficient distribution channels. Apple is gaining market share in personal computers due to the high levels of innovation in its products. The company that has been gaining market share most rapidly in personal computers over the past two years has been Acer—it has become the second-largest vendor on a global basis in unit volumes of personal computers.[2] Acer has acquired three smaller U.S. personal computer companies: Gateway, eMachines, and Packard Bell.[3]

HP and Dell have a high market share in notebook computers, but they have strong competition from Sony, Toshiba, ASUS, and Acer. Samsung is increasing its market share in notebook computers too.

While a large number of companies participate in the new netbook computer market, a shakeout is expected as the market matures. Companies that have achieved low costs because of their efficient supply chains and strong distribution channels will dominate the netbook market. Brand recognition will also be important.

The U.S. computer companies have also been highly innovative in adopting new business models—such as having telecommunciations companies offer netbooks with heavily discounted pricing if buyers commit to long-term service contracts—and in being cost leaders. Their emphasis on innovative and compelling features is necessary to capture global market share leadership.

While personal computer companies from Japan and Europe have tried to compete against U.S. companies, success has been modest or nonexistent. The superior performance of U.S. products is one factor, but the most important attribute of the U.S. companies is the cost competitiveness of their supply chains. The American PC vendors were early users of contract manufacturers. The combination of low-cost manufacturing, low R&D costs (technology was available from Intel, Microsoft, and other companies), and very low overhead costs made companies such as Dell and the HP personal computer division cost competitive on a global basis. This is how American computer companies adapted effectively to global competitive pressures.

Processors

Processor engines are the key building blocks in all computers. Fortunately for the United States, the American companies Intel, AMD, and IBM dominate the global microprocessor market. However, the British company ARM is making inroads in the market. It sells microprocessor designs for others to build at outsourced factories in Taiwan and elsewhere. It is possible that processors from ARM can gain inroads into the new netbook computer market in the future, which would enable other U.S. semiconductor makers such as Qualcomm, NVIDIA, and potentially Broadcom, to become major players in the global market. Consequently, U.S. computer companies have shown strong performance by both developing low-cost products through their use of efficient supply chains and distribution channels and their ability to control key building blocks, such as processors. The combination gives the U.S. companies major competitive advantages.

Imagine how much different the competitive environment would be for the U.S. automobile industry if engines and transmissions were manufactured by specialized companies, rather than each major automobile company's having its own engine and transmission capability. The economies of scale enjoyed by specialists would mean lower costs and more advanced technologies deployed even faster.

However, new competitive threats loom large in parts of the computer market. This isn't a surprise because the widespread availability of components such as microprocessors, memory chips, and disk drives lowers the barriers to entry.

New PC Threats

The computer companies in Taiwan are coming on strong. Acer and ASUS are taking advantage of their own efficient supply chains and their expanding customer bases. For example, 90 percent of the global computer circuit board design and manufacturing for desktop and laptop PCs is based in Taiwan.[4] In the future, Taiwanese companies will try to move up the value chain, including the production of processor engines, thanks to availability of the ARM design. However, even with the strengthening of the Taiwanese companies in personal computers, it is likely that the U.S. computer companies will maintain a substantial global market share for the next few years.

To date, Chinese computer companies have not represented major competitive challenges to the U.S. companies. Lenovo is the largest Chinese PC company. It tried to strengthen its position in the computer business through the acquisition of the PC business of IBM. However, after some initial success, Lenovo lost momentum as it couldn't keep up with the sharp price declines in the market. Lenovo wasn't able to reduce its costs to keep in step with its much larger competitors, which had lower unit costs due to their economies of scale. Lenovo changed its CEO early in 2009,[5] and it is increasing its emphasis on the China market.[6]

The Downside of Success

A key part of the success of the U.S. computer industry is its low cost. Low costs have been achieved through the outsourcing of manufacturing to the Far East and the use of contract manufacturers. Contract manufacturers are independent companies that provide global economies of scale to produce computers, telephones, consumer entertainment devices, and other products.

However, a consequence of outsourcing to contract manufacturers is the loss of jobs in the United States. A large percentage of the manufacturing of computers, as well as the components and subassemblies, such as displays, is conducted in the Far East. While it is better from a balance-of-trade perspective that a U.S. consumer buys a computer manufactured by an American company than by an Asian firm, there are balance-of-trade deficits associated with most of the computers of U.S. companies sold in the U.S. market. There is, however, a positive balance of trade for the computers of U.S. companies that are sold into other geographic regions, such as Latin America.

Without the use of third-party contract manufacturers, the U.S. computer companies would not be cost competitive and would have closed. Consequently, a balance must exist between manufacturing products in low-cost geographic regions and having corporations that are profitable and are able to hire managers and engineers in the United States.

Strong leaders in the U.S. computer industry, including Michael Dell, Steve Jobs of Apple, and Mark Hurd of HP, have succeeded in managing that balance for their stockholders. While these leaders and others have limited the number of manufacturing jobs in the United States, overall they have improved America's balance of trade.

The willingness of visionary CEOs, entrepreneurs, and investors to commit to new areas of computer technologies has been another key area of strength for the United States. Google is a great example of a company that in less than 10 years became a household word around the world and a major player in the computer industry. Computer manufacturers have also been willing to change business models and compete in multiple geographic regions, due to a strong commitment to achieving and maintaining global market leadership.

The short-term prospects for the U.S. computer companies are positive. There are, however, new opportunities and challenges.

Internet-based hardware devices that rely on new technologies from Intel and other companies will create new markets. However, these new handheld computerlike devices are expected to be made by companies from Taiwan, South Korea, and China. Nokia also is developing a range of these devices, and it announced the Booklet 3G in August 2009.[7]

Component Challenges

Key components of computers are the flat-panel displays, which are manufactured almost exclusively in South Korea, Taiwan, and Japan. However, China is currently developing the capacity to manufacture flat-panel displays. Because of the need for large capital expenditures, U.S. corporations have not established flat-panel display manufacturing facilities, even though many of the early technologies were developed in the United States.

The computer industry also depends on peripherals, such as hard disk drives, optical drives, printers, and portable memory devices. The U.S. companies Seagate and Western Digital are the global leaders in hard disk drives, but that market is notorious for steep price declines and poor margins due to rapid product obsolescence. Hard disk drives are manufactured almost exclusively in the Far East.

Indeed, a large amount of hard disk drive technology was developed by IBM, but IBM sold its business to Hitachi due to the financial challenges of managing this particular line of products. It is, however, likely that Hitachi will either sell off or close down a large part of the hard disk drive business it acquired from IBM due to difficulties in competing against Seagate and Western Digital, according to International Business Strategies (IBS) analyses. The Japanese hard disk drive industry has become financially weak as well: the hard disk drive business of Fujitsu has been acquired by Toshiba.

A competing technology to hard disk drives is that of solid-state drives. Several companies build memory devices without moving parts (hence, the phrase *solid state*), using the same memory chips found in thumb drives and camera memory cards. Most of these devices are made in Asia, although a U.S. company, SanDisk, has a strong patent position.

The U.S. companies do not have strong positions in optical drives, including the Blu-ray, but these product areas are not strategic.

It's All about the Software

The most important trend in the computer industry since the 1990s is that software and services are more important than hardware. Microsoft, IBM, Oracle, salesforce.com, and others are global leaders in the new software and services environment.

While a number of U.S. companies have software development activities in the United States, extensive software development occurs in India, Russia, and elsewhere. The use of low-cost software developers follows the same outsourcing pattern exhibited by Dell, HP, and other computer hardware manufacturers.

The evolution of IBM from hardware to software to services is an example of how a large company has changed its business model and regained strong financial performance. A high percentage of the growth of the services revenues of IBM is in geographic regions outside of the United States. To meet the overseas demand, IBM is increasing its head count in these geographic regions while reducing its head count in the United States.[8]

The services business model is human resource–intensive, so the employment implications of this shift to services is huge. The head count of IBM employees in Brazil, Russia, India, and China (BRIC) was close to 100,000[9] at the end of 2008, compared to 85,000 at the end of 2006.[10] IBM had approximately 73,000[11] employees in India at the end of 2007. At the end of 2008, IBM had 115,000 employees in the United States, but it announced additional layoffs in early 2009.

Corporations such as IBM, Dell, and HP will continue to seek a profitable equilibrium between domestic and overseas employment because they are driven by profit motives, not altruism or patriotism. It will be up to governments to support programs that encourage employment in their home markets. The U.S. government should focus on finding ways to support the next generation of computerlike devices as a way to foster more domestic employment and exports.

The computer industry is one domino that has not fallen. It is important that there is continued support for the growth of the computer industry in the United States to keep this domino upright.

Consumer Electronics

The U.S. consumer electronics industry has weakened significantly since the 1960s and 1970s. For example, currently, there are no large U.S. television vendors even though companies such as RCA and Zenith were television pioneers. Today, these companies barely exist in the minds of consumers.

In the twenty-first century, the model for consumer electronics development can be best understood through the rise of TV maker VIZIO. The headquarters of VIZIO is in the United States (Irvine, California), the engineers of the company are in Taiwan, and the manufacturing is done in Chinese factories owned by a Taiwanese company. Roughly one quarter of VIZIO is owned by its Taiwanese supplier of critical parts.[12] VIZIO has been able to gain one of the largest shares of the low end of the U.S. television market by having a low-cost business model that attracted discounters such as Walmart and others as distribution channels. In addition to low prices, it also made savvy inventory and marketing decisions in 2009, according to *Forbes* magazine.

It's not clear how profitable VIZIO is, but it is clear that its competitors are hurting. Large, Japanese television manufacturers, such as Sony, Panasonic, and Sharp, are losing money according to their consolidated income statements for the quarter ended October 30, 2009, for Sony, and September 30 for both Panasonic and Sharp. Niche players in the TV business include Toshiba, Philips, Hitachi, and Mitsubishi. These companies are also losing money or are drastically reducing the size of their businesses. It is unlikely that all these companies will stay in the television business in the long term due to the impact of the new low-cost vendors in China, Taiwan, and South Korea. Pioneer has already announced its withdrawal from the television market, although it plans to partner with Chinese retailer Suning Appliance, who may be able to use the Pioneer brand for flat-panel TVs in China.[13]

Samsung, LG Electronics, and VIZIO are well positioned to dominate that mainstream television market in the next few years.

The number of televisions manufactured by Chinese companies is increasing, as Haier, TCL (joint venture with Thomson), Hisense, and others are stepping up production. While the initial emphasis of the Chinese manufacturers was on their local market, they have increased their emphasis on exports.

The key semiconductor components for televisions are manufactured by vendors, such as MediaTek, STMicroelectronics, Broadcom, and MStar. The use of integrated circuits from independent companies is different from the past, when the semiconductors were manufactured by television companies such as Sony, Panasonic, Philips, Hitachi, and Toshiba.

With the availability of semiconductor components, companies that do not have engineering strengths can manufacture televisions that are competitive in performance with the legacy vendors such as Sony and Panasonic. The key factors for success are styling and low-cost distribution channels. Low-cost manufacturing can be provided by outsourcers such as Foxconn.

Since no televisions are manufactured in the United States, there is a large negative balance of trade when televisions are purchased by U.S. consumers. However, changes are occurring in the business that can benefit U.S. companies. One change is the convergence between the game consoles, televisions, cable TV set-top boxes, and computer functionality. These formerly separate and distinct devices are being combined into a new consumer multifunction platform. This relatively complex, computerlike platform plays into the design and software strengths of the U.S. chip and computer companies.

Apple is attempting to support this convergence. Its TV devices haven't been successes in the marketplace, but they are harbingers of what is to come. And Apple's stellar design, consumer interface, and marketing skills undoubtedly will increase interest in this category over time. Unfortunately, most of Apple's products are manufactured in China, by Foxconn.

Microsoft's Xbox 360 game console emphasizes interactivity, which could be extended to the new consumer multifunction platforms. However, Flextronics and other contract manufacturers produce the consoles for Microsoft.

Set-top boxes from Cisco, Motorola, and others can also perform as convergence platforms. These companies are driving the adoption of new Internet access concepts as well as interactively including video-conferencing. Cisco has already announced a commitment to the consumer market, buying Pure Digital Technologies, the company that introduced the Flip video recorder.[14] Motorola, however, is primarily focused on trying to regain market share for its wireless handset business, and it had announced it may sell or spin off its set-top box business,[15] although this decision has since been reversed.

The electronics industry continues to be characterized by new opportunities based on new technologies and new business concepts. A key requirement is to have corporations positioned to take advantage of the new growth opportunities. They have to be willing to make the required expenditures to build market positions in global markets as well as in their local markets.

Apple had tremendous success with the iPod and its derivatives, which demonstrates the success an innovative company can achieve if it has a strong understanding of consumer needs. Apple focused on ease of use and establishing a content infrastructure for the iPod, which is radically different from designing and building hardware. A key attribute of Apple is having a universal user-friendly interface so that consumers in many geographic regions and at many skill levels can use its products. A similar approach made the iPhone a breakthrough product and success as well.

However, Apple products and the Microsoft Xbox are manufactured in the Far East, driven by the need for these products to be low cost. Apple is a unique company, with a strong commitment to global leadership for its products. Also, Apple is led by an innovative leader who is willing to drive the adoption of new concepts and is not limited by legacy approaches and business models. However, despite the activities of Apple and Microsoft, the United States has a large balance-of-payments deficit in consumer products.

Future Consumer Electronics Opportunities

There are market opportunities for new consumer products that involve support of high-definition video and the associated services. The leveraging of the combination of content and platforms is one way for the United States to build new corporations.

However, for this market opportunity to materialize, the developers of movies and other content need to rethink and rework their business models. Just as Steve Jobs and Apple helped the recording industry escape the abyss of music piracy thanks to the iTunes online model, executives of the Hollywood studies and the leaders of the computer and consumer electronics industries have to work together to unlock the potential of a huge new global video marketplace. To date, the movie industry has resisted easy and universal access to much of its new content, and it continues to try to optimize revenues from its legacy distribution channels.

Strong leadership and a compelling vision of the opportunities from Internet-based content distribution and consumption, including interactivity, could enable the U.S. electronics industry to reverse the downward trend of the past. New devices based on a wide range of new technologies could provide the United States with the equivalent of 10 new iPhone and iPod industries.

Cell Phones

The U.S. cell phone hardware industry consists of Motorola, Apple, and Palm.

Motorola was the global market share leader in mobile telephones in the past, and it is credited with inventing the mobile telephone. Motorola dropped from being the second-largest vendor globally in 2005 to the fifth-largest vendor, behind Nokia, Samsung, LG Electronics, and Sony/Ericsson in the fourth quarter of 2009. While it once had more than half the market, at the end of the fourth quarter of 2009, Motorola had less than 10 percent of the market, compared to Nokia's 30-plus percent.[16]

It is possible for Motorola to recover market share in the wireless handset market based on its new family of cell phones. The Android platform, with software developed by Google, is a strong competitor. While the hardware and software were designed in the United States, manufacturing is primarily in the Far East.

Apple is increasing its market share with its iPhone family. According to IBS estimates, Apple had about 2.6 percent of the global market at the end of Q4/2009, and it could have between 15 and 20 percent of the market by 2011. Apple is complementing its iPhone products with the iPad, which released in April 2010.[17]

Research in Motion (RIM), a Canadian company focused on the e-mail segment of the mobile platform market, is experiencing solid success within its areas of focus. RIM has shown strong performance in the corporate e-mail market. It pioneered an effective user interface for this type of application, and it has become the standard cell phone for businesspeople in many organizations.

Palm was a pioneer in the mobile platform market, but other companies quickly overtook it. While the company introduced the innovative Palm Pre phone with a touchscreen and a slide-out keyboard in 2009, market share is likely to remain low for the company.

Standards Battles in Wireless Communications

The wireless communications market represents a strategic capability in many geographic areas. It is a huge market, and it is poised to become even larger as more countries build the infrastructure to communicate voice and data without cables. The demand for wireless telephone and data services is widespread: 4G wireless services can improve the productivity of individuals and businesses, enhance public safety, reduce energy consumption, and entertain as well as inform individuals.

Improving the coverage and performance of wireless networks is the focal point of a global standards war. European countries and companies have driven the adoption of several standards that covered prior generations of cell phone voice and data services. Standards such as GSM, GPRS, EDGE, and W-CDMA have become global standards. A U.S. company, Qualcomm, drove the adoption of its cdma2000 protocol, but with South Korea rather than the United States being the initial adopter of this protocol. Later the U.S. cell phone giant Verizon Wireless adopted the Qualcomm protocol. Subsequently, China and India also adopted the Qualcomm protocol.

However, some Chinese government and industry leaders launched extensive activities in China to develop a new proprietary protocol for a more powerful wireless technology, while also adopting the European and Qualcomm protocols.

It is significant that, in China, there are major initiatives to provide broadband wireless capabilities to hundreds of millions of people by the end of 2012. There are no comparable activities in the United States. While wireless communications is a strategic capability for U.S. businesses and consumers, there is no real vision and leadership in terms of how the United States can be the global leader in broadband wireless communications. The March 2010 National Broadband Plan from the Federal Communications Commission of the U.S. government is far less ambitious and limited than what the Chinese are already implementing and will not help the United States become a global leader in broadband wireless.

The United States is lagging in a number of geographic regions in the quality of broadband communications infrastructure, both wireless and wired. Cable TV customers and smart phone owners in Japan, South Korea, and parts of Europe have 3 or 5 or 10 times faster connections than are available to U.S. consumers.[18] The availability of high-bandwidth capabilities in the United States is slowed by the inertia of the carriers, which are highly focused on short-term profits.

Verizon, AT&T, T-Mobile, and to a lesser extent Sprint, are not driving the adoption of the higher-speed wireless standards aggressively enough to give the U.S. global leadership. These companies control the wireless airwaves, and the lack of competition protects them from pressure to provide faster bandwidth to their consumers. The result is a low level of service for the U.S. consumers and missed job opportunities. Essentially, wireless communications infrastructure in the United States is comparable to that in developing nations.

Little U.S.-Made Cell Phone Equipment

Wireless communications infrastructure equipment sold to the telecom providers and large companies are an area in which the United States has dramatically underperformed other countries, even though there has been technology leadership in the United States. The lack of strong wireless infrastructure equipment companies in the United States is indicative of the low level of emphasis in the United States on strategic communications capabilities. For example, Motorola's wireless infrastructure business is not a market share leader.

The leaders in the wireless infrastructure market are Ericsson, Huawei, Alcatel/Lucent, Nokia Siemens Networks, and ZTE. Huawei and ZTE are Chinese companies that have gained substantial market share rapidly. In fact, Huawei has become highly competitive in advanced cell phone technologies on a global basis. While Huawei has sold its systems based on cost leadership in the past, the present emphasis of the company is on providing better services and lower operating costs compared to its competitors.

With China having advanced cell phone technology in the near term, and with over 50 percent of the infrastructure being provided by Chinese companies, it is likely that Huawei will become the global market share leader in cell phone infrastructure equipment in the next year or two.

However, a few American companies are investing in next-generation wireless data and voice communications equipment. Intel has taken the initiative to promote WiMAX, a technology that provides the next generation of wireless data transmission speeds. Clearwire (a joint venture with Sprint) is establishing WiMAX infrastructures in Baltimore, Maryland, and Portland, Oregon, but it is unlikely that WiMAX will be more than a niche capability. It is likely that the equipment market for the next-generation mainstream cell phone technology, called LTE, will be dominated by non-U.S. companies.

By not having the appropriate emphasis on wireless communications, the United States does not have the high employment in wireless communications that it could have if it were the global leader. So it's not a surprise that the balance of trade for wireless is negative: the United States imports wireless handsets, as well as the necessary infrastructure equipment, from the Far East and Europe.

Another domino has fallen, with no major response from Washington. In reality, it is likely that Washington will place more emphasis on growing the peanut industry, via farm subsidies, than on wireless handsets in the next few years.

Semiconductors

The United States was the leader in the global semiconductor market until the late 1970s and early 1980s, when the Japanese took over leadership. The area of strength of the Japanese companies was in memory chips. The key memory product was invented by Intel.

However, poor financial returns in the early 1980s led the Japanese companies to reduce their expenditures in expanding manufacturing capacity in advanced semiconductor technology. The South Korean companies Samsung and Hynix (combination of the memory businesses of LG Electronics and Hyundai Electronics) saw an opportunity, made the investments, and won memory market share leadership.

Samsung, in particular, made large expenditures (almost $4 billion in 2009[19]) in expanding its manufacturing capacity to become the global market share leader in memory products.

A few U.S. memory chip companies remain, but they are struggling financially. Micron was a chronic money loser until the end of 2009. Another memory chip company called Spansion filed for bankruptcy protection (it is a joint venture between AMD and Fujitsu). IM Flash, a joint venture between Micron and Intel, also has not been profitable until recently. Micron is trying to link its memory chip activities with those of the Taiwanese vendors, specifically Nanya.

The U.S. semiconductor companies, however, have adapted to global semiconductor competition by developing leadership products such as microprocessors, as noted earlier. Intel, AMD, and IBM adopted a strategy of focusing on the most advanced type of chips and product areas where Asian competitors were weak.

Intel is the largest semiconductor company in the world because of its dominant position in microprocessors. Its revenues are almost twice as large as the second-largest semiconductor company, Samsung. The reason for the high revenues and high profits of Intel: strong leadership and control of 80 percent of the market for processors for computers.[20]

Intel also had a close relationship with Microsoft, which allowed Intel to have control over the processor architectures for the Microsoft operating systems software. The combination of Intel and Microsoft has been a key factor in the United States' continuing to dominate the computer industry and Intel's dominating the processor market. Another reason for Intel's success: its prices relate to the value of the end equipment, not its costs.

AMD has most of the remaining 20 percent of the processor market. Two U.S. companies—Intel and AMD—dominate the processor market for computing applications. IBM, Freescale, Texas Instruments, Analog Devices, and a few other companies also make processors, but only for niche applications.

Because U.S. firms created the integrated-circuit industry in the 1950s and still dominate the market for the most valuable type of chip, microprocessors, it is not surprising that most people assume American companies are the market share and technology leaders in the overall semiconductor industry. While U.S. companies dominate chip supply, manufacturing is done in Asia.

Furthermore, in the IC industry, the rates at which the United States is declining and China is consuming a high percentage of chips is shown in Figure 4.1.

In 2000, the United States consumed 31 percent of the worldwide market for semiconductors, and China 17 percent. In 2015, the United States will absorb 14 percent of the worldwide production while China will use almost 50 percent.

If China has the largest market segment, semiconductor companies that have close relationships with the equipment manufacturers in China will have competitive advantages. This does not augur well for U.S. companies in any high-tech sector.

FIGURE 4.1

IC Market by Geographic Region

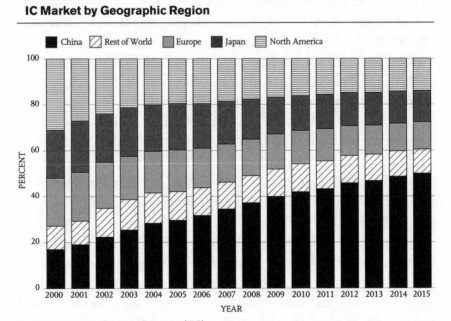

Source: International Business Strategies (IBS)

Semiconductors represent a key building block function of electronic systems. Leadership in semiconductors is a key factor in participation in many high-growth applications within the electronics industry. It is, consequently, critical for the United States to maintain leadership in technology and market share within key segments of the semiconductor industry if it is to control the supply chain of many electronics products in the future.

It is ironic that the United States supplies the brains of the electronics equipment, but other countries provide the electronics equipment. The U.S. companies make the brains, but others make the torso, arms, and legs. If U.S. companies were also assembling the equipment, they would gain a dominant percentage of the value of the equipment. It used to be this way. In the past, the semiconductor industry was characterized by vertical integration. Chip companies created the silicon wafers, etched the chips on the wafers, put the silicon slivers into packages, and tested the chips. And then they would insert the finished components into their computers, test equipment, data communications gear, or other end user products. Today, few chip companies remain fully vertically integrated.

While Intel, IBM, Texas Instruments (TI), and Micron retain most of the aspects of vertical integration, the U.S. semiconductor companies are primarily using wafers from the foundry vendors for most of their chips. Even TI, a $10 billion+ IC vendor,[21] uses wafers from foundry suppliers for its most advanced chips.

The wafer foundry vendor base is primarily in Taiwan. The Taiwan Semiconductor Manufacturing Company (TSMC) has almost 50 percent[22] of the pure-play wafer foundry market. TSMC is to silicon wafers what Saudi Arabia is to crude oil. Even Intel, with its wafer fabrication facilities in Arizona, New Mexico, and Oregon, relies on assembly and test facilities in the Far East.

In fact, the vast bulk of employment in the electronics industry is in the Far East, though most of the core technological foundation of the industry is concentrated in the United States. This is another example of how America has failed to gain the full value of the employment and exports after establishing technological leadership.

The foundry base for global chip supply should be in the United States. While the United States set up a strategic petroleum reserve (SPR) to hoard supplies of crude oil in the event of embargoes or other supply chain disruptions from the overseas suppliers of crude oil, no one has recognized the strategic importance of having domestic suppliers of semiconductor wafers. Those silver disks are worth their weight in gold and are more valuable than tanks or submarines.

The U.S. semiconductor industry is expected to remain strong on a global basis, but it is leaning a bit. The domino tilted in the early 1980s, but it recovered through the innovative leadership of corporations such as Intel. IBM also contributed to the recovery of the U.S. semiconductor industry through its Common Platform initiatives.

But the American semiconductor industry must be protected so that it doesn't fall.

Aircraft Manufacturing

Boeing and McDonnell Douglas had dominant market positions in the commercial aircraft market in the 1960s, 1970s, and 1980s. The emergence of the European consortium Airbus, however, caused McDonnell Douglas to weaken, and the company merged with Boeing in 1997.[23] Although Boeing has had some down phases, the company is currently strong in the global air transport market.

While Boeing is increasing its level of outsourcing, it is unlikely that the competitive position of the company will be challenged (other than by Airbus) in the next decade. The employment base in air transport at Boeing is not large compared to the total working population in the United States, but the industry continues to be strategic and generate exports. Indeed, Boeing is one of America's strongest exporters.

However, China will emerge as a builder of aircraft in the future. The country is undertaking a range of projects to gain access to and develop commercial air transport technologies; for example, it is building a made-in-China jumbo jet.[24]

Defense Industry

The U.S. defense industry continues to be the global leader, with large budgets in many areas of electronics. There will be no major challenger to the U.S. military in advanced technologies in the next decade. There are U.S. exports of military equipment, but many of the exports involve offset agreements.

Agriculture

The United States continues to be an exporter of many types of agricultural products. With increased demand for crops to support energy production, such as corn for ethanol, the U.S. agricultural industry is in a growth mode.

With its large land area, fertile soil, and access to a large water supply, the U.S. agricultural industry has been an exporter for decades. The United States should continue to be a net exporter of agricultural products.

However, a potential problem is that there are increased purchases of U.S. farmlands by foreigners—specifically, Asians. This is in stark contrast to land management in China, where all land is owned by the government. While it is not recommended that the U.S. government buy land or prohibit its purchase by foreigners, it is important to understand the strategic value of land and agriculture.

Pharmaceuticals

The United States is also strong in pharmaceuticals, but it has tough competitors in Europe and Japan. American pharmaceutical companies have a high market share and strong brand recognition in prescription and over-the-counter drugs as well as toiletries. However, U.S. companies such as Procter & Gamble and others that have established strong overseas operations increasingly rely on manufacturing outside of the United States, including in China.

Summary

While it is important not to underestimate the strengths of U.S. corporations, it is also critical to understand the reasons for the weaknesses in many industries. In many cases, the competitiveness of U.S. companies has weakened because subsidies have been provided to competitors in other geographic regions. In addition, preferential treatment is given to local vendors in local markets in a number of countries. The role of government is to ensure that their corporations (their wealth creation armies) do not face large competitive barriers.

My analysis of the activities of the U.S. corporations shows that success is often based on the willingness to change business models in response to competitive pressures. The willingness to change business models is more common in new industries, such as electronics, than it is in older industries, such as automobiles. New business models are also more readily adopted by new companies than by the mature companies.

It is critical to be low cost compared to competitors, which generally requires flexibility in manufacturing strategies. Companies with rigid manufacturing strategies and high costs inevitably experience large losses. So it is important to use offshore manufacturing capacity to be price competitive, but it is equally important for U.S. companies to produce enough exports to offset these imports.

American corporations have not been regarded as assets that not only protect local markets but also effectively gain high market share globally. The proper role of corporations in the twenty-first century has not been understood. Too few citizens and policymakers have recognized that the aggregate output has to support both local demand and global demand.

The large expenditures made to import manufactured products such as automobiles and consumer products, as well as commodities, such as oil and gas, have not been matched by large and thriving exports. Instead, the U.S. government's industrial strategy has been to stimulate consumption for short-term satisfaction.

The United States has gone from an environment (30 or 40 years ago) of having dominant corporations in many strategic industries to being the leader in a relatively narrow range of industries. As we have seen, U.S. companies are market leaders in computers, software, semiconductors, air transport, and other areas. Yes, the United States is also strong in data networking and large storage devices, but these markets are small compared to automobiles and consumer electronics. In addition, the markets for many of these high-complexity electronic products outside of the United States are relatively modest, limiting the export leverage. Also, with the manufacturing of most of the electronics equipment for most applications being outside of the United States, the trade balance value of data networking and storage devices is low.

Many critics say it is impossible for manufacturers in developed countries to compete against firms in lower-wage areas. But there are ways for manufacturers to do so. For example, camera, printer, copier, and scanner maker Canon of Japan is an example of a company's taking the automation approach. It has a high global market share in digital cameras, camcorders, and copy machines. Canon has a strong CEO who is committed to maintaining manufacturing in Japan as well as in other locations to maintain high quality. To support the growth opportunities in China, Canon is also establishing automated manufacturing factories in China.

Leadership in some sectors is one area of significant strength for the U.S. economy and its companies. While the weakening of U.S. banks after the 2008 Wall Street meltdown makes investments in capital-intensive areas more difficult, a reviving stock market and a recovering venture capitalist industry offer some hope.

The United States is characterized by strong entrepreneurs in a number of key areas, but many lack focus on how to utilize their strengths to increase the wealth of the country. In reality, if there are too many players in any specific domestic market, they can become too weak to compete effectively in global markets. This type of problem is a characteristic of a number of Japanese companies—they have become too weak to compete effectively in global markets because of their intense home market competition.

Government policies remain an issue. The United States spends tens of billions of dollars each year to build advanced military aircraft, submarines, and other weapons, but it allocates a relative pittance of the federal budget to improving the wireless communications infrastructure in the United States. The priorities of spending support in the United States are based on legacy priorities and lobbying activities rather than on the need to make the corporations the conquering forces for the generation of wealth.

The industrial base in the United States has weakened significantly in the last 30 to 40 years on a global competitiveness basis. The weakening will continue unless there are major changes in industrial policies. If the U.S. industrial base weakens, the wealth of the United States will decline even further.

5

THE ROLE OF GOVERNMENT IN U.S. INDUSTRY

SINCE THE CIVIL WAR, the growth of the U.S. economy has been based on the successful exploitation of a range of natural resources. Fertile soil, millions of acres of trees, numerous rivers, and an enormous supply of coal have provided the ideal environment for the growth of American corporations. In addition, public support of primary and secondary education, as well as government funding of land grant colleges, helped a hungry and ambitious population to use the natural resources to build a strong industrial base. As a result, U.S. corporations became global leaders in a number of market segments.

Government policies were generally pro-industry to help build national wealth. Industry created jobs, which provided tax revenues, which provided resources to create more jobs and improve the standard of living for its citizens. The role of government also included the support of the military, which in some cases provided funding for corporations. Defense Department–funded research provided at least part of the foundation for several industries, including nuclear power, integrated circuits, and jet aircraft engines.

A major part of the United States' wealth was built on the success of the U.S. corporations' access to raw materials and freedom from burdensome regulation. Manufacturers in this country enjoyed almost unlimited access to the coal, iron ore, copper, alumina, wood, crude oil, and other natural resources, as long as they paid the property owners. Railroads were given land grants to reward their expansion plans throughout the West.

American financial institutions were able to become global giants too. The country's banks, insurance companies, money management firms, and securities brokerages were the envy of the rest of the world. They created scores of innovations that helped to propel the rest of the country. Everything from money market checking accounts and mutual funds to the venture capital that funded Apple, Google, and other economic powerhouses can be attributed to the wizards of Wall Street.

And when the captains of industry went too far, creating great public pain, government stepped in to limit their activities. Scandals in food preparation, polluted rivers and land, and repeated boom and bust economic cycles triggered new regulations beginning early in the twentieth century. Sometimes the new regulations were relatively effective over the long term (food and drugs) while other regulations were circumvented by ever more ingenious creativity left unfettered by weak regulators.

Prior financial calamities in the early 1900s and the Great Depression of the late 1920s through the 1930s led to the creation of the Federal Reserve Board to regulate banks, the Federal Deposit Insurance Corporation to protect bank depositors, and the Securities and Exchange Commission to regulate stock and bond brokerages. Deregulation of industries was in vogue in the 1980s, leading to the breakup of the AT&T telephone monopoly, increased competition among the airlines, and fewer controls over financial services firms. The act by Congress to reverse the key provisions of the Depression-era Glass-Steagall Act, which separated the banking and securities industries, was heavily promoted by Republicans and signed by President Bill Clinton in 1999. Less than a decade later Wall Street collapsed, pushing major banks to the brink of collapse. Only a rescue by the U.S. government prevented a financial Armageddon.

The meltdown of the financial services industry in 2007 and 2008 made a number of these companies a large drain on the economy. The American International Group (AIG) bailout cost the taxpayers $180 billion+ in loans.[1] The cost of saving Citigroup required an investment of $25 billion and a guarantee on the toxic assets. Fortunately, the U.S. government's $45 billion investment in the Bank of America (BoA) to help the BoA absorb Merrill Lynch and recover from other toxic investments turned a profit—the bank bought back the preferred stock invested by the U.S. Treasury in December 2009 and sold stock purchase warrants for more than $1.5 billion in March 2010.[2]

The $700 billion Troubled Asset Relief Program (TARP)[3] has been used to solve a variety of problems within financial institutions with mixed results. While the financial institutions are recovering, several are only beginning to repay the federal government for the government's loans and equity investments. The ultimate cost to the taxpayers remains to be seen.[4]

The financial crisis in the United States has required that draconian measures be taken, and there will be the need to pay back the money borrowed to fund the programs. Since it is unlikely that the government or the politicians will have the ability to reduce government programs or otherwise economize, the only source of cash to pay down the debt will be through higher taxes. Increasing taxes on the high wage earners has always been the typical answer to this challenge. However, that is not a good answer because the high wage earners are also the investors who have stimulated the growth of the economy in the past. It is not a good idea to reduce their ability to help fund the next Google, Apple, or Cisco.

Obama at the Steering Wheel

With its latest policies, the U.S. government has become the largest share owner of the U.S. automobile industry in addition to one of the largest stockholders of the financial services companies. Interesting times. No one is happy with a U.S. president at the steering wheel.

It is not uncommon for socialist and communist government agencies to own businesses or portions of businesses. Even some European governments also own either a stake or controlling interest in corporations. For example, France and Spain own a piece of the European Aeronautic Defence and Space Company N.V., the builder of the Airbus commercial aircraft that competes against Boeing. Indeed, many non-U.S. airlines are either partially or completely owned by government—Air France, for example, is partially owned by the French government. The government of Singapore also has ownership stakes in a number of industries, and while success to date has been good, the government has very tight control over the population of Singapore. That model would not be successful in the United States because of the traditions of freedom enjoyed by the American people. Can you imagine trying to ban chewing gum in the United States, as the Singaporean government did for 12 years?

While government ownership can subsidize industries considered to be strategic, there are relatively few examples of governments being successful in managing businesses over many decades. Political interference will prevent an enterprise from focusing on maximizing profit. There is a need to balance the responsibilities to the employees and the shareholders when the government is an owner and the owners are in one sense the employees. In many cases, capitalism places too much emphasis on the shareholders. Socialism, on the other hand, tends to place too much emphasis on the employees.

The United States is clearly migrating from a capitalistic philosophy to a socialistic philosophy but without the strategies in place to build new industries and expand employment within these industries. While the government ownership of equity stakes in financial services firms and automakers is supposed to be temporary, it has established a precedent. Also, the Obama administration and the Democratic Party are committed to national health care coverage, which almost certainly will mean more government involvement in the funding and management of the medical establishment.

There has to be a new philosophy that balances the relationships between capitalism and socialism. The new approach should be based on one key metric: the growth of the wealth of the country over an extended timeframe.

Government should be supportive of corporations and ensure that there is a level playing field in the global competitive environment. The right kind of financial incentives (tax breaks, R&D support, and infrastructure investments) and more effective trade policies can empower U.S. companies to better compete. A problem, however, is that the U.S. government has little understanding of the global competitive environment. Instead, it is focused almost exclusively on local issues, the factors that enable reelection.

Meanwhile, U.S. companies find that their access to certain overseas markets is restricted or essentially closed, and the U.S. government has not taken the required actions to protect its corporations from operating in situations where they are at strong competitive disadvantages due to unfair trade practices.

Reducing the Cost of Doing Business

A key problem in the United States is the lack of mechanisms to control the increases in corporations' nonproduction costs. Increased taxes to support increasing legions of government employees, higher taxes to pay for universal health care, and higher taxes to pay the deficits accumulated during the period from 2000 to the present hinder the ability of U.S. companies to be competitive in world markets. Corporate profits drained to pay higher taxes will further deplete research spending and diminish the ardor for new product development and introductions.

The potential cost of universal health care coverage is particularly frightening. Providing universal health care coverage in the United States not only will increase the operating costs of companies but it will also add to the government's deficits. After many years of watching government employees, especially elected officials, enjoy superior health care benefits, the population now insists that it should also have comparable health care coverage. Unfortunately, better health care will result in the higher cost of government.

Increased spending on social benefits and social programs will deny that funding to improve road, air, and rail infrastructure in the United States, unless additional deficit spending is approved. Improving the transportation infrastructure in this country, especially mass transit, provides substantial benefits to employers. The increased efficiency of the working population is a proven benefit of the taxpayer-financed low-cost transit systems in Europe. If taxes support the increased cost of operating the government and public welfare programs, the result will be that the country becomes more inefficient in the use of its people resources and other assets. More tax dollars going into welfare programs means fewer tax dollars going into the building of corporations and the generating of actual wealth.

The United States is operating with short-term metrics. Addressing the current economic downturn through increased consumption is not a long-term solution to the country's problems. Indeed, there have been no major initiatives to address the long-term factors that allow exports to be increased and the balance-of-payments deficits to be reduced.

The balance of payments is a key metric for evaluating the ability to build wealth over the long term and to determine the ability of a country to compete against global competitors. The recent TARP and stimulus programs do not help the United States reduce its trade deficits or otherwise improve its competitiveness in global markets.

The lack of long-term strategies for reducing operating costs, building employment, and stimulating exports has resulted in the disappearance of a number of manufacturing sectors in the United States, such as textiles, clothing, shoes, and television sets. The predominant trend for U.S. consumers is to buy lower-cost products from corporations based in other geographic regions because those manufacturers have been willing to make large expenditures in manufacturing capacity and take long-term perspectives on the financial returns. While it is important to allow consumers to buy the lowest-cost and best goods, it is critical to have strategies to compensate for the abundance of imports with an equal measure of exports.

The U.S. market is open to foreign companies, and in many cases there are low barriers to participation in the U.S. market. The trade barriers that have been established are oftentimes due to the pressures from special-interest groups rather than from strategic industries. Duties imposed on imported tires in September 2009 were put in place because of union pressures rather than pressures from the tire companies. A similar situation has occurred in steel piping, which accounts for a very small percentage of steel imports but nevertheless has resulted in a substantial amount of trade friction. The markets in other countries, however, are not as open as in the United States, and as a result, the local companies are able to build a high market share in their home market and use this strength to gain a high market share in the United States.

When the United States was the dominant vendor in global markets, it was able to take a magnanimous approach to allowing competitors to have open access to the U.S. market and to protect their local markets.

In the present environment, in which the U.S. corporations have weakened dramatically in many industries, the United States needs to take much more proactive approaches to ensure that its corporations are competing on an equal level with competitors in both the United States and other countries.

Industrial Decisions Affected by Politics

The level of long-term planning for strategic industries in the United States by leaders has been and continues to be low, but there have been some exceptions—namely, those clearly identified with national security. Politicians have protected military contractors by providing them with generous contracts and barriers against foreign military equipment. The barriers have also prevented the U.S. military from being held hostage by a foreign government if a vital piece of equipment were withheld. And as part of a long-term plan to develop alternative energy sources as a defense against Arab oil embargoes or other disruptions to imported oil flows, they also established a strategic petroleum reserve (SPR) to provide oil refiners with raw materials. Unfortunately, only the SPR has been funded appropriately—solar, geothermal, and other nascent energy sources have not received enough support.

The lack of top-level strategic vision within U.S. government organizations is partly related to the election process for the politicians. Presidents and other senior elected officials focus on what can be accomplished before the next election. A key factor enabling the reelection of politicians (a high percentage of politicians are reelected) is that of obtaining federal funding for new projects for the politicians' local constituents. This focus on "pork-barrel politics" has a higher priority than the long-term strength of the economy. The redistribution of tax funds sought by most politicians is driven by their motivation to gain votes instead of building long-term employment and having a positive balance of trade.

There has also been and continues to be a lack of deep business and technology expertise among the politicians in Washington and in the state legislatures. Consequently, political leaders in the United States generally underestimate the strength of the country's global competitors. The leaders fail to realize, or refuse to acknowledge, the extent of the direct and indirect support provided by other governments to their own countries' companies. The paucity of spending on the U.S. infrastructure in recent years is an important example.

A low percentage of the taxes collected in the United States has been used to strengthen the country's infrastructure. This is a shortsighted budgeting practice because an efficient and modern infrastructure can make a country's companies and workers more efficient. America's shortfalls in infrastructure investments are in direct contrast to China's spending. China makes very large expenditures to enhance its infrastructures and makes very low expenditures on welfare and other social programs. While the infrastructure in China has remained inferior to that of the United States through the early years of the twenty-first century, the infrastructure in China will be much stronger by 2020.

In fact, U.S. infrastructure maintenance and improvement have been underfunded for decades. Bridge repair is underfunded and behind schedule in most states. The 2007 collapse of a bridge in Minnesota due to inadequate maintenance and poor design is one example of a larger national problem.[5] Without major changes, the infrastructure in the United States will continue to disintegrate.

Until the 2007 and 2008 bailouts of the financial institutions and automobile industry, governmental and political meddling in corporate activities was actively discouraged. It is ironic that a key motivation for the automobile industry bailout was to protect employment and the industry's pension obligations. All of a sudden government meddling in private industry was applauded.

Prior government support has been usually narrowly targeted on specific areas that were viewed as politically expedient. The reality of the environment in the United States is that unless there is an impact on the tax base or campaign funding, the politicians do not take an active leadership role in business issues.

For example, support for alternative energy programs waxes and wanes based on the price and availability of gasoline. Only when the price is high or fuel is scarce do politicians respond with announcements about new programs to develop energy independence. Stimulants for establishing alternate fuel sources, such as solar energy and windmills, began more than 30 years ago in the wake of the first Arab oil embargo. The solar energy market provides some employment, but there are no large exports to date as the market remains small. Ironically, the recent boom in windmill development in the United States will increase imports since one of the major equipment suppliers is Vestas, a Danish company. And while solar energy installations reduce our use of imported oil, the benefits have been negligible so far. Additional government support of the solar energy industry will have a low impact on oil imports for the next few decades.

In the United States, industries such as agriculture are protected due to the senatorial power structure. Sparsely populated states such as Iowa, Montana, Idaho, Wyoming, Kansas, and Nebraska have a disproportionate amount of political clout in Washington, D.C.—they have more senators than the four high-tech states (Massachusetts, California, Texas, and North Carolina). With agriculture being a key industry within these low-population states, their politicians promote and protect agriculture to be reelected. Also, pro-farming bills are passed, such as those mandating an increased use of ethanol, without full understanding of the longer-term implications on the cost of food and cost of energy. The skyrocketing cost of corn in 2007 was directly attributed to the diversion of millions of bushels of the grain to create ethanol.

In the United States, the reality is that the agricultural industry, which is concentrated in the Midwest, has had more political power than the electronics industries concentrated in California and Massachusetts. The exception is electronics for the defense and aerospace industries, which are located in many states because of political clout. It is no accident that a lot of NASA operations are in Texas, the home state of Lyndon Johnson, a powerful senator and later president who was a champion of the space agency as well as a hungry consumer of space agency pork.

California and Massachusetts have historically had a strong Democratic Party presence in Washington and in their local legislatures. The Democratic Party has not supported the electronics industry to the same extent that it has supported the automotive industry because high-tech companies are unlikely to have strong trade union representation. With few exceptions, trade unions have not been able to recruit high-tech workers because their pay and benefits have been already high. Without the political clout of votes to protect its self-interest, high taxes are levied on the electronics industry. The most onerous taxes are usually the state levies based on the value of property. The cost of an electronics industry factory is typically $4 billion or more, due to the expensive equipment and precise specifications required to make chips. The tax that is placed on assets (equipment) by municipalities in California is one of the reasons that manufacturing of electronics products has left the Golden State.

Due to the lack of unions and the politicians who support them, changing employment patterns within the U.S. electronics industries has both helped and harmed the American economy. The outsourcing of manufacturing to the Far East by U.S. electronics companies was easy to do because labor does not wield the same level of political power in the Far East that it does in the United States. The electronics industry and corporations were able to shut manufacturing facilities with little financial penalty. While there was the ability to gain access to low-cost goods, there was a reduction in the manufacturing base in the United States.

Contrast the wholesale departure of electronics assembly in the United States with the situation in Europe. In France, Germany, and elsewhere, the costs of shutting down manufacturing facilities are high. This barrier to exit has kept a number of high-cost facilities open, producing goods that have not been cost competitive. The union support and extensive regulations protecting manufacturing jobs have decimated the consumer electronics corporations in Europe.

The lessons of the demise of the California and French high-tech manufacturing centers are clear—there is a need to balance the cost of manufacturing, employment, taxes, imports, and exports. So the U.S. government, the unions, and the industries have to work together to devise an industrial policy that does not throw good money after bad. It is not appropriate to promote employment of low-skill, high-volume factory work in the United States, but it is important to promote the building of high-technology industries that provide the combination of high employment and large exports.

A paradox in the United States is the perception that as long as an industry is strong and very profitable, it doesn't need protection by the government. Also, companies within most industries want limited government involvement because the executives at most companies believe that all government does is impose restrictions and add costs. Furthermore, many industry officials naively believe their competitors in other geographic regions share the same beliefs. However, in many cases, this assumption is a major error because a wide range of subsidies is provided to support corporations in many countries.

The lack of understanding by U.S. government officials and corporations of global competitive threats is partly due to the heritage of the United States as being a leader. Most of the time companies in other geographic regions have been the followers in technology, so the officials in most U.S. companies are not familiar with being the underdog.

When industries in the United States become decimated—no profitability, declining market share, low revenues, and low employment levels—the political power of these industries becomes weak. Elected officials don't pay a lot of attention to companies with little to no money and/or votes to donate to political campaigns.

The appliance industry is likely to be one of the next areas where the U.S. corporations will lose competitiveness. The wave of South Korean and Chinese manufacturers of air conditioners, washing machines, and refrigerators with advanced features and low prices has proven to be a huge challenge to domestic manufacturers. The industry has already consolidated—Whirlpool has acquired Maytag, Amana, Jenn-Air, KitchenAid, and other brands in an attempt to achieve economies of scale. General Electric, built by inventor Thomas Edison, has attempted to sell its appliance division, with companies outside of the United States as the most probable buyers.

When foreign buyers purchase businesses in the United States, many of the employees are initially kept, but over time, employment is reduced and the factories are closed. Zenith was once the largest manufacturer of televisions, but its factories and employees are long gone. The brand lives on, though, as a product line of the South Korean company LG Electronics. Another example of the downfall of a U.S. high-tech company is AT&T's Lucent equipment business, which is now controlled by a French company. The brands continue, but not the factories or the jobs.

A number of countries, including the United States, have projected a philosophy of supporting free trade, but in reality, there is no such thing as entirely unlimited access to a country. Many of the decisions regarding trade in the United States are based on the effectiveness of the lobbying activities of the representatives of industries and local communities. The political power of the states, as well as the communities that businesses are located in, has had a major impact on the decisions made by U.S. politicians.

The United States lacks a coherent approach to building strategic industries that will contribute to national wealth on a long-term basis. Efforts to provide employment are focused on short-term expediency when an election is near. Americans are too busy enjoying all of the low-cost goods from China to complain to their senators and members of Congress about the devastating impact of our trade imbalance.

A fundamental belief in the United States is that the strongest competitors will win by having the best products and lowest costs. This is an appropriate philosophy if there is open competition. The reality is that other countries do not have the same openness to business and consumer buying patterns. The result is that the competitive environment is not a level playing field for U.S. companies.

The United States is also operating in an environment where past success is considered to be indicative of future success within many industries. The reality is that many of the business concepts that were effective in the past are no longer applicable within the global competitive environment.

Weak Support for Capital-Intensive Industries

A key characteristic of U.S. industry in the twenty-first century is its low level of expenditures on capital-intensive factories. There are exceptions, such as the aerospace industry, but even Boeing increased its level of outsourcing for the 787 commercial jet rather than making capital-intensive investments to enable its manufacture in the United States.

The reason for the low expenditures in capital-intensive facilities is concern over the financial impact of these facilities operating at low levels of capacity utilization. Short-term financial metrics are given priority over long-term strategic implications because of shareholder and lender priorities.

In addition to electronics, companies in the heavy industries in the United States, such as steel, are also underinvesting compared to competitors in other geographic regions.

Examples of industries in which U.S. companies are not making the levels of investment required to remain competitive on a global basis include the following.

Wafer Fabrication Facilities for Semiconductor Supply

Within the United States, the only American company that has aggressive wafer fab capacity expansion strategies is Intel. The company is also building wafer fab capacity outside of the United States, with advanced facilities in Israel and Ireland. Note that the action of the European Commission (EC) to impose a fine of more than $1.4 billion[6] on Intel is likely to reduce future investments by Intel in Europe.

In addition to the already mentioned New York State wafer fabrication facility being built with financial support by the Abu Dhabi oil kingdom, Samsung has built an advanced facility[7] in Austin, Texas. It is, however, unlikely that Samsung will build another wafer fab facility in the United States.

IM Flash, a joint venture between Intel and a memory chip company in Idaho named Micron, was planning to build an advanced wafer fabrication facility in Singapore. However, this facility has been postponed due to the pricing pressures in its market. In fact, the long-term financial viability of IM Flash is unclear.

IBM has an advanced wafer factory in Fishkill, New York, but it is not likely to increase capacity. In fact, there is the strong possibility that IBM will try to sell this facility.

Not only are there relatively few factories in the United States that can make the most advanced semiconductors, earlier-generation factories will be closing over the next 5 to 10 years. For example, National has announced the closing of a fabrication facility in Austin, Texas. The U.S. semiconductor industry essentially is adopting the outsourcing business model for wafer supply. Imagine ExxonMobil saying it wasn't interested in exploring for crude oil anymore and would instead buy all of its requirements from other companies.

Roughly 80 percent of the wafer supplies for U.S. companies other than Intel and AMD will be from Taiwan. The balance will be primarily imported from Singapore and South Korea.

Consider the myriad risks and vulnerabilities for the U.S. economy. Any major political or other problem in Taiwan, such as a major earthquake, could cripple the U.S. semiconductor and electronics industries. When China succeeds in its unification plans with Taiwan, China will control the supply of wafers to most of the U.S. semiconductor industry.

While the United States is highly concerned with the supply of oil and other natural resources, these resources are much more fragmented from a geographic supply perspective than are wafer foundries. Wafer supply for the American electronics industry should be under the control of the U.S. corporations. This is an area where the United States needs to make the required expenditures to gain global market share leadership.

There is a lesson to be learned about how the Taiwanese companies came to dominate this capital-intensive industry. To encourage the building of wafer fab facilities for the support of local wafer supply as well as for participation in the global foundry market, a number of incentives have been provided by the Taiwanese government to local companies. As a result, there is large wafer fab capacity in Taiwan.

Incentives are being provided to chip makers by some of the states in the United States. In addition to the New York support of Globalfoundries, Texas is helping Samsung, while Arizona, New Mexico, and Oregon are contributing to various Intel projects. The problem is the limited scope of the states' vision: these efforts are attempts to provide local employment and ultimately tax revenue rather than being part of a comprehensive strategy of having a domestic wafer supply.

The United States has the technology, financial resources, and market demand to warrant expanding its wafer fabrication capacity, but it is taking a passive approach to doing so. The result is its increasing dependence on external suppliers, primarily those in Taiwan. With the need to import wafers, there will be a negative balance of trade as well as a loss of employment for the United States. There will also not be the employment base that would be possible if the U.S. semiconductor industry were self-sufficient from a wafer supply perspective.

The United States has the technology base to be the leader in the manufacturing of the wafers needed by the electronics industry, but there are no incentives (similar to those in other countries) to set up the manufacturing facilities.

Flat-Panel Displays for Televisions and Computers

As noted in an earlier chapter, flat-panel displays are almost exclusively manufactured in Asia. Many flat-panel display factories are in Japan. Sharp is collaborating with Toshiba and Sony on a new liquid crystal display (LCD) manufacturing facility. Panasonic will build an advanced-generation facility, in collaboration with Hitachi and Canon. Sony will also continue to collaborate with Samsung on expanding its LCD manufacturing capacity.

BOE Technology, with the support of the Beijing government, is committing $4 billion[8] to a new LCD facility in China. Samsung, LG Electronics, and Sharp are also committing multiple billions of dollars each to setting up new LCD facilities in China.

No U.S. company or government agency has made a commitment to the manufacturing capacity for flat-panel displays because the financial returns have the potential for high risk. There are also no commitments to flat-panel display manufacturing in Europe either.

It is understandable to be afraid of the financial risks. As display technologies become more complex, the construction cost of a new factory will be in excess of $5 billion. Consequently, the number of companies with the financial resources to build these new factories will be small.

One of the few examples of a company with the financial wherewithal and courage is Samsung of South Korea. That has made the company a strong contender for market share leadership in flat-panel displays and in other capital-intensive industries.

The supply of flat panels will be split between Taiwan, South Korea, and China in the next decade. While the strategic value of display technology is not as high as that of semiconductor wafer supply, the flat-panel displays are another example of a failure to take action to reduce a coming flood of imports, as well as an opportunity to build employment.

It is important to note that missing the LCD production wave also means losing the opportunity to gain important knowledge about large-scale flat-panel display manufacturing. If this knowledge base is not continuously updated, there is the potential for a loss of global competitiveness in other electronics technologies as well. If a generation of technology is missed, it becomes very difficult to build facilities in the more advanced technologies.

In addition to the Asian challenge in capital-intensive industries, there are signs that other aspects of the high-tech industry also are vulnerable. While the United States is a bastion of strength in software- and Internet-centric companies, such as Microsoft, Google, Oracle, Yahoo!, and VMware, Asian competition is looming in this sector as well.

It is significant that the Chinese search engine Baidu has higher market share in China than Google. Learn the following lessons from this startling development: (1) Even though new concepts and technologies are developed in the United States, they are emulated in other geographic regions within short timeframes. (2) The strength of global competitors is increasing, even in an area that many thought would be dominated by U.S. companies for generations.

The key challenge for the United States is to build up its employment base in highly skilled, low-capital-intensive industries rapidly enough to compensate for the decline in the high-capital-intensive industries. In addition, consider some segments of the capital-intensive industries as being strategic and stimulate the required investments.

Outsourcing of Manufacturing

The electronics companies in the United States, Japan, and Europe reduced costs in the 1970s and 1980s by hiring other companies to assemble products for them or setting up company-owned assembly facilities in the Far East. These facilities gave access to low-cost labor, but in many cases, the facilities were small and relatively inefficient.

The next phase in the quest for lower costs was to transfer the company-owned manufacturing facilities to contract manufacturers such as Solectron and Flextronics. Then the large brand companies (HP, IBM, Dell, and others) subcontracted the assembly services to the acquiring companies. In most cases, the smaller facilities were shut down and the manufacturing was transferred to large centralized facilities.

Consolidating work into massive facilities provided the contract manufacturers with huge economies of scale, especially with many of the large facilities being established in China. By outsourcing manufacturing, the U.S. companies also did not have to make expenditures in a new generation of high-cost electronics assembly equipment. So outsourcing helped them avoid more capital investments as well as higher labor costs.

There was a general acceptance of the concept that a large facility in the Far East with low-cost assembly workers as well as low-cost overhead could be more efficient than smaller facilities that were spread over many geographic regions.

The setting up of the large capital-intensive manufacturing facilities resulted in high revenue growth for contract manufacturers such as Solectron and Flextronics.

A key characteristic of Solectron, which was one of the early contract manufacturers, was to have product quality that was comparable to that which could be obtained from the Japanese manufacturers. The Japanese manufacturers were the global leaders in quality. In addition to having quality that was comparable to the quality of the products of the Japanese companies, Solectron also was low cost, which gave competitive advantages to the customers of Solectron. The capabilities of Solectron and smaller companies were some of the factors that resulted in the weakening of the competitiveness of some of the Japanese electronics companies.

The transfer of production facilities to the contract manufacturers enabled the U.S. and European corporations to focus on product design, especially the design of products that would be inexpensive to produce. The equipment produced by the U.S. electronics equipment companies using the contract manufacturers was competitive in cost, quality, and features on a global basis.

The next phase was the dramatic growth of the Taiwanese contract manufacturers as designers as well as assemblers. While Flextronics has acquired Solectron and remains competitive, there has been a significant weakening of the market share of the non-Taiwanese contract manufacturers.

The Taiwanese contract manufacturers have low overhead and highly efficient manufacturing facilities. In many cases, these facilities are located in the low-cost regions of China. The result of the migration of assembly facilities to the Far East was to reduce the employment of assembly workers in the United States as well as contribute to the demise of the support infrastructures around the manufacturing facilities that were located in the United States. The support infrastructures included the equipment maintenance support as well as the engineers and technicians who were experts in their respective fields. These invaluable capabilities have been dissipated.

Also, as the assembly operations have become more complex and the capital equipment expenditure requirements for the new generations of technology have increased, it is not likely that new manufacturing facilities will be located in the United States or Europe. As a result, the percentage of employees of U.S. high-tech companies that are located in the United States will continue to decline.

There continues to be relatively strong manufacturing technologies in Japan, but it is likely that these skills will dissipate over the next 5 to 15 years too, as there is the increased use of low-cost facilities in China and other low-cost regions. There are, however, exceptions such as Canon, which is trying to protect its technology base in Japan. As noted previously, Canon has set up highly automated manufacturing facilities with tight control over the product quality.

The outsourcing of manufacturing has been necessary for the U.S. electronics equipment companies to remain cost competitive, but there is also the need to stimulate other industries to provide growth of employment in order to offset the losses of employment from the outsourcing. Coordinated planning based on a long-term vision of employment opportunities is required.

It is significant that companies such as IBM, which had global leadership in manufacturing technologies in the past, have migrated away from manufacturing to emphasizing design services and software development. Although manufacturing of complex systems was an area of major competitive strength for IBM up through the 1990s, most of the manufacturing facilities that IBM had in the United States have since been shut. While IBM has maintained a large employee base, a high percentage of the employment is outside of the United States. It can be claimed that the U.S. electronics industry has a viable long-term approach to achieving sustainability by migrating to software and services development, with manufacturing capabilities and materials technologies supported by the contract manufacturers. However, there is a huge risk in pursuing this strategy because it depends on access to large manufacturing capacity offering low-cost production and enough competition to keep the manufacturing costs from the Far East, including China, low.

If monopolies occur and competition disappears, U.S. companies will have little control over the prices of the services they are buying. Higher-cost products will result in a lot of unhappy U.S. consumers. The area of concern regarding the potential concentration of supply is in the capital-intensive industries.

The Support Infrastructures around Core Industries

Most industries, including electronics and automobiles, have large support structures around the core industries. Steel, wire, tires, batteries, and other crucial parts of an automobile are not made by GM, Ford, or Honda. The vendors of these components and services support local communities to a much larger degree than their core customers, the original equipment manufacturers.

Building support infrastructures around core industries can take decades, and it represents an extension of technology and employment to the core industry. Automobiles, electronics, aircraft, appliances, and other large manufactured products have established large support industries around them. As noted before, the head count in the support industries can be four to five times that in the core industry. As the manufacturing base of the core industries declines, the requirements for the support industries are also reduced, with a loss of employment.

There is the underlying view by venture capitalists and others in the United States that by moving up the value chain, new revenue streams can be generated that are much larger than the revenues from selling hardware. The best example is the cell phone industry, where the revenues recorded by the telephone carriers Verizon, AT&T, Sprint, T-Mobile, and others are much higher than the revenues of their hardware partners. Or consider the video game business—the games are more valuable than the console. It is the old story of the men's razors— the blade business is more valuable than the razor business.

However, what most venture capitalists and others forget is that to obtain value for the content in the games, there is the need to establish a large base of hardware. The strategies of the game console companies, such as Nintendo, Sony, and Microsoft, have been to lose money on hardware to obtain high revenues and high profits from software.

An example of the importance of the hardware platform: prior to the establishment of an installed base of personal computers, there was not a large market for the operating systems and application software, such as those provided by Microsoft.

Once the base of personal computers was built, a large market developed for software.

Without access to the operating system software, a large installed base of personal computers could not be established. The *combination* of the software and hardware capabilities resulted in a large market for personal computers.

Apple is establishing a base of software and content around the iPhone. As of February 2010, Apple's App Store has approximately

150,000 programs, and the company is developing a strong third-party base. The iPod is closely linked to Apple's iTunes, which has stimulated the sales of iPod platforms and also content material.

China is following the Apple model. It is spending $59 billion[9] to upgrade its wireless infrastructure to stimulate the sales of smart phones. This infrastructure investment will trigger dramatic growth for downloaded Internet content.

Unfortunately, the United States does not have the vision to drive the adoption of the next generation of wireless data and voice communication to stimulate the growth of new broadband Internet-based services.

Another example of infrastructure building is Google. It has had high growth due to the large installed base of Internet users and a huge investment in data centers around the globe. The Internet user base has become larger due to the combination of hardware and software as well as the availability of broadband communications.

Google is viewed as a company that developed business models to offer better access to content. Google also manages content, which has very high growth potential: the amount of content is expanding rapidly and is unstructured.

The synergy effects of the support infrastructures represent major opportunities. It is, consequently, important for the United States to focus on industries that not only have the core businesses but also have the large and growing support infrastructures.

The Decline of Research Activities

The United States was the top research center globally in the 1960s through the 1990s, but there was a decline in funding on new areas of technology by the U.S. government and industry in the 1990s and the early years of the twenty-first century (see Figure 5.1). Without access to leadership technologies, the competitiveness of U.S. industry will weaken because the U.S. corporations are high cost compared to those in developing countries.

FIGURE 5.1

R&D Spending Is Flat in the United States, but It Is Rising in China

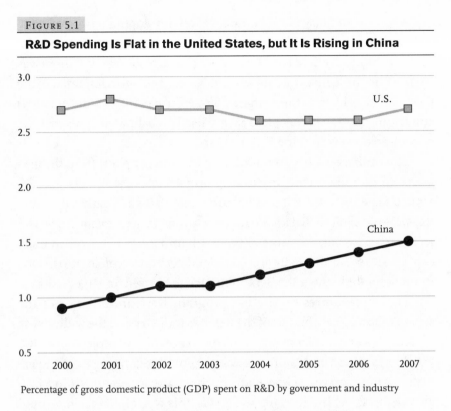

Percentage of gross domestic product (GDP) spent on R&D by government and industry

Source: United Nations Educational, Scientific, and Cultural Organization (UNESCO)

The leverage of technology from the military and aerospace industries to the commercial sector also slowed.

After World War II, the United States had the image of being very strong from a military perspective. The Cold War with the Soviet Union resulted in relatively large military spending in the United States, with the development and production of high-performance military hardware.

The strength of the U.S. military was a major factor in giving the United States a strong political position in the global arena. Also, the United States had to be superior to the Soviet Union in military power so that the United States was not directly threatened. No one in the American government wanted a repeat of the Cuban Missile Crisis of 1962.

The U.S. military placed emphasis on developing advanced technologies rather than on having a large number of troops. The technology leadership required commitments of large resources, but there was payback on these investments when these technologies migrated to the commercial sectors of the economy. For example, many of the wireless communications technologies that are used globally at the present time were developed within the U.S. military.

The military-centric corporations had strong support from the government and undertook speculative projects. An example is that the United States built the B-1 bomber in the late 1970s and early 1980s, and this project required that a wide range of advanced technologies be used. In reality, however, the value of the B-1 bomber has been low in most conflict situations due to improved radar detection technologies. In fact, its predecessor bomber the B-52 continued to be used for large payloads.

The expenditures on the B-1 program were an indicator of the strong lobbying capabilities of the defense industry and the willingness of Congress to make large expenditures in speculative projects. The B-1 bomber is an example of the development of technologies at the expense of the taxpayers without any major strategic benefits from a military perspective. In the 1970s and 1980s, this type of inefficiency could be absorbed by the United States without a significant impact on consumers' standard of living due to the strengths of the U.S. economy.

A number of U.S. corporations, including Lockheed, Northrop, Boeing, Rockwell, Raytheon, Hughes, Litton, and General Dynamics, obtained technological knowhow and other benefits from the military spending. In addition, the spending led to employment for a large number of engineers and managers as well as for the assembly line workers for the military programs.

There were benefits to the semiconductor industry as well. In fact, a key part of the strategies of a number of semiconductor companies during the early 1970s and 1980s was to focus on military programs. Texas Instruments is an example of a chip company that had a substantial amount of Defense Department business, and it leveraged that funding for commercial success.

While spending within the military is high, the dominant percentage of expenditures is currently on the deployment of technology rather than the development of technology. The emphasis on off-the-shelf devices reduced the military's costs, but it also reduced the overall rate of breakthrough research funded by the Defense Department. The changes in the military spending patterns and its reduced emphasis on the development of advanced technologies are areas in which the United States has gone through major changes in the past 20 to 30 years.

The loss of the military in driving the development of new technologies is not good for the U.S. electronics industries. The reduced leverage of military technologies into commercial applications is evident in the low profile of commercial business groups within the defense and aerospace industry, including companies such as Lockheed and Boeing.

The low level of commitments to long-term research projects (10 years or longer) in the United States has resulted in advanced research facilities at a number of organizations being shrunk or closed.

The decline in Bell Labs over the last 20 years has been dramatic. Bell Labs was one of the leading research centers globally, with a number of Nobel Laureates. The transistor was developed there, along with a host of other technologies vital to our day-to-day lives and businesses. At the present time, Bell Labs is a shell of its former capabilities. There has also been a reduction of advanced research at Xerox and other organizations once known as prominent research organizations.

When AT&T was a monopoly, U.S. consumers had access to leadership communication capabilities, but with high costs. Those monopoly telephone call costs provided AT&T with the ability to support Bell Labs.

With deregulation, the cost of communications to the consumer has been dramatically reduced. The other impact, however, is that the technologies available to the consumer, such as high bandwidth access, are much more limited than those available in other countries. The manufacturing arm of AT&T has been acquired by Alcatel, an acquisition that was accompanied by large reductions in the head count in the United States with large pressure to protect the number of jobs in Europe.

Having strong advanced technology centers can provide access to a wide range of new products. Key personal computer innovations by Apple can be traced to the pioneering work done by the Palo Alto Research Center (PARC) operated by Xerox in the 1970s and early 1980s.

Microsoft has expanded its research organization, but with a focus on the strategic products of Microsoft. Google has established advanced research capabilities, but the head count is relatively small. There is also advanced research at HP, but, again, the head count is low.

There has been an increased role of universities in developing and commercializing research in the United States, but universities are primarily teaching institutions. The level of expenditures on research projects in universities is relatively low.

Albany NanoTech has been established in New York, but there has been a reduction in process technology R&D at many companies in the United States.

There are extensive activities in the United States in software development, and the United States clearly remains the global leader in software development. There is, however, increasing competition in software development from companies in India and China. While the past emphasis in India was to develop software based on contracts from foreign companies, the level of sophistication in software development has increased rapidly in India, with the establishment of companies that are competitive globally in a number of areas.

The United Kingdom is an example of a country that placed a low level of emphasis on high technology. Consequently, there are limited opportunities for engineers to find jobs at U.K. companies. Ireland has had a strong commitment to supporting technology companies, but the lower costs involved with Asian companies' production have diminished R&D and high-tech operations in the Emerald Isle. The economy of the United Kingdom has relied on financial services as a key area of wealth generation, but this segment of the economy has weakened dramatically.

It is significant that Germany is experiencing a declining interest by students in engineering disciplines. They perceive that engineering does not have a good future.[10] Germany, however, continues to depend on leadership technologies in areas such as automobiles for employment and exports.

Japan is also experiencing a decline in the number of engineering students. And these students are not keen to work for the large Japanese electronics companies. This is, again, related to the expectation of potential weaknesses in job opportunities in the future.

The trends in Germany and Japan in engineering could be early indicators that the economies of these countries could continue to weaken in the future. Japan is already becoming weak.

Having advanced research centers provides employment for top scientists and engineers. There are also incentives for universities to have advanced technologies training because their top graduates can find stimulating careers.

While exports are not generated from research institutes in the near term, they can still generate new businesses. The founders of Google did their pioneering Internet search research while getting their doctorates at Stanford University.[11] In fact, much of the chip technology developed in the Silicon Valley in the 1980s can be directly connected to research conducted at nearby Stanford.

In the future, the reduction in basic R&D within the United States will reduce the ability of U.S. companies to obtain price premiums for their products based on technology leadership.

The Effect of Foreign-Born Leaders on U.S. Industries

Within the U.S. electronics industry, a number of leaders of corporations were born outside of the United States, with many being Indian or Chinese. Many of the leaders of the U.S. electronics industry came to the United States as students and stayed after graduation.

Examples of leaders in the electronics industry who were born outside of the United States include Andrew Grove of Intel, Jen-Hsun Huang of NVIDIA, Sehat Sutardja of Marvell, Wilfred Corrigan of LSI Logic, and Willem Roelandts of Xilinx.

A characteristic of the U.S. electronics corporations has been the willingness to bring in outsiders. In the 1960s and 1970s, many of the outsiders came from Europe, with relatively easy assimilation into the U.S. culture. Some were running away from prejudice, dictatorships, poverty, or other problems in Europe or Russia. Only a small percentage of engineers and managers who emigrated from Europe to the United States had considerations of returning to Europe. Very few wanted to work for European corporations.

The willingness to bring in outsiders was also conducive to the acceptance of new business and technology concepts. An example is that many of the new business concepts within Intel were conceived and implemented by Grove.

The high mobility of senior managers between corporations led ultimately to the leveraging of new concepts. In many older industries, companies become resistant to change: it is easier to establish new business concepts and new products in new corporations. The managerial mobility in the Silicon Valley was one of the key factors that allowed a large number of new companies to start.

The First Asian Invasion

In the 1970s and 1980s, many Japanese companies expanded their facilities in the United States. A large number of Japanese engineers and managers were dispatched to the United States, but a very high percentage returned to Japan after their assignments. The Japanese engineers and managers considered that being in the United States was a temporary assignment. A key part of their motivation to accept temporary relocation was to obtain higher positions when they returned to Japan. The result was that Japanese companies did not absorb a significant amount of the business cultures common in the United States. The Japanese companies continue to be dominated by business concepts and organizational structures that have been in place for decades.

In the 1980s and 1990s, many of the new engineers and managers within the electronics industry came from the Far East, which included

India and Taiwan. While the engineers from India and Taiwan provided very high levels of technology and business abilities, there was generally not the same level of absorption into the U.S. society as there had been for the European engineers and managers.

Many of the Indian and Chinese engineers and managers maintained close links to their families. They established strong involvement in their ethnic social circles and community groups in the United States. With the growth of electronics industries in Taiwan and India, the engineers from Taiwan and India in the United States were a natural bridge to the new companies in these geographic regions.

The linking into the U.S. businesses has been a key factor in the growth of corporations in India and Taiwan. A similar bridge is currently occurring between Taiwan and China and also between China and the United States.

The United States has, however, changed its visa policies, and it has become more difficult for graduates to stay in the United States. This is a major strategic error. It hampers our ability to build strong industries in the United States because of the loss of access to very bright engineers. The engineers from Taiwan and India educated in the United States are able to return and find lucrative positions in their countries. The result is that U.S. companies lose strong technical talent, which will weaken the competitiveness of U.S. companies in the future while strengthening the competitiveness of the overseas companies hiring those engineers turned away by the U.S. immigration policies.

Meanwhile, it is relatively easy for relatives of people who have emigrated to the United States and have minimal formal education to emigrate to the United States. In many cases, these immigrants access a wide range of social services, at a substantial cost to the U.S. taxpayers. But the immigrants who can contribute to the wealth of the United States are often declined access.

Recruiting strong talent from the outside to complement the capabilities within the United States in the past has proven to greatly enhance American competitiveness. Unfortunately, the present immigration policies in the United States are working with different priorities. So, again, the United States is not taking the appropriate approaches to building its corporations for the future and optimizing the approaches that have had good success in the past.

The United States clearly does not have immigration policies that support the long-term goals of the United States, which are to increase employment and improve the balance of trade. The political decisions within the United States are based on short-term expediency rather than on the key steps and actions required to build wealth.

The Poor Use of Profits

The profits and cash generation capabilities of U.S. companies have been very strong over the past few years, even though there has been a significant weakening due to the impact of the global recession. Without these profits, investors won't invest. And without investors, it is very hard to build national wealth.

In many cases, shareholders have short-term metrics. They demand increased earnings per share and revenue growth each quarter. These short-term metrics place strong pressures on the corporations to limit spending in areas that require long-term investments.

The compensation of CEOs, senior managers, and the boards of directors of U.S. corporations is closely linked to the increase in stock prices, which are, in turn, linked to profits and the generation of cash.

The bonuses that have been obtained through stock options have been very high for many top executives of U.S. corporations over the past decade. This has led to an environment where the emphasis was on increasing stock prices rather than on building corporations for long-term growth.

As corporations generate cash, the cash can be used to fund additional new product development, pay dividends, buy companies, or buy back shares. Companies can also build up their cash reserves. With the expectation that stock prices will increase if earnings per share increase due to the lower number of shares, many companies in the United

States have been very active in buying back shares. A number of companies claim that buying back shares is an investment in their company.

While there are regulations regarding the dilution of shares to employees, the buying back of shares allows an increase in earnings per share, which benefits the stock options held by management.

If the earnings per share increase and the price of the stock increases, the investors are happy. There is, consequently, a conflicting decision for management between using the cash to buy back stock, increasing the stock price in the short term, and investing in new products or other strategies that can provide revenues and profits in 5 to 10 years. The result, however, is that many companies have been buying back stock, which reduces the funds available to invest in the longer-term opportunities.

The impact of the stock option and share buyback activities of U.S. companies is that compensation levels of executives have been very high ($230 million[12] for the CEO of Yahoo! in 2006). If there is high compensation for executives of companies for 2 to 5 years, there is no need for them to worry about the fate of their employers during the next 10 to 20 years. It is significant that the CEO of Yahoo! in 2006 has subsequently been replaced and that his contribution to Yahoo! is not considered significant. There are clearly many other cases in which the compensation of CEOs does not have a close link with their contribution to building a company effective in competing in global markets.

It is significant that companies such as Nokia and Samsung are global leaders and that the compensation levels of senior management do not have the same multiples of the compensation of lower levels of management as would be the case for U.S. companies.

There is the need for the electronics industry in the United States to have compensation structures consistent with building companies for the long term. Their goal should be to obtain high market share in global markets and build the wealth of the successful leaders. While it is not appropriate to constrain the financial performance of corporations, there can be additional incentives to increase R&D expenditures, have longer-term vesting of stock options, and other tactics to better align the long-term goals of the company, its leaders, and its investors and other stakeholders.

Guidelines can be established such that there is the ability to support the building of wealth for the country as well as rewarding the managers and engineers who build large and successful corporations.

It is important that corporations not be vehicles for financial institutions and senior management to use to take out a much higher percentage of wealth than their contributions actually generated. Compensation of top managers should be based on longer-term contributions; it should not be hundreds of millions of dollars of compensation based on two to five years of work.

There continue to be many strong U.S. corporations and many strong business leaders. These are the armies and generals that can be used to generate wealth, but it is important that they operate within a compensation structure that benefits the country as well as their own specific areas.

Key Trends in U.S. Wealth Creation

The following is a summary of U.S. wealth trends:

- The United States has been wealthy for 100 years, and there's a cultural assumption that the United States will continue to be wealthy. People assume that when the economic recession is over, the United States will return to strong economic vitality. However, the United States is likely to experience a decline in wealth over the next decade due to the rise of China and other factors noted earlier.
- Unemployment in the United States, especially in the nongovernment sector, is very high. The reason is that a number of U.S. corporations, such as the automakers, have declined and have reduced their head counts in the United States. According to their respective annual reports, the companies that are strong in global markets, such as Cisco, Microsoft, HP, and IBM, are, however, increasing employment outside of the United States rather than in the United States.

The employment in the government sector will increase, which will require additional tax funds to pay for, which will need to be covered by a private employment base that is potentially shrinking. Also, because of the generous retirement packages of the government employees as well as the increase in the size of the government, the cost of government will take over an increasing percentage of taxes in the future.

It will be very difficult to slow the increase in the cost of government.

- The United States is operating with large internal deficits, which are occurring because of the funds used to resolve the financial services sector crisis and to try to stimulate consumption. The stimulation of consumption makes the people feel secure in the short term, but it aggravates the weaknesses of the economy in the long term because increased consumption means more imports.

  The cost of the government's stimulus packages will need to be covered through either increasing taxes or commandeering significant tax revenues from needed infrastructure and other long-term wealth creation government investments.

  Additional programs, such as those related to universal health care, will increase taxes and deficits in the United States.

- The balance of trade of the United States is negative, is very large, and is growing. Without the building of a manufacturing base, the trade deficits will continue to increase.

- The United States is borrowing from China, Japan, Germany, the oil exporters, and other countries to fund the deficit, maintain the value of the dollar, and maintain buying power. The borrowing is unsustainable. The dollar reserves of foreign countries are being used to buy assets: China is buying companies that own rights to raw materials.

  To try to ensure that the internal deficits do not consume a high percentage of taxes, the United States is forced to keep interest payments low. By keeping interest payments low, the U.S. dollar will weaken over the long term.

- To build wealth, the United States will need to increase its exports. Exports are increased by developing and manufacturing products that can be exported. Most of the global exports are hardware products, such as automobiles, televisions, mobile telephones, and other products, but software products can also be exported. The United States is high cost, and there is, consequently, the need to manufacture products that can support high price premiums. Low-cost manufacturing can also be obtained through high levels of automation.

  The design and manufacturing of very high fuel-efficiency automobiles are an option for the building of a new industrial base.

  Another area that has high growth potential is advanced medical technologies. They can provide both social and financial benefits.

  The United States is the leader in technologies in a number of areas, but there is the need to accelerate the building of businesses that can leverage the value of the technologies in global markets. There is the need to take the same approach to building corporations as there was to the building of the military.

  The reality is that the government in Washington appears to be against corporations and for labor unions and the protection of the legacy infrastructures. The reality is that without strong corporations, there is no growth of employment for the manufacturing of goods that can be exported.

  The actions of Washington after the economic meltdown of 2008 will increase taxes on corporations with operations outside of the United States. While many of the tax laws in the United States are ludicrous, the general approach should be that of reducing the overall taxes and also reducing the cost of government so that a higher percentage of taxes is used to support the growth of areas that contribute to the generation of wealth.

- The United States is living in a world of illusion regarding the level of consumption realistic for its population. There is a lack of understanding of the strengths of the external threats and the capabilities of corporations from other countries. And there is a lack of understanding of how foreign governments are supporting their local corporations in protecting local markets and competing in local as well as global markets.

The United States is operating on the illusion that its superior strengths will win the war on wealth. The United States is, however, operating with visions of the past, when a competitor could be intimidated. What worked against Japan in the 1970s and 1980s won't work with China in 2015. There is also a lack of understanding that global markets have to be addressed and that the U.S. market is a part of a larger entity.

China is emerging as a world power. It supplies a high percentage of the products consumed in the United States. China has been relatively passive to date about its growing economic and political power, but there is increased pressure inside China to resist U.S. political and economic requests. China is likely to become increasingly assertive, and while military conflicts will not be the key battles, there will be key battles for raw materials and supply chains for the manufacturing of products.

As the middle class in China, India, and other countries grows, there will be increased consumption of many products. The result will be increased demand for raw materials, which will drive up prices and potentially result in shortages.

The strain on the supply of a range of raw materials will increase. The countries that have the financial strengths to control the supply chain of raw materials will be those that can manage the growth of wealth.

The analysis of the United States needs to take into account the weakening of the internal structures from the impact of increasing costs of taxes and government. There are also the external competitive pressures, which are getting stronger. China will be one of the external forces that will accelerate the weakening of the United States.

It is important for the United States to understand the strategies of China, but it is also important for the United States to remain strong and to cooperate with China. This way both countries gain in wealth. It is important for the United States to have a strong military force, but it is equally or more important that it have strong corporations that have high market shares of global markets, which includes the China market.

It is important to note that the weakening of the United States is not the fault of China. Rather, it is the result of greed existing within U.S. society. It is the internal weakening of the oak tree that allows the storms to accelerate the deterioration and loss of tree limbs.

The next chapter describes how and why China came to become the new superpower.

PART III

CHINA: THE GROWING GIANT

Prosperity and Poverty

ARRIVING IN CHINA THROUGH the airports of Beijing or Shanghai, you enter a spacious and ultramodern terminal. The building is clean. There are large open spaces and soaring ceilings. Everything appears efficient and contemporary—no different from terminals in Zurich, Tokyo, or New York City. It's easy to get through baggage claim and customs fast. Gateways have always been important in Chinese culture as a way of protecting the interior as well as impressing visitors with their splendor, and these portals to modern China initially impress you as well-planned, twenty-first-century hubs.

Yet driving into the large cities, another less-favorable impression intrudes. The traffic becomes heavy. Gridlock, or the threat of it, looms at a lot of intersections. Many vehicles are old, spewing black smoke. The air is heavy with pollution. There is a small truck filled with cages of squawking chickens. There is another truck with cages of young pigs. Suddenly, you are not hungry.

A confusing picture begins to develop. China seems modern and efficient but also filled with people suffering with poverty, ignored in plain sight in the workday traffic of the upwardly mobile. Although some of the vehicles are antiquated, they are making deliveries to large new department stores like those in New York City or Los Angeles.

Off the main roads, there are many low houses that are not old but are in poor condition. They were built in a hurry, cheaply. The side streets are narrow and clogged with people. Some are walking and some are on bicycles. The clothes of many are torn and dirty. There are drying clothes hanging all over. There is a lot of movement. It appears chaotic.

Arriving at the hotel, the feeling of orderliness resumes. The lobby is clean, and it has high ceilings. Service is efficient. There are smiling, comfortingly English-speaking people at the reception desk. Again, everything is reassuringly contemporary. In a short time, there has been a transition from order to chaos to order.

Settings change rapidly in China. It's as if unseen stagehands were switching the backgrounds and props as directed by an invisible stage manager. China is 5,000 years old. Confucius lived and taught more than 2,500 years ago. There is a picturesque and impressive exterior that China wants you to perceive. The Chinese want visitors to think that the picturesque and impressive sites are indicative of the entire country, instead of just being a pretty façade masking a crowded and once-impoverished country. Famous sites, such as the Forbidden City and the Great Wall, overwhelm visitors with their beauty and size. But there is another reality, clamorous and struggling, that we have to go offstage and into the back alleys to see and touch.

China is complex, and its moods can change rapidly. It can be sunny and positive, but also dark and hard to interpret. A lot depends upon location. Approximately 700 million[1] people live in the country-side. There, people appear more relaxed. They'll stop to talk to each other. In the cities, people rush, and their purposeful hurry creates a wake of isolation in the midst of a crowd. They think they are in control of their destinies.

However, in China, the government exerts very strong control. Even with the relaxation of restraints that happened lately, the policies of the government affect almost every aspect of life. Those policies are as ubiquitous as the weather. The one-child-per-couple limit imposed beginning in 1979 is the most famous of government restrictions on individual rights.

In addition to the government, there are many other forces driving change. The young are adapting to the changes, but many of the middle-aged and older population are resisting or ignoring the changes. (The Chinese people have a great aptitude for sidestepping change.) Because of the large number of people, the Chinese have developed skills to shut others out. They also shut out foreigners unless there is a need to interact.

China is like the body of a person, where the arms and hands and fingers and legs can move at different speeds. The countryside of China is the torso, and the cities are the arms and legs. China's brain is the central government. China also has a heart, which is the underlying warmth of the people.

When traveling to the north, to cities such as Beijing and Tianjin, one can sense a feeling of high-energy aggressiveness. Much of the unrest and fighting in China throughout its history occurred because of invasions from the north. There is a wariness of outsiders there. In the south, in Shanghai, for example, people have welcomed outsiders and developed the ability to trade with them. There is a greater disposition to be hospitable, and greater prosperity because of it.

China is going through a world-renowned, perhaps unprecedented industrialization. Although its economy is only 30 percent of the U.S. economy (the GDP of the United States in 2008 was $14.44 trillion[2]), China is building factories on a monumental scale to produce goods for export as well as for local consumption. In 2008 China's GDP was $4.404 trillion.[3] China's exports that year amounted to $1.43 trillion,[4] or roughly one third of its GDP. Around a fifth of China's exports— more than $300 billion[5]—were to the United States in 2008. While China is depicted as a voracious consumer of natural resources and commodities, almost a third of its GDP is exported: merchandise that is bought for use, ultimately, in other countries.

The country operates with five-year plans that set many of the government's economic goals. The government appears strong, but its top-down control is coming under increasing stress as the number and financial clout of entrepreneurs grow. More and more the factories in China are owned by businesses whose managers do not want to be controlled by the central government. Nor do these managers want to pay the central government's high taxes. China's entrepreneurs, small business owners, and farmers want to operate without constraints. They want to start the businesses that they conceive, plant the crops they know how to grow, and negotiate prices on their own. The government, however, keeps a tight rein on industrial policy. Priorities are based on the need to sell an enormous amount of exports, even if that emphasis limits the amount of goods available for local consumption, and therefore limits the citizens' standard of living. Not surprisingly, the government feels that only it sees the big picture. It presumes that it alone knows what's best for the entire country.

Beauty and Ugliness

China is like a kaleidoscope. Twist it and a new image appears. Some regions are beautiful, such as the mountains and rivers of the Yunnan province in the southwest and Guangxi in the southeast. The temples and historical buildings, such as those in the Forbidden City in Beijing and the buried Terra Cotta Warriors near Xi'an, are awe-inspiring. But rivers elsewhere are being choked with pollution, and there are millions of rundown buildings in the older cities, where the population of rats appears as numerous as the human population.

Yet China is a proud country, and its growing success is fueling this pride. The Chinese are willing to submit to government control as long as they feel that their country's wealth is growing. They take great pride that China appears to be succeeding. That growing pride and the reassurance that their national wealth is accruing has tempered the people's restiveness.

The Chinese are deeply superstitious and skeptical of outsiders. Winning their trust requires a lot of effort. Whether China is a friend or an enemy of the United States depends on how the goals of China and the Chinese are being met. China can be an ally or an opponent. Understanding the growing might of China is indispensable to building a working relationship that endures.

6

WHAT IS
CHINA TODAY?

CHINA HAS MADE DRAMATIC PROGRESS in a number of industries since 2000. With Taiwanese partners, China will be poised to compete strongly for market share in a number of strategic global markets, as well as to maintain control of its domestic market. At the same time, all the nations with which China competes also will pursue both defensive and offensive strategies. They will try to protect their home markets while trying to gain share in foreign markets. The United States and other countries will try to obtain open access to segments of the Chinese market.

The difference between China and its competitors is that China's competitors strive to offer themselves as open markets or at least purport to cherish that as an ideal. China doesn't. It is critical to understand that China has established a range of control mechanisms that regulate access to the China market. For example, licenses for manufacturing products, such as cars, are given only to selected companies, and those have to be controlled by Chinese majority owners.

The long-term implications of a strong industrial base in China must be understood. To have worldwide prosperity—in China, the United States, and their other trading partners—

is certainly an objective worth saluting and striving for. In actual practice, however, economic outcomes customarily are not so benign. In a competitive environment, there are winners and losers.

China is operating with well-defined goals. Its large population is an asset, if well utilized. In China, the population is primarily used for building the manufacturing base and increasing output.

In the United States, the emphasis is on consumption, which, in effect, depletes wealth, especially when the consumers make their purchases using credit that they cannot repay. The United States at the present is trying to manage its way out of the problems caused by the excessive leverage of its financial institutions and consumers. Meanwhile, China is building up its industrial base and the factors that promote the building of wealth.

Consumption is being stimulated in China. It increases economic activity and especially employment. But consumption is also at the same time being managed by the central government in China to ensure that long-term, economy-strengthening objectives are being met and are not being sacrificed for the public's short-term material gratifications. That's why China is determined to sustain its overwhelmingly positive balance of trade with the rest of the developed world.

The global recession has had a significant deleterious impact on China. But China has managed the downturn better than Western nations. One reason is that China has not been burdened with large deficits and excessive leverage. It can pay for its stimulus packages. Its stimulus actions have not been financed by creating or enlarging deficits. China didn't have deficits at the beginning of the recession, and it doesn't have them now. So it will have that advantage too when it comes out of the recession.

Economy

China's population is 1.3 billion[1] to 1.5 billion people, depending on how you do the counting. The country has more people than the combined populations of Europe, the United States, Japan, and several other industrialized nations.

Many Chinese now know what astronauts feel like after blast-off. Economic development in China has been on a rocketlike trajectory. The Chinese people inhabit a country that is transforming itself at breathtaking speed from being rural and poor to becoming a major industrial giant.

Industrialization in the West occurred over a period of roughly 200 years. The industrialization of China is being compressed into a period of roughly 20 years. In the process the country is changing its social structure and economy drastically. The annual growth of the GDP in China over the past 20 years has averaged almost 10 percent (see Figure 6.1). Double-digit annual average GDP growth for two decades is unique among nations in modern times.

The growth of China's economy can be characterized as follows.

In 1980, the GDP per person in China was just a little over $300 per year,[2] less than 86 cents per day per person. In 2008, the GDP per person (assuming a population of 1.5 billion) was almost $3,000,[3] or over $8 *per day* per person.

FIGURE 6.1

China's GDP Growth

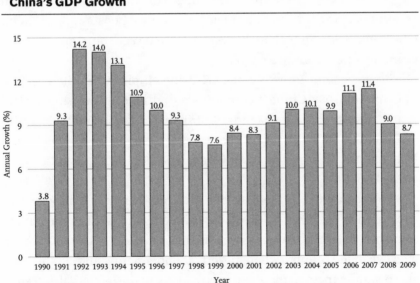

Source: China National Bureau of Statistics

Even in 2009, a year of recession for China's trading partners, China had an estimated GDP growth of 8.0 percent,[4] according to the National Bureau of Statistics of China. While there was a decline in the rate of growth of exports in 2008[5] as well as in 2009,[6] exports still account for almost a third of the GDP.[7]

Meanwhile, consumption has been growing, but not as fast as the GDP has grown. Retail sales in China have increased at a 17 percent rate each year since 2008, according to the National Bureau of Statistics of China. Auto sales accelerated 40 percent in 2009, according to an article in the *New York Times*.[8] While consumers are buying more, overall consumption as a share of the GDP has fallen for the last 10 years.[9] It now accounts for roughly 35 percent, half the percentage in the United States.[10] (In the 1980s, consumption in China was more than 50 percent of its GDP.[11]) In part, this is attributable to thrift. Most Chinese are prudent, precautionary savers, and they live on a fraction of their take-home pay. In the aggregate, consumers and institutions in China save around $2.5 trillion every year.[12]

As the GDP grows, the population of the middle class gets bigger, which increases consumption. The added consumer demand—a form of human growth hormone for an economy—boosts employment, which injects additional buying power into the economy, spurring the economy into an upward spiral.

Because of the growth in the GDP and employment, the standard of living in urban China has improved dramatically over the past 15 years. Nevertheless, the standard of living of the average person in China still is far below that of the average person in the United States. Note that the GDP per capita of China is $6,000[13] compared to America's $47,500.[14]

The people living in regions of rural China continue to be very poor compared to the large cities. There is an enormous difference in the standards of living between city residents and most of the 700 million who live in the country, where poverty is endemic and abject. There are also big differences in the standards of living of the industrial entrepreneurs and the lowest-paid factory workers. This is producing multiple economic classes in China, with the tensions and class antagonisms such divisions breed.

Exports drive the growth of China. Surging exports are the basis for China's positive trade balances. Increasing exports is one of the main goals of the Chinese government's industrial policy.

China's positive balance of trade has been created by a number of factors working in concert. In the first place, the central government promotes industries that generate exports. Second, consumers exhibit relatively high savings rates. Chinese households in late 2009 were estimated to be saving up to 40 percent of their income, according to an article in the *New York Times*. Third, the Chinese use credit far less than Western consumers. Fourth, wages have been kept low. According to James Surowiecki, the financial columnist for the *New Yorker*: "While [China's] boom has been extraordinary, ordinary workers have not reaped the gains one might expect. In the past decade, . . . the share of GDP that goes to wages has actually fallen."[15]

So domestic consumption has been held down, and it continues to be only a small percentage of the GDP compared to the share that consumption represents in Western economies. The result of this emphasis on exports and restrained consumption is that as of December 2009, China has built dollar reserves of almost $2.4 trillion.[16] China also has 1,054 tons[17] of gold in its reserves, which is an increase of 454 tons since 2003.

China is building its employment base by focusing on making things that it can sell abroad. To sustain its large export industry, China needs its major trading partners, such as Japan, Taiwan, Korea, and the United States, to remain large consumers of its products. So it must make sure that such customers are able to afford and continue to buy the merchandise manufactured in China.

But while the government is committed to building the wealth of China, it also will act out of other political convictions in its dealings with the United States. Japan, South Korea, and European countries have conducted trade with the United States while viewing it as a political and military ally. American rifles guard their borders. By contrast,

Chinese leaders view their country as competing with the United States for superpower status, not as a U.S. protectorate. Certainly, China is nobody's colony anymore. China's leaders always view the commercial competition between the two countries, especially in key industries, as a political threat as well as an economic one.

American businesspeople and political leaders need to understand the dualism of the Chinese perspective toward the United States. If the United States acts with consideration and finesse, the Chinese market can be an open and lucrative opportunity. But if the United States acts in a bullying, self-righteous, or unfair way, it is likely that the Chinese market will not be as advantageous as America would like. Meanwhile Chinese corporations will gain increasing shares of global markets.

Employment

According to the National Bureau of Statistics in China, in 1996, 688 million[18] people were employed in China. By 2008 that had grown to 780 million[19] (see Figure 6.2).

Almost 100 million people entered the Chinese labor force in 12 years, an amount equivalent to almost two thirds of the entire U.S. workforce. As with so much else in China, this engagement of so many was not spontaneous. The absorption and placement of new workers was coordinated and guided by government policies to expand the employment base. Such administration includes the training of managers, engineers, technicians, and assembly workers in industries of strategic importance such as automotive, electronics, and pharmaceuticals.

Joint ventures between Chinese and Western companies are used extensively. They boost employment and management expertise as well as bring in technology. Also, government policies encourage entrepreneurialism, especially in instances where the funding comes from outside. When that happens, China expands its employment with other people's money.

China must sharply increase its industrial base to accommodate the approximately 200 million additional workers expected to be look-

FIGURE 6.2

China's Employment Growth

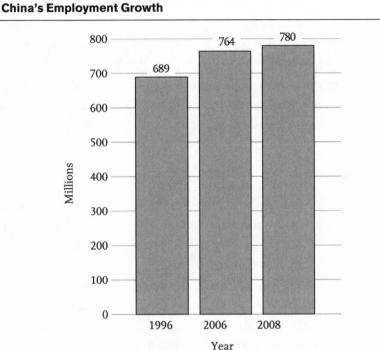

Source: Chinese government reports and the U.S. Central Intelligence Agency's (CIA) *World Factbook*, various years

ing for employment by 2020. The slowing of the rate of growth of exports because of the global recession has increased unemployment in China. A number of recent graduates have had trouble finding jobs, according to an article based on a government agency announce-ment.[20] The current difficulties for the new graduates are concern-worthy because the number of new graduates will continue to increase. At the same time the recession has slowed China's evolution from being a cheap labor economy to one capable of employing a wide diver-sity of skilled laborers. In the past, low-skill manufacturing and construction workers predominated in the workforce. In the future, China will need to provide jobs for a large number of engineering and management workers.

As the recession wanes and employment builds in China's major industries, it's expected to lead to an increase in employment in support industries. The buildup of suppliers in industries such as automobile manufacturing is being encouraged by a range of incentives such as tax breaks for buyers.[21] If things go according to plan, such development of support industries will improve China's self-sufficiency in the supply of components used in automobiles as well as sharply increase automotive industry employment.

Migration

The industrialization of China has resulted in a dramatic migration from the rural areas into the cities. In 1980, 80.4 percent[22] of the population was rural; by 2008 the percentage of the population in rural areas was approximately 54 percent.[23]

The migration of hundreds of millions of workers from the rural areas into the cities has led to the establishment of megacities such as Shenzhen, where the population has grown from 4 million in 1998 to 19 million now (approximately 10 million are unrecorded immigrants), according to government data. Around 10 million of the 19 million are migrant workers. Shenzhen was established as a Specialized Economic Zone (SEZ) in 1979. At that time it was a coastal village whose main distinction was that it was close to Hong Kong.

Today Shenzhen is a gigantic hive of transient labor, with transport geared to getting workers from the bunk beds in their barracks to the job sites. Three workers use the same bunk bed every 24 hours. There has also been a large increase in the population of cities such as Shanghai and Guangzhou (formerly known as Canton).

While the skylines of the cities display modern high-rise buildings, there are sections of these cities where 10 or more people live in a room. With the global recession, there has been a large increase in unemployment in many of the large industrial cities. The benefits provided to the unemployed are meager. Many of the unemployed have to be supported by their families (another motivation for precautionary saving). The crucial requirements are food and a bed. Other amenities are discretionary.

Of the half of the Chinese population that live in rural areas, 140 million[24] travel from their homes to work in large cities on a monthly or weekly basis.

The large number of migrant workers shows the willingness of the Chinese to make sacrifices to have jobs and support their families. These migrant workers represent a major asset if there is a need for their skills. They represent a liability if there isn't. So it's important that the construction and other industries that employ the migrant workers remain active and are able to employ hundreds of millions of workers.

If the economy of China continues its robust growth and employment keeps up with the population growth, many of the workers in China will continue to make large sacrifices because of their belief in a better China. If the economy in China does not keep growing, it is likely that there will be increased dissatisfaction.

Even with the worker migration, there is still a rural population of around 700 million.[25] While there have been attempts to increase jobs in rural areas, the results have been mixed. Many of the rural areas have not been able to establish strong industrial bases.[26]

Some rural cities, such as Hefei, have set up industrial parks. They have confiscated land, built roads, and erected the exteriors of buildings. Many of the buildings are empty, and there is a large amount of overgrown unused land. Yet, as the industrial base in China grows, these building shells will be used. In the eyes of Chinese planners, the question is when they are filled rather than if.

7

CHINESE
CULTURE

POLYGLOT SOCIETY FREEDOM and free enterprise. Diversity. Checks and balances to limit government interference in personal life. Straightforward outspoken entrepreneurship. Pioneers crossing the untamed wilderness.

To understand a country's business practices, you have to understand its culture. American culture is built on the foundation of a polyglot society whose members enjoy personal freedom, whose government consists of built-in checks and balances among its various branches. It is that foundation from which free enterprise and employment diversity practices originate. American culture embraced the pioneer spirit crossing the untamed western wilderness 150 years ago—a clear precursor to the entrepreneurial spirit in the Silicon Valley, Boston, Texas, and elsewhere.

Just as the culture in the United States shapes its business practices, so does the culture of China's people shape its business practices.

The Chinese are proud people, who place a strong emphasis on protecting their cultural values. Polishing its proud image is an indispensable part of the growth of the political and economic power of China. The hosting of the

Olympic Games in 2008 gave China the opportunity to demonstrate its ability to stage an important world event for which the planning was excellent. The opening ceremony was spectacular, and there were no major security problems.

The new buildings in the large cities, such as Shanghai and Beijing, provide images of growth and modernity. The industrial parks in Pudong, which was a marsh 20 years ago, are clearly major achievements, and they project strongly the image of a country that is dynamic and thriving.

The Inscrutable Chinese Personality

The population of China has been conditioned by centuries of internal strife because competition for survival was intense. If a small mistake was made, such as publicly disagreeing with a superior, the penalty was often death, which made the Chinese very cautious. Even though the present environment does not impose a death penalty for mistakes, the survival habits learned when the death penalty was prevalent remain ingrained in the people.

The extensive conflicts in China and the opportunities for one ruler to overthrow another also provided opportunities for people with initiative and aggressiveness to gain power rapidly and gain wealth. There is, consequently, a duality in China: a combination of caution on the one hand and aggressiveness on the other. It manifests itself these days such that some people are willing to take big gambles while others are not and prefer to stay within their comfort zones, being very cautious to ensure their own survival.

The combination of caution and aggressiveness is the result of thousands of years of history. Unlike some of the Western civilizations in which there was the perception of the divine right of kings to rule, in China, the emperors or leaders had to have the faith and support of the people to continue to rule. Competition among power groups, including siblings of the previous emperors, resulted in leaders' being frequently overthrown. The dynasties have also had subdynasties within the main grouping, as territories were split by siblings of the emperor.

To keep control, emperors established a management style called "fighting at home." Subordinates were encouraged to compete with each other for wealth, power, and positions by monitoring each other. Emperors could not monitor a large number of subordinates with different responsibilities scattered among many cities.

By having competing groups monitor each other, the emperor was able to obtain information from one group on the weaknesses and problems of another group. By having this type of hierarchical system in which there existed many levels of competing infrastructure that monitored each other, an emperor was able to achieve control over large and diverse groups and areas.

However, the emperors had to provide rewards as incentives to their subordinates to ensure their loyalty. Consequently, the emperors needed to have access to wealth, so they could reward their subordinates based on the benefits that the subordinates could convey to the emperors.

This type of environment protects the power of an individual leader, but it is not always conducive to safeguarding the common good and building a strong society. Yet Chinese leaders today believe the approach does have value—many of the top leaders in China use the approach of fragmenting the responsibilities of their subordinates to maintain strong control.

The net impact of the competition among the groups historically was that it was difficult for the emperors and others in power to know whom to trust because allegiances could change rapidly. One of the results of the constant tension and court intrigue was that it became a habit for people to mask their true feelings about other people until they felt they could trust the other people. Over time, the Chinese perfected the art of not only masking their true intentions but also of saying one thing while secretly thinking the opposite. This ability is not viewed negatively; indeed, it is considered an admirable quality.

A Hostile View of Hostiles

While internal conflicts shaped the societies in China, external pressures and invasions also played a strong role. The Great Wall of China was built to keep out the northern invaders. Even that marvelous edifice was breached through treachery, though, more than 500 years ago, when a general allowed enemies to pass in retaliation for a stolen concubine. Needing to respond to and protect against both external and internal threats is a recurring theme in China's history.

The strengthening of the internal operating structures of society combined with the building of resistance to external threats have been key drivers for the philosophies and strategies that are common in China at the present time. The military conflicts and the resulting changes in the power structures have over centuries been factors that have conditioned both the cautious and ambitious sides of the Chinese.

The Individualism of the Chinese People

The commonly held perception of the Chinese is that they are conformists and are willing to work in cohesive environments. But the reality is that the Chinese are highly individualistic and are driven to succeed. In the past, Chinese people had to project an image of conformity to the superiors, and that image is still there. But the real feelings under the surface are different. Conformity is a façade in China. This type of duality has always been and still is common when the Chinese interact with outsiders.

The individualism in China in the past was demonstrated through the creativity of many Chinese inventions. Individuals developed the abacus, irrigation systems, compass, woodblock printing presses, and other inventions that were crucial to China's development. One can see the individuality and creativity in the art of China, especially in their potteries and bronzes.

The strategies in Sun Tzu's *The Art of War*, written in the sixth century BCE, are highly original. The level of strategic thinking in China continues to be very strong, and while many of the techniques were applied in the past to war, some of them are effective in corporate battles.

That there are hundreds of millions of small business owners in China, including the shopkeepers and restaurant owners, testifies to the individualism in China. The haggling approach of many of the Chinese small business owners testifies to the entrepreneurship of the Chinese.

The other picture is that of the large factories in Shenzhen with tens of thousands of young female workers laboring for 10 to 12 hours a day, six days a week, in conditions that would not be tolerated in the United States. This harsh work environment is reminiscent of armies in the past where tens of thousands, and even hundreds of thousands, of foot soldiers were sacrificed. The level of efficiency of the large factories in China is impressive and is indicative of the willingness of the Chinese people's generosity in making sacrifices so they will have work and therefore be able to care for their families.

The willingness to sacrifice the masses for the good of the few individuals was a common theme in the past in China. There have been many military battles in China, where hundreds of thousands of warriors were killed. People are an asset that is replaceable. Wait a few years, and another large group of soldiers or assembly workers becomes available.

Old and New Generations

In China, it is common for young children to be brought up by their grandparents while both parents work. If the parents work in a city and the grandparents live in a rural area, the parents might see their child only once a year during the Chinese New Year.

The child-care security provided by the grandparents is important for the young who migrate to the cities, start businesses, and take risks. If they fail, they can go back to their rural hometowns to live again with their parents. This family safety net is important for the migrant workers who commit their lives to enable their children to have an education and a better future.

The roles of the grandparents, parents, and children in Chinese family life offer an explanation as to how the high opportunity and risk of the modern cities is offset by the greater levels of stability maintained in the rural areas.

Education and Demographics

In 2008, China's colleges and universities saw 600,000 engineers graduate, up from 200,000 in 2000. In contrast, the United States had approximately 474,000 engineering students enrolled in 2006;[1] however, they have, on average, better training than most of the engineering graduates in China. There are enormous differences in the quality of training among the newly graduated engineers in China, due to the wide variations in the quality of the colleges. A few Chinese colleges are on a par with the best in the United States, but most colleges in China do not provide an education comparable to what is received in most U.S. colleges.

The Chinese realize how important it is to improve the skills of their graduates. There are plans in China to graduate 1 million engineers per year by 2015 and to ensure that their training is consistently high and is as good as those graduating anywhere else.

The Chinese also acknowledge that it is imperative to align the numbers of graduates with the job opportunities available. As the education and training of engineers in China improves over the next 10 to 20 years, the engineering base in China will represent a major asset—if the industrial sectors also prosper and expand so that there is employment for the graduates. That's a big if.

Having the ability to dominate the local market to employ such students is crucial for China's companies. They need the high volumes that can be had from controlling the local market to justify hiring a lot of workers. As a result, Chinese social planners are supporting the development of corporations that have a high market share in China as well as those that have a high market share in external markets.

The battle for market share in China has a range of strategic implications that are demographic as well as commercial. So the Chinese government is extremely active in controlling access to the China market, to create a society that offers employment for future Chinese graduates with homegrown firms. The development of domestic corporations to offer employment to new graduates is of great importance in China.

The Chinese have always placed a high value on education. It's part of the country's cultural heritage. Families make enormous sacrifices to send their children to expensive universities. But, beyond appreciation for scholarship, the government in China also supports education because it's crucial to its plans to expand the middle class.

The development of a large middle class involves many challenges, including providing the housing and infrastructure demanded by an educated population. Another occupational requirement for the middle class is to have access to a sufficient number of mid- and high-level management jobs. More affluent, better-educated managers will expect their jobs eventually to offer promotions.

Such needs are embodied in the goals prescribed in the government's five-year plan. The plan requires that a range of industries be established, which will require increased skills in high technology and access to trained technologists. As with the development of suppliers for automobile manufacturers, many of the major industries have to be developed in coordination with other industries. That requires careful planning. Chinese government leaders believe it is not appropriate to allow market forces alone to guide the growth of industries because they view market forces as being very short term and changeable.

Well-educated managers begin to develop five-year plans of their own. It will be harder to manage the middle class in the future, and not just because it will be bigger. They have a wider-ranging, more cosmopolitan perspective—and they know that their education and management skills would enable them to work somewhere else. The methods that have been used to control the population in the last 10 to 20 years might not work with them.

As the middle class becomes more aware of life as it's lived elsewhere—because they will see it on TV, in the movies, and via the Internet—in many cases they will want to live that way. The same goes for autonomy. When they see people in other countries running their own lives, they will want to do it too. The Chinese leadership will need to balance open access to such images of material fulfillment and freedom with the need to guide the economy. Nevertheless, China's leaders believe that there is a need to control the growth of wealth, which means that consumption inside China will need to be restrained and rationed so that the balance of trade will continue to be positive.

One reason China is very conscious of the importance of increasing exports is that its leaders presume that, as the middle class grows, consumption of both domestic and foreign products (brands such as Nokia, Apple, Gucci, Cartier, Mercedes-Benz, and BMW) will increase. As China increases imports, it will need to export more to pay for the imports.

China's cultural heritage influences many of its decisions. For example, the way China conducts its foreign trade is attributable, in part, to its deeply engrained aversion to personal debt. Borrowing is despicable to many Chinese because it allows creditors to have control over the one who owes. Personal debt is viewed as a failure. This view may become a problem in that the young are developing buying habits more comparable to those in the West, which is resulting in some culture conflict in China.

A Youth Culture

The upward mobility of the young within corporations is high. This is radically different from Japan, where one's level of responsibility is customarily related to one's seniority. In Chinese firms, often there is no group of older, experienced managers to serve as mentors for young managers.

Many of the most successful businesses in China have been built by young entrepreneurs. A number of billionaires in China, such as Ma Huateng of Tencent, Robin Li of Baidu, Jason Jiang of Focus Media, and Jack Ma of Alibaba Group, founded their companies when they were 35 years old or younger. A key to the success of these young entrepreneurs is that they have applied market technology concepts developed in the United States, Japan, and Europe while incorporating features unique to China.

For example, Alibaba Group is the operator of Alibaba.com, a business-to-business online trading company that connects buyers directly with suppliers, cutting out the brokers and other intermediaries. Alibaba is an example of a business that combines Internet technology concepts from outside China with features unique to China. Not unlike a commercial Amazon.com, Alibaba offers a supply chain networking platform. But because credit and debit cards are not as widely used in China, Alibaba has developed a PayPal-like payment technology, called Alipay, that is unique to China in that it is escrow based.

Another company that has established a business model that is unique to China is Focus Media. The company installed flat-panel advertising displays in elevators and other public places. The advertising content is changed by people who go from location to location on bicycles to plug in new cards or DVDs. This way of updating content clearly would not be practical in most Western cities.

While updating ad content by using bicycle technicians may seem oddly old-fashioned, it is cost effective in China where the supply of unskilled labor is high. But China is also emphasizing the development of advanced technologies both within corporations such as Huawei and within universities and research institutes. The Shenzhen Institute of Advanced Technology (SIAT) is an example of the advanced technology research centers in China.

Consumer Lifestyles

The increases in the wealth of a large number of people in China over the past 15 years have been dramatic. This improvement in purchasing power has been concentrated in the large cities, such as Shanghai, Beijing, and Guangzhou.

Consumers in such cities have developed buying patterns and lifestyles similar to those in large cities in other developed countries. The new department stores in the large cities in China are indistinguishable from those in many larger Western cities. They feature the same brands: Gucci, Louis Vuitton, and Ralph Lauren. This adoption of Western consumption patterns happened fast. It shows the willingness of the young to adapt to new, non-Chinese lifestyles.

The smaller cities and villages in China, however, continue to be very poor. There, change is occurring slowly. In the smaller cities there are numerous one- or two-story strip malls where food and supplies are sold.

The contrast between the lifestyles in the major coastal cities and the interior is dramatic. In some rural areas, lifestyles have not changed significantly in 30 to 40 years.

Chinese Philosophy and Its Impact on Business

While the Confucian philosophy is to try to respect authority and to be ambitious in setting goals, the Taoism philosophy is to have harmonious resolution and to have happiness from the inner feelings. The result is that there are both conflicts and escape mechanisms in Chinese philosophies, which have similar characteristics to some of the Western religions.

The different approaches to philosophy of life add an additional dimension to Chinese society. For previous generations, the willingness to sacrifice in the present to get a reward in the future was a key part of Chinese philosophy. But most of the young people in China today are not as patient as their parents. They are less willing to wait decades to be rewarded for their work and sacrifices.

Conflict in Business Approaches

There are more than 1 billion customers in China, but there are tens of millions of competitors for these customers. While China appears to outsiders as a very cohesive social and political environment, in reality, the Chinese people are intensely competitive. One Chinese business leader has said that the Chinese are like crabs trying to get out of a basket, climbing on top of each other to get out.

China's government will need to harness that individualistic, entrepreneurial character of the Chinese if it is going to continue to succeed in building large enterprises that are disciplined and capable of competing in global markets.

While many top-level political leaders in China have long-term goals, many business leaders in China have only short-term goals. Meeting short-term financial objectives enables the founders of companies to become wealthy.

The short-term perspective is also related to the intense competitive pressures in most market segments in China and in global markets. It is important to react rapidly to competitive changes.

China's leaders are trying to change the state-owned enterprises (SOEs) into more entrepreneurial enterprises. This is being done to gain access to additional financial resources as well as to bring in more free-thinking outsiders into the management.

Nevertheless, very conservative management perspectives predominate at a number of the SOEs. For years the perpetuation of employment for some of the senior managers has had a higher value than generating profits and being responsive to change.

With the now-closer relationships between the SOEs and various government agencies, the top managers of the SOEs have to be politically astute. Ensuring the continued support from government agencies can be more important than getting optimal results in the domestic market.

Many of the SOEs' top managers are older and have been trained within a rigid hierarchical structure. Their careers have not prepared them for the competitive pressures they must cope with to operate effectively in the global market.

For example, China Mobile, China Telecom, and China Unicom have done well as wireless carriers in China. However, the fact that China Mobile has 500 million subscribers in China does not necessarily mean that the company can compete strongly in markets outside of China.

Many successful Chinese companies, such as Tencent, Baidu, Alibaba, Focus Media, and others, have been founded by entrepreneurs who were age 35 or younger. The ability of young managers to establish successful companies in China is a hopeful sign of the opportunities in China for innovative entrepreneurs.

One of the pernicious legacies of the Cultural Revolution is that China does not have a strong base of experienced managers. Therefore, it is important that a steady stream of new companies be established by young entrepreneurs, so they'll have ventures in which to train themselves. The number of new companies that will arise in China will depend crucially on the availability of liquidity from investors to fund such ventures.

The track record for new Chinese ventures, especially those in high tech, has been unencouraging. Many companies in the electronics industry hit severe financial problems after their promising initial phase. Some of those problems arose because they couldn't develop appealing follow-on products.

One problem faced by start-up companies is that the domestic market is highly volatile and intensely focused on low prices. That makes it difficult to generate profits and invest in developing new products.

Companies in Taiwan went through similar phases in their development of the electronics industry. It took 5 to 10 years for companies such as Acer, Foxconn, and MediaTek to establish winning business models. But now the electronics industry in Taiwan is very competitive in technology and in manufacturing costs. It is able to compete anywhere.

It is likely that one or two more iterations of business models will be needed before a number of the Chinese companies become successful in the global market. However, it's reassuring to consider that the China market for many products will be 50 to 60 percent of the global market in 2015, according to International Business Strategies' (IBS) projections. How protectionist China's government continues to be will play an important role in the country's long-term competitiveness. And China's protectionism may not ultimately help it (protectionism has sometimes bred weaklings).

China's leaders hope to conquer external markets, but now they are also putting more emphasis on building domestic markets as well. This is in contrast to the U.S. industrial machine, which is large but is becoming inefficient and is not supported by government initiatives to increase employment and exports.

The challenges facing China are enormous, and its progress has been excellent. However, most of the growth in China has resulted from the access it offers to low-cost manufacturing.

The growth of the GDP in China will result in the expansion of its middle class. That will increase consumption of a wide range of goods and services. Similar patterns are also expected in India, Brazil, and other developing countries. That will increase worldwide demand pressure for oil, steel, and copper as well as food. And that will bring China into a high-impact collision against the United States, Japan, and the European Union.

At some point the government in China will have to divert resources into controlling and, perhaps, remediating pollution. This is unavoidable because pollution is damaging China's water supply, perhaps irreparably.

China also needs to deal with the imbalance of employment. Around half of China's GDP is produced in the industrial coastal zone,[2] which represents approximately only 14 percent of China's land area.[3] China will need to take steps to improve the employment situation throughout the rest of the country.

8

CHINESE
GOVERNMENT
POLICIES

UNLIKE GOVERNMENTS IN DEVELOPED countries where private sector leaders do not view elected officials and bureaucrats as friends of business, in China the government effectively runs the economy and most companies. Think of the various political leaders in China as a supervisory board for the nation's companies.

The Chinese economy is managed through a succession of five-year plans, which set many specific goals. These five-year plans form China's industrial policy and are a key contributor to the country's growth. Central to the five-year plans is an emphasis on exports over local consumption, to achieve a positive trade balance. This emphasis builds industries and corporations to generate the employment base and the manufacturing of goods that provide good economic returns.

The leadership, however, is pragmatic enough that as the global competitive environment changes, it is able to modify some of its goals.

For example, as the reality of the 2008 to 2009 global recession set in, government policies were modified to increase local consumption. An impressive part of the Chinese government policies is the leadership's ability and willingness to change as the economic environment evolves.

This type of centralized control over commercial enterprises has been aided by the educational backgrounds of China's leaders.

China's Technocrat Leadership

A high percentage of the top leaders of China are engineers. The educational pedigrees of the Chinese leadership are shown in Table 8.1, which was assembled from the Central People's Government Web site as well as Xinhuanet, the Xinhua News Agency's online presence.

The high levels of education of the Chinese leaders and the engineering background many of them have enable them to understand the technical and business issues important for competitiveness. A number of the top leaders attended Tsinghua University, which has extremely high admissions standards. This elite group has developed and implemented economic policies that have proved to be constructive.

While China is making large expenditures now in infrastructure to become more efficient, China's industrial success has been fairly recent. In fact, as recently as 2003 China received \$1.3 billion[1] in foreign aid. The transformation of China from being a nation in need of foreign support to one that is financially powerful has occurred in only the last eight or nine years.

The Government's Attitude toward Its Citizens

The social contract between the Chinese people and their government is drastically different from that in Europe and the United States. In the West, the population is given benefits based on their needs and voting power—the Great Society welfare programs launched by Lyndon Johnson in the late 1960s were in part a response to the increased number of registered minority voters. In China, the paramount metric for determining the value of people is their contribution to building

TABLE 8.1

Educational Backgrounds of Top Leaders in China

Name	Position	Hometown	Year Born	Education
Hu Jintao	President of People's Republic of China Chief secretary of CPC Central Committee Chairman of Central Military Commission	Jixi of Anhui Province	1942	Conservancy project of Tsinghua University in Beijing, undergraduate degree in engineering
Wen Jiabao	Premier of State Council Member of Standing Committee of Political Bureau of CPC Central Committee Secretary of Leading Party Members' Group	Tianjin city	1942	Beijing Institute of Geology and master's degree in geology
Wu Bangguo	Member of Standing Committee of Political Bureau of CPC Central Committee Chairman of Standing Committee of Tenth National People's Congress Secretary of Leading Party Members' Group	Feidong of Anhui Province	1941	Department of Radio and Electronics of Tsinghua University, undergraduate degree in engineering
Jia Qinglin	Chairman of National Committee of Chinese People's Political Consultative Conference	Botou of Hebei Province	1940	Department of Electric Power of Hebei Engineering College, undergraduate degree in advanced engineering
Li Changchun	Member of Standing Committee of Political Bureau of CPC Central Committee	Dalian of Liaoning Province	1944	Industrial Enterprise Automation of Department of Electric Machinery of Harbin Institute of Technology, undergraduate degree in engineering

(continued on next page)

143

TABLE 8.1

Educational Backgrounds of Top Leaders in China (continued)

Name	Position	Hometown	Year Born	Education
Xi Jinping	Vice chairman Member of Standing Committee of Political Bureau of CPC Central Committee Member of Secretariat of CPC Central Committee Secretary of CPC Shanghai Municipal Committee	Fuping of Shaanxi Province	1953	School of Humanities and Social Services of Tsinghua University in Beijing, Ph.D. of law
Li Keqiang	Vice prime minister Member of Standing Committee of Political Bureau of CPC Central Committee Secretary of CPC Liaoning Provincial Committee Chairman of Standing Committee of Liaoning Provincial People's Congress	Dingyuan of Anhui Province	1955	School of Economics of Peking University, Ph.D. in economics (also studied law at Peking University)
He Guoqiang	Secretary of Central Commission for Discipline Inspection of CPC Central Committee Member of Political Bureau Member of Secretariat of CPC Central Committee Head of Organization Department of CPC Central Committee	Xiangxiang of Hunan Province	1943	Inorganic Chemistry Department of Beijing Institute of Chemical Engineering in Beijing, undergraduate degree in advanced engineering

Name	Position	Birthplace	Year	Education
Zhou Yongkang	Secretary of Political and Legislative Affairs Committee of CPC Central Committee Member of Standing Committee of Political Bureau State councilor and member of Leading Party Members' Group of State Council Minister and Party Secretary of Ministry of Public Security	Wuxi of Jiangsu Province	1942	Exploration Department of Beijing Petroleum Institute, undergraduate degree in advanced engineering
Hui Liangyu	Vice premier of State Council Member of Political Bureau of CPC Central Committee	Yushu of Jilin Province	1944	College degree from Jilin Provincial Party School, economist
Zhang Dejiang	Vice premier Member of Political Bureau of CPC Central Committee Secretary of Zhejiang Provincial Party Committee	Tai'an of Liaoning Province	1946	Economics Department of Kim Il Sung Comprehensive University in North Korea, undergraduate degree in economics
Wang Qishan	Vice premier Member of Political Bureau of CPC Central Committee Deputy secretary of CPC Beijing Municipal Committee Mayor of Beijing Executive chairman of Beijing Organizing Committee for XXIX Olympiad Deputy secretary of Leading Party Members' Group	Tianzhen of Shaanxi Province	1948	Department of History of Northwest University in Xi'an, undergraduate degree in economics

the country's wealth. People are considered as resources in China, and its leaders take the same calculating squint at people that they would take toward an iron ore deposit, a fattened pig, or a piece of production equipment. People are something to be managed so they can be productive. They are nurtured and cultivated if and as long as they are productive. As they age, the value of people as a resource goes down. They are a depreciating asset. When their ability to contribute to the national wealth has reached the point of diminishing returns, they are expendable. But their loss to the labor force won't be lamented. There are millions to take their place.

China is willing to provide education to the young because it is expecting a payback: their eventual productivity. On the other hand, providing pensions to the elderly is a low priority, even if they have worked hard their whole lives. That's another reason why the Chinese people save money so diligently. They know or they fear that they will have to fend for themselves when they are elderly and tired. The ruling consideration is to use the population as an asset to build wealth.

China plans to spend \$124 billion[2] to improve its health care system. The funds will go to building new teaching centers to graduate more physicians, building hospitals, and setting up clinics. The building of the medical care infrastructure can increase the employment base in China, but it will not provide exports. Nevertheless, healthy workers are productive workers.

There is a lesson in how China treats its people: it shows how China will treat outsiders. If the Chinese leaders view Chinese citizens as expendable, it's no surprise that those leaders would consider foreign countries and corporations to be worthwhile if and only as long as they are useful. If the benefits to China are high, the Chinese leaders will cultivate a relationship with a foreign country or corporation. If the benefits to China are low, the leaders will not have a rationale for maintaining the relationship.

The education, training, and contribution of the population are critical parts of the building of wealth in China. If you were to ask a planner from the central government if this was a callous way to view and treat human beings, the likely response would be that, with such a gigantic population, there would be an enormous difference in the ability to build wealth between an efficient and an inefficient use of the population.

The Government's Top-Level Guidance of Business Growth

The growth of China's economy is guided by detailed five-year plans established by the National People's Congress. Table 8.2 shows the top tier of the Chinese government hierarchy that administers the plan.

There are a number of important issues that pertain to or are an outgrowth of the government structure in China, as described below.

The top-level ministries are very powerful and have the ultimate authority to mandate what actions are needed to govern economic affairs.

According to the National Bureau of Statistics of China, there are approximately 100 million people employed by the government, which represents approximately 15 percent of the GDP. That 100 million is also approximately 15 percent of the workforce in China.

There is no counterforce to the decisions of the top ministries. Their rulings have the force of unappealable law, even if what they are trying to achieve may not be realistic. For China to strengthen its industrial base within such a short time, it needs an efficient decision process and rapid implementation. Trying to have a consensus approach to administration probably would result in slow decision processes and perhaps a wasteful fragmentation of resources.

While China's leaders would acknowledge and accept that mistakes are being and will be made, nevertheless the growth of the GDP in China is rapid and is being accomplished without creating large deficits.

The management of the growth of China involves a wide range of bureaucracies. It is often unclear, to outsiders as well as the Chinese, who the actual decision makers are. But to judge by results, the skills of the top-level government officials in China are improving. Certainly many of the highest goals are clear and are being persuasively communicated.

TABLE 8.2

State Structure of China

The National People's Congress (NPC)	The President Head of State	The State Council	The Central Military Commission (CMC)	The Supreme People's Court	The Supreme People's Procuratorate
Highest organization of state power	Supreme representative both internally and externally Responsible for commanding Armed Forces	Also called the Central People's Government Highest executive organization Highest organization of state administration	Highest state military organization	Highest trial organization	Highest legal supervision organization of state
Ministry of Foreign Affairs		Ministry of Supervision		Ministry of Railways	
Ministry of National Defense		Ministry of Civil Affairs		Ministry of Water Resources	
National Development and Reform Commission		Ministry of Justice		Ministry of Agriculture	
Ministry of Education		Ministry of Finance		Ministry of Commerce	
Ministry of Science and Technology		Ministry of Human Resources and Social Security		Ministry of Culture	
Ministry of Industry and Information Technology		Ministry of Land and Resources		Ministry of Health	
State Ethnic Affairs Commission		Ministry of Environmental Protection		National Population and Family Planning Commission	
Ministry of Public Security		Ministry of Housing and Urban-Rural Development		People's Bank of China	
Ministry of State Security		Ministry of Transport		National Audit Office	

Corrupt Government-Owned Companies and the Impact of Bureaucracy

Many large companies in China are either entirely or partially owned by the government. These companies are major enterprises of the industrial infrastructure, and they handle the supply of water and electricity. In other industries, such as oil and telecom, the government's ownership is still dominant even if the firms are not completely owned by the government.

These types of companies do not have limitations on the prices that they charge for their goods and services. So they can generate very high profits because they are quasi-monopolies.

In the past, these types of companies did not provide high compensation. With the ability to sell a percentage of their stock, the market valuations of these companies became very high. So there is the ability to pay very high levels of compensation via stock. With their very lucrative compensation structures, jobs at these companies have become much sought after by new graduates. Many of the most sought after positions at these companies are given to children of government bureaucrats.

If unemployment increases in China, specifically for new college graduates, and people have been learning about the behind-the-scenes employment practices of these quasi-government organizations, there could be growing disillusionment with the system. This type of corruption can result in growing inefficiency within strategically important industries in China. And outrage has been festering among the public.

The bureaucracy in China is relatively new. Many of the government agencies became business centric only after 1976. The tendency for bureaucracies is to become self-preserving and to focus on their own benefits as opposed to being committed to improving the wealth of the country. Corruption in China tends to increase as the distance from the seat of the central government increases or as the control of the top-level leadership is reduced. Where such powerful, monopolistic government utilities are concerned, an increased measure of vigilance would be warranted.

As in any society where enormous power is concentrated among a few, it is crucial to ensure that corruption is controlled and that the top leaders conduct themselves as fiduciaries of the people's wealth rather than amassing wealth of their own or of their offspring. At the very top levels, it appears that corruption is under control.

The Government's Large Investments in Industrial Growth

The Chinese government is conservative in many of its political decisions. But it is willing to make enormous long-term investments for promoting economic development. It appears capable of boldness to ensure that there is rapid progress in strengthening industry, even if that creates some waste. China is in a hurry, but at least it is hurrying with well-defined plans and is monitoring its progress.

Three of the largest expenditures have been made for infrastructure projects—the dam known as the Three Gorges Project, Beijing Capital International Airport, and the high-speed rail link between Beijing and Guangzhou via Shanghai.

These and other large projects are improving the efficiency of China's industries and provide massive short-term employment. They also enable China to increase its expertise in managing large complex projects. China was very proud of the opening of Terminal 2 in Shanghai, with no lost bags or flight delays.

Many of the high-growth opportunities for businesses are in high technology. This creates many opportunities, but it also represents an area in which China will compete directly with the United States. However, while many high-tech U.S. corporations are successful in global markets, in China they are competing against a cartel composed of Chinese corporations and their supportive government connections.

Industrial Growth in the Provinces

China is a large country. There are 32 provinces as well as what are called *autonomous zones*. Many of the provinces and large cities, such as Shanghai, have their own industrialization agendas. A common goal of many of the provinces and cities is to grow employment by encouraging the establishment of companies or company facilities in their regions. That employment increases the tax base.

The provinces and cities, as well as the central government, are active in the expansion of strategic industries. The provinces are encouraged by the central government to specialize in specific industries. Some of the larger cities such as Shanghai, Beijing, and Shenzhen have their own industrial agendas. The provinces and cities may exercise some autonomy. Since there are currently around 62 cities[3] with a population of more than 1 million, there is the potential for a huge number of duplicative initiatives.

So it is no surprise that redundant initiatives have led to a duplication of industries in a number of areas. For example, small independent automobile companies have been set up in a number of provinces. In some cases the output capacity of these companies has been too low for long-term survival. To encourage the automobile companies to reach critical mass, the central government has been trying to consolidate the industry into three to five larger companies. The automobile industry is considered strategically important in China because of the large employment base that it establishes.

Redundant industrial specialization cannot be supported. The central government decides which cities receive support for certain industries or transportation systems. There is intense competition among the cities for government support. Autonomy notwithstanding, the central government sweetens its subsidies to provinces and cities that support its top-level goals.

By forcing the cities and provinces to compete for funds, the central government is able to have strong control over the cities. Fewer larger automobile companies will be easier for the central government to control and protect. Competition among these few stronger contenders will help them all become stronger. Meanwhile China imposes large tariffs on imported automobiles, which helps protect the local producers. While the Chinese automobile companies compete aggressively against each other, they benefit from strong protection from outsiders.

The activities in the provinces and industrial zones also are partly controlled by the central government through the granting of manufacturing licenses. This gives the government the ability to set priorities for the different regions and promote initiatives that support its plans for long-term growth in employment and exports. Licensing also controls the number and type of foreign companies allowed to operate in the provinces via joint ventures.

Some cities and provinces have achieved a large measure of success in building their employment base in electronics. For example, in the Wuhan East Lake New Technology Zone in the Hubei Province, the provincial government has built and is the owner of a plant that produces integrated circuits (ICs). These semiconductor chips are the brains of computers, cell phones, and other devices. They are created by imprinting the circuits on 300-mm-diameter circular wafers of semiconductor material. (A 300-mm wafer is about 12 inches in diameter, or smaller than a small pizza.) This production of IC wafers is the most advanced commercial IC manufacturing technology. The plant is being operated by the Semiconductor Manufacturing International Corporation (SMIC), a semiconductor manufacturer based in Shanghai. The expectation is that the wafer manufacturing facility will generate employment both within the facility as well as in supporting industries. SMIC sells over 60 percent of its output to North American companies.[4]

While it is important for cities to have autonomy, it is also important that their investment decisions support the long-term, government-promulgated overall strategies for industrialization. Shanghai has encouraged the establishment of an industrial and financial base in Pudong, and many foreign and Chinese companies have set up manufacturing facilities there. While Shanghai tries to have a high level of autonomy in its decision making, it is important that it coordinates its activities with other large cities so it doesn't create overcapacity in manufacturing for specific products.

China is an appealing place for foreign companies to establish manufacturing facilities because it provides them access to low-cost labor and potential access to Chinese customers. The central government has provided low-cost land for building factories, and it has made the approval process for setting up new manufacturing businesses relatively easy. Industrial zones often provide electricity, water, and other services at low cost. Companies can establish factories with low initial costs, and the cost of manufacturing products within those factories will be low. However, the government may require that the company operating the plant be majority owned by a Chinese partner or that a very high percentage of the output be exported.

By owning the land, the central government in China has control over the future use of the land and the buildings on the land. While it is likely that leases will be offered and then extended for businesses that are strategic, the government will usually retain the right to terminate the leases.

The government is always, in effect, a silent but extremely influential partner in any dealings of foreign companies within China. It's a partner with its own agenda, one that will always outrank yours if the agendas conflict. The government will be generous if your agenda meshes with its goals. If not, that support can be withdrawn quickly.

Building Infrastructure

China is renowned for building mammoth infrastructure projects. The Great Wall is almost 4,000 miles long, not including trenches and other natural defense barriers such as rivers and hills. Another large project was the Grand Canal, which stretches 1,085 miles from near Beijing to Hangzhou.[5] Today the infrastructure projects are most often roads, railroads, power grids, and power plants.

China plans to build 30,000 miles of highways from 2005 to 2020.[6] The roads are needed to support the large number of vehicles that are expected to be manufactured.

China has embarked on a $585 billion stimulus package focused on improving the transportation and communications infrastructure.[7] The stimuli also are providing well-defined, short-term employment, especially for migrant workers.

High-speed rail systems are being built for passengers and freight for many of the inland centers as well as the coastal areas, such as the Wuhan-Guangzhou bullet train line, which opened in December 2009. Another standout example is the construction of a high-speed rail link between Beijing and Shanghai. That is employing 110,000 workers.[8] These new rail lines are the primary transportation links for the country in the future, just as the navigable rivers of the United States led to the commercial development from the colonial period to the Civil War. Subway systems are being expanded in cities such as Shanghai and Beijing. New subway systems are being built in cities such as Xi'an. Roads are also being built and improved to accommodate the large increase in automobiles that will be manufactured and purchased in China. China is also expanding its oil refining as well as promoting initiatives to increase fuel efficiency. All of this infrastructure will enhance the ability of China's migrant workers to travel to urban employment areas.

While China continues to lag the United States and other developed countries in infrastructure and transportation, it is catching up fast. In another 10 to 20 years China is expected to make the same amount of progress as the United States did in 50 years.[9] (The U.S. interstate highway system took almost five decades to complete.)

Since the government owns the land, it is relatively easy to obtain the required rights of way. In many cases buildings have to be demolished and people have to be moved in order to build the infrastructure. In most cases the government has ranked the value of economic development for the entire country above the rights of individual property owners. The preferences and entitlements of individuals customarily have low value compared to those of society. However, as in all countries, there are occasional exceptions. A high-speed train line between Shanghai's Pudong Airport and Hangzhou had its route changed because of protests.

Recently there have been airport expansions, such as those in Beijing and Shanghai. There are also plans to build an additional 97 airports in China by 2020.[10] However, air travel will be given lower priority than rail travel in most of China. When the high-speed train service between Beijing and Shanghai, a distance of almost 1,500 kilometers or more than 900 miles, starts in 2011, it is likely that a high percentage of travelers between the two cities will travel by train.[11]

Power Supplies

Improving the supply of power has been one of the preoccupations of infrastructure planners in China. Electricity generation capacity is being increased, and the grid is being improved.

Coal is the principal fuel for generating electricity in China. An enduring problem with using coal is that the main sources of the ore, in Shanxi and Shaanxi, are long distances from the centers of population. New railroads for transporting heavy freight such as coal are being built to improve efficiency.

The Chinese are also increasing their nuclear power generating capacity, with no outcry from citizens regarding safety. France, which is one of the world leaders in the building of nuclear power stations, has not been awarded large contracts in China because of their political differences, especially those regarding China's occupation of Tibet. More recently France has been trying to improve relationships with China, and it is likely to get some contracts for nuclear power facilities. As the French have learned, political conflict with China can penalize their business interests.

There are concerns with pollution in China. However, pollution and the environment will be a lower priority than the growth of employment and industry. If pollution were to reduce industrial productivity or the competitiveness of exports, then actions would be taken promptly to reduce pollution.

China is, however, very conscious of the need to build large electricity generation capacity. If electric vehicles become important in the future, it is important to have adequate electricity.

Water Shortages

Water supply is a major present problem. The pollution of rivers and lakes is taking a terrible toll on the water supply of China. Aqueducts have been built to increase the amount of water supplied to large cities such as Beijing, but even with these recourses, it is likely that parts of China will have shortages of water in the future.

There are already water shortages in the north, especially in the northwest. An example is Xi'an. It had eight rivers during the Tang dynasty (618 to 907 AD) when Xi'an was the capital of China and China was the strongest nation in the world. Today, Xi'an has two rivers that have hardly any water.

Rainfall is uneven over China, and better management of the water supply is required. The water problems are made more complicated because some areas with large populations, such as Beijing, are also areas that have low rainfall.

Ensuring adequate water is one of the challenges facing China. As the industrial base and the middle class grow, they will both need more water. Because rainfall is uneven and inadequate in some of the larger cities, China will have to move water or people. Moving water will cost less than moving people, but probably both options will be used.

Moving the People

Moving people daily to deploy them as labor is another pressing issue. It is not realistic to expect or allow large cities such as Beijing, Shanghai, Guangzhou, and Shenzhen to grow as rapidly as they have in the past 5 to 10 years. Even with the building of subways, the transportation networks within these cities are overloaded.

There has also been a big rise in the value of houses in the large cities, which drives up the cost of living for the residents and leads workers to press for more pay. This trend could lead large cities to focus on more advanced technologies. Meanwhile less populous cities in the interior can focus on staffing high-volume, labor-intensive factories.

China's social planners are offering incentives for companies to establish factories in or near smaller cities in the interior. Such relocations would allow employees to live in or much closer to their hometowns, which could promote a more stable social environment. The pay scales in the interior cities are much lower than they are in the coastal cities and in areas such as Guangzhou and Shanghai. There is also lower employee turnover in smaller inland cities. More industrial employment venues in the interior would also reduce the number of migrant workers straining transportation capacity to, from, and within the big cities, especially during the Chinese New Year.

While market forces can effect such changes in the distribution and transportation of industrial labor, this evolution can take time and the process can be inefficient. So the central government is involved in relocating as well as allocating labor resources as sensibly as possible. This not only improves efficiency and reduces costs but it also has the side benefit of keeping many parents, who had been migrant workers, much closer to their children and extended families.

9

CHINESE ECONOMIC PHILOSOPHIES

CENTURIES OF EXPLOITATION and foreign domination, as recently as World War II when it was invaded and occupied brutally by Japan, have made the Chinese extremely concerned to maintain their independence and to cultivate their power and competitive advantages. A major goal of the Chinese is to be free of foreign domination. Many of its experiences, even with supposedly friendly foreign countries in the nineteenth century,[1] have been distasteful and shameful for the Chinese people. The Communist Party constantly reiterates that it will ensure that China will never be dominated by foreigners.

The government is also protective of China's productive assets. It tries to ensure that they cannot be exploited by foreigners. Toward that end, for example, the central government owns all land and controls its leasing. That enables the government to determine and supervise what the land is used for. That also enables the government to quickly provide the rights-of-way for new roads, new railway lines, and new airports.

Protecting assets also extends to corporations. Such protectionism is currently justified by claims that Chinese corporations are weak and need to build up. There are limits on foreign ownership of corporations in a number of industries. Manufacturing licenses for products such as automobiles are granted only if the government has been assured that a Chinese partner has majority ownership of a business entity or joint venture.

The Chinese also see markets as assets. Even as Chinese corporations strengthen, it's foreseeable that the Chinese will protect their markets, at least for many strategic products. The protection will be direct, such as requiring government-granted manufacturing licenses, or it may be indirect, such as finding fault with imported products and communicating that fault via propaganda or by imposing tariffs.

After more than 5,000 years of wars and other conflicts, the Chinese have learned to be long-term strategic thinkers and to develop their competitive advantages. Originally China's strategies were developed for armies; now many of the strategies are being applied to corporations and local markets. Because the United States is currently the second-largest market for its exports,[2] China will ensure U.S. demand remains undiminished, at least for the next few years. The Chinese refrain from attacking a strong adversary. Better to wait until the opponent becomes weak. Because it views the United States as its main competitor as a global superpower, China will wait until the United States becomes weaker before it does anything more assertive. For now China's emphasis is on nurturing its industrial strength: making sure foreign corporations are unable to dominate Chinese corporations within China's market. The goal of the next phase will be for Chinese corporations to gain high market shares in foreign markets.

The success of Huawei Technologies in the global wireless communications infrastructure market shows the ability of Chinese corporations to build a strong technology base and to gain high market share in high-technology markets outside of China. Established in 1988, Huawei specializes in the development, production, and sale of communications equipment. It is considered to be among the global leaders in data and voice communications gear for telephone operators and large companies. In 2008 it claimed revenues in excess of $18 billion.[3]

China's leaders would probably view Huawei Technologies' progress as a vindication of their attempts to run China as a giant, protective incubator for its businesses. In fact, other Chinese companies are expected to emulate the Huawei tactics of developing the local market and then attacking overseas markets with advanced technology products.

That protective mindset also extends to the country's capital markets. For example, there are restrictions on foreign ownership of stock. China requires there to be two classes of stock for its publicly traded companies. One class confers voting rights that ensure its shareholders retain majority control. Foreigners cannot amass such stock but can own the second tier shares which offer the potential for capital appreciation.This way China controls investments by outsiders and ensures that foreign shareholders cannot interfere with strategies the government has planned for various industries. Sinopec is one example of a Chinese company with a two-stock class structure. There are many benefits for China in its controlling the use of the money that is generated within its borders. One benefit is that it enables China to promote its manufacturing base. Protectionism is one of the tools China is using to protect its assets, which include its corporate armies. Protectionism also often shelters and sustains uncompetitive, poorly managed, and inflexible domestic companies. How that plays out will be demonstrated in markets outside China.

Access to Raw Materials

For China to increase its GDP and continue to strengthen its industrial employment, it needs to import enormous amounts of raw materials, including oil, copper, and iron ore. While in the near future the emphasis will be on ensuring enough low-cost raw materials for immediate use, the government is also carrying out initiatives to ensure access to the resources that will be needed in the next 20 to 50 years.

The worldwide demand for raw materials will increase as countries such as China, India, Indonesia, and Brazil increase the standards of living of their middle class and overall populations.

Even in 2006 China's consumption of raw materials was a substantial portion of overall global demand. It consumed 45 percent of the cement, 30 percent of the steel, iron, and coal, 20 percent of the copper, and 20 percent of the aluminum.[4]

China's consumption of annual worldwide oil production—only 10 percent in 2007—will be low for only a short time.[5] Automobile production in China is forecast to be 20 million vehicles annually by 2020. Meanwhile India is developing $2,500 automobiles. Because of India and China, global demand for oil will increase enormously in the future, even with the development of autos that are more energy efficient.

The large consumption of materials by China is for exports as well as the domestic market. As corporations in China strengthen and the size of the middle class increases, there will be a marked increase in domestic consumption of end products and, therefore, the natural resources that are incorporated in that merchandise.

The industrial world has never experienced a phenomenon like China, where growth has been as rapid, where more than a billion people are trying to become middle class in a breathtakingly short time. Because of its size and growth rate, China's consumption of natural resources from 2012 to 2015 will be much larger than its demand from 2007 through early 2008, when shortages in copper, steel, and other vital materials were already happening.

China clearly understands the need to ensure its access to natural resources, and it is actively trying to acquire companies (or substantial partial ownership in them) that have raw materials. This is consistent with the Chinese disposition to own tangible assets. The Chinese value factories that produce things, and they are suspicious of industries that do not have and use tangible assets.

The competition for natural resources will require the use of several strategies. One key requirement is to have large financial resources to be able to pay or acquire suppliers. With its large dollar reserves and overwhelmingly positive trade balance, the financial resources of China are strong and will continue to strengthen while the financial resources of the United States will weaken.

Besides the need to pay for the raw materials, countries competing for natural resources need the political influence to negotiate favorable terms with foreign governments that, in many cases, control supplies. When there are shortages, such influence can be crucial to ensure adequate supplies. By buying companies with mineral rights now, the Chinese are proactively establishing and ensuring their future supply base.

Selective Breeding in the Chinese Economy

While there are more than a billion customers in China (seemingly more than enough customers to go around), there is also intense competition among Chinese companies. As some domestic companies fail, others are started—by entrepreneurs who have learned from past failures. Survival skills are learned and spread. The result is a steady building of expertise in China. Each wave of new corporations is stronger than the preceding one.

Another rarely noted weapon in China's competitive arsenal is its use of tax policy for economic development. The tax system in China has been revised and implemented to be conducive to industrial growth. A high percentage of tax revenues are committed to the building of employment.

For example, taxes on cigarettes are high in China, as much as 65 percent of retail prices. The taxes on cigarettes provide support for construction, education, consumption, and other socially useful purposes. The total tax revenues from cigarettes are $293 billion per year. There are approximately 350 million smokers in China.[6]

The competitive threat from China's economy does not come from just a few world-class corporations. Rather, it comes from the combination of corporations (some of them sponsored and/or partially owned by the government) plus central government agencies, provincial governments, and other local groups, all of which are working together to strengthen the capabilities of Chinese corporations to gain market share in the domestic as well as export markets. There is even competition between the provinces to support their local industries because of the need to provide employment for new graduates as well as assembly workers within those provinces. The internal competition will winnow out the losers, so only the best will survive and address the export market.

This combination of demand from a gigantic population, government control and guidance, and protection from much foreign competition, all of which are enhanced by provincial support and challenged by domestic competition—all these factors constitute, in effect, a deliberate selective breeding program for Chinese companies. Not surprisingly, they have evolved, changing from firms that depend primarily on their low-cost labor to resourceful producers capable of succeeding throughout China's markets. This transformation has occurred largely in the past five years. The next phase is to build companies that can compete worldwide.

Certain geopolitical advantages also may help China's economic ambitions. One of China's aims is to try not to have major political enemies. This is in contrast to the United States, which made many enemies during the George W. Bush presidency. This avoidance of foreign conflict is consistent with historical strategic thinking in China. If a nation creates enemies, those enemies could form an alliance and combine their resources. That could result in a strong adversary. If enemies or competitors are divided, or, better yet, not created in the first place, then it is easier to prevail over them.

The Progress of Industrialization in China as Seen in the Textile Industry

While China started its industrialization after 1976, most of the high-growth activities in China have occurred since 1986. During the past 20 years China has established a large base of heavy industries, such as steel, construction equipment, factory machinery, ship building, and coal mining.

In addition to developing the various heavy industries, China has also built the necessary infrastructure. This is the industrial equivalent of being at sea and building both the dry dock and the boat at the same time. India has taken the same approach.

At the same time, China has been establishing industries that are labor intensive: textiles, clothing, and furniture, among others. This phase is continuing in China, although now the Chinese have competition from other low-labor-cost countries, such as Vietnam. These other countries do not have the vast number of workers or the financial resources that China has. The textile industry in China continues to employ a large number of workers. It serves as an occupational opportunity for many young women who have great dexterity but little education or technical expertise.

The initial phase of textile manufacturing in China used equipment imported from the United States, Europe, and Japan to set up large manufacturing facilities. Low-cost labor and management were the main competitive advantages then.

Beginning in the late 1990s, though, the manufacturing equipment was produced in China. As China built up its textile manufacturing equipment, companies in other countries shut down. This was a critical phase because the Chinese learned to control all the facets of the industry. If another country wants to get into textiles now, it would have to buy the equipment from China.

The skills that were developed in the United States, Europe, and Japan for the design and supply of the textile equipment have been transferred to China. It would be difficult to reclaim that expertise because it's the Chinese now who are best acquainted with the increasingly complex equipment.

China provides clothes for retailers such as the Gap, Lands' End, Walmart, and Costco, and also companies in Japan, Europe, and elsewhere.

Because the U.S., European, and Japanese retailers contracted for massive volumes of clothes, Chinese suppliers didn't particularly need marketing skills. On the other hand, the demand for certain merchandise could be highly volatile. The loyalty of specific customers was low. But the Chinese learned to understand them all. Japanese customers were much more demanding about quality. U.S. customers accepted low quality but wanted very low prices.

As China changes, it has become necessary to move textile and clothing factories from the higher-cost coastal cities, such as Shanghai, into lower-cost interior regions. Even with the improvement in the education system, there is a large population of uneducated females in China. It has been important to provide employment opportunities for them.

While the initial emphasis of the textile industry in China was on the export market, now, as the population becomes wealthier and more discerning, there is more demand for clothes in a variety of up-to-date styles in China.

Many famous designer clothing brands have a presence in China, but domestic brands account for more than 80 percent of consumption in China. The local brands have names that are similar to the well-known foreign brands (often one letter in the name might be changed, for example, "Guchi" instead of "Gucci"). Many of the marketing concepts in China are primitive, but here, as in other aspects of the business, the Chinese have steadily developed their expertise. Besides copying approaches that have succeeded for foreign clothing companies, the Chinese are trying new approaches.

The young in China want to wear the latest designer fashions, which increases the demand for clothes. The young in urban areas tend to spend most of their income; they are very different from the older Chinese who are frugal and continue to save a relatively high percentage of their earnings.

The retail environment has provided the textile industry with a tremendous domestic outlet. The new shopping centers in China have characteristics and prices similar to those in developed countries. In many cases, small business owners rent space in a store, and these businesses are responsible for their own inventory and they pay a percentage of their revenues to the building owners. This allows the number of stores to grow rapidly, enabling a single retail unit to offer many different types of products. Stores within stores and other more modern versions of the pushcarts used by immigrants on the Lower East Side at the dawn of the twentieth century in New York City show the entrepreneurial characteristics of the Chinese. GOME is an example of a company that has used this approach in the electronics industry.

The textile industry in China has become so strong that the United States and European Union have established import quotas. Because of these limitations, the textile industries in India, Indonesia, Pakistan, Malaysia, and Vietnam have gained an advantageous opportunity.

The textile industries in the United States, Japan, and most parts of Europe, including Italy, have been severely wounded by Chinese exports, especially at the low end of the market.[7] It is unlikely that programs will be established in the United States, Europe, or Japan to rebuild the textile and clothing industries even though there is the potential to have large employment and the potential for reducing imports and increasing exports.

A similar situation can apply to shoes and furniture, where it is not likely that financial incentives will be provided to allow these types of industries to recover in the United States, Europe, or Japan, other than potentially in the high-end niche segments.

The textile and clothing industry in China has become large and powerful. However, the textile industry is generally viewed by government officials as low tech. While the textile and clothing industries provide employment for many, they are regarded as not offering high-level employment in significant numbers for engineers and technicians.

Government Involvement in Compensation

In industries that have a large number of workers and for factories owned by foreign companies, the Chinese government is becoming more active in determining compensation and employment conditions. The result is that labor costs are increasing for the foreign companies.

The establishing of labor contracts in China can result in additional costs for foreign manufacturers while providing competitive advantages for Chinese manufacturers. The use of the labor contracts indicates that government officials want to exert control over who manufactures products. It also indicates that government officials want to extend control over foreign companies.

Because of its ability to influence employment contracts, the Chinese government will be able to decide in which industries local manufacturers will be supported and to choose which joint ventures it will support and/or encourage.

It is unlikely that strong trade unions will be established in China because trade unions could foreseeably challenge the authority of the central government. The officially sanctioned trade union, which is called the All-China Federation of Trade Unions (ACFTU), is controlled by the government.

One well-known Chinese strategy that it uses in competitive situations is to choose weak opponents or to do what is necessary to make opponents weaker. That approach extends to preventing opponents from forming alliances with those who have similar interests. *The 36 Strategies* is a collection of ancient tactical proverbs by General Wang Jingze. It places a strong emphasis on the ways to divide opponents and ensure that they do not combine their strengths. This approach will be used to prevent trade unions from becoming strong in China.

While the Chinese government can allow wages and benefits to increase, its more fundamental goals are to increase employment and exports. Also, Chinese policy planners are reluctant to increase wages until industrial production has expanded to the point that domestic factories can produce enough goods for both local consumption and exports.

The industrial base in China will continue to grow in areas that are labor and capital intensive. The next phase is to grow industries that are brain power intensive.

Contract Manufacturing Activities

In the 1990s, China was a favored location of a number of the electronics contract manufacturers because of its large pool of low-cost labor.

Contract manufacturers assemble products for companies such as Hewlett-Packard, IBM, Apple, Sony, Phillips, and Cisco. The ink-jet printers or laptop computers found in American homes and offices often have been assembled by contract manufacturers such as Solectron and Flextronics. These electronics suppliers found China appealing because the cost to set up manufacturing facilities was low. The land-lease costs were low or free, and the buildings were also provided at low cost or were free. Most of the output from the contract manufacturers was exported.

While the initial social benefit of these manufacturing facilities was to provide employment for assembly workers (untrained and uneducated young workers), their operations led to improvement in manufacturing skills in China. There continues to be a large contract manufacturing industry in China because of the need to continue to employ a large number of uneducated workers.

A more recent trend in China has been the proliferation of contract manufacturing facilities in China owned by Taiwanese companies. One outstanding example is Hon Hai (also known as Foxconn), which employs more than 500,000 workers, even after the 2008 and 2009 recession.

In addition to Hon Hai, other Taiwanese manufacturers established large manufacturing facilities in China. The common language between Taiwan and China is a major asset in setting up such businesses in China.

While China provides its labor pool, a high percentage of the investments for setting up manufacturing facilities comes from external sources. The technology and training also come from outside of China. Its suspicion of outsiders notwithstanding, China has been willing to accept investments from foreign sources along with whatever else might be useful for economic development. The result is that China has gained access to foreign manufacturing expertise at low cost, while it has developed a large and ongoing employment base that has served as an occupational home for its managers as well as its assembly workers.

As the corporations in China mature and the value of the products that they manufacture increases, such progress leads to the training of a large number of managers, supervisors, engineers, and technicians.

This expanding pool of trained supervisors enables new businesses to be started, which further increases output.

The many joint ventures that have been started also provide access to the technologies, products, and management skills of foreign companies. As the Chinese develop technologies and learn management skills, the value to them of being involved in joint ventures declines. Once the Chinese have absorbed the knowledge, they have the tendency to discard their partners.

Besides low-cost labor, another compelling motivation of the foreign companies to set up facilities in China has been the chance to sell their products to the enormous Chinese market. Meeting this goal has usually required most multinational corporations to have China-centric market strategies.

The experience of many foreign corporations is that it has been difficult to penetrate the Chinese market without a Chinese partner. Even when the foreign corporations have been able to find Chinese partners, such joint ventures have had mixed results for the foreign companies. When these joint ventures have not done well selling products from their base in China, it has often been because they did not develop an understanding of the decision processes of their Chinese partners. Foreign companies need to understand the strategies and goals of their Chinese partners. How a win-win situation is perceived in China can be radically different from how it is perceived in the United States.

Chinese companies are very flexible in the business models they support, and this willingness to be flexible represents a key competitive strength of China. The flexibility also means that, if a business is not growing as expected, Chinese partners are quick to make changes. Besides being less doctrinaire about the business models they pursue, Chinese partners usually are more concerned with achieving long-term goals than with achieving short-term objectives. However, in other cases, Chinese partners show less regard for the long-term objective than for the short-term success. The flexibility of thinking and strategies of Chinese managers can sometimes be difficult to comprehend.

It is important to analyze Chinese companies and market sectors on a case-by-case basis and to have an in-depth understanding of the goals, strengths, and weaknesses of the Chinese partners or competitors.

For many Chinese businesspeople and government planners, the long term is longer than that of their Western counterparts. China's planners presume it will take another 10 to 20 years for China to be able to compete in the sophisticated markets in developed countries. And they are prepared for very slow progress.

Confucius said: "It does not matter how slowly you go [as] long as you do not stop." The history of China shows a willingness to work tirelessly for years to build strengths that can be used to dominate an enemy or competitor. The relentless way that China is building its strengths should not be underestimated. It is building its strength in a very methodical way, and it won't stop until it is a formidable competitor.

State-Owned Enterprises

Besides the industrial zones, a number of state-owned enterprises (SOEs) have been established in China to support the development of industries that are strategic (oil, steel, communications, and automotive, for example). Through the SOEs, the Chinese are able to make long-term commitments to the development of technologies and the building of management expertise in industries in which the time to profit can be long. There are different types of SOEs, but a common characteristic is that some substantial percentage of control is maintained by the government.

Some state-owned enterprises in China are shown in Table 9.1. The list shown was assembled from their individual company Web sites as well as the Shanghai and Shenzhen stock exchanges.

Some of the SOEs have public shareholders. Nevertheless, the firms are controlled from the top by government ministries. For example, even though China Mobile is a public company, the CEO of the company is chosen by the government. Also, the communications protocols that are utilized by the company are selected by the government. That

TABLE 9.1

Government Ownership of Selected Chinese Companies

Company	2004 Sales (B CNY)*	2008 Sales (B CNY)*	Business	Share Owned by Government 2004 (%)	Share Owned by Government 2008 (%)
Baoshan Iron & Steel	162	245	Steel	85.00	73.97
Changhong Electric	12	28	Consumer electronics, appliances	53.63	30.64
China Life	77	341	Insurance	73.00	68.36
China Merchants Bank	15	55	Bank	48.91	31.15
China Minmetals	123	156	Metallurgy materials, steel trade	100.00	100.00
China Mobile	192	412	Cellular operator	75.50	74.24
China Telecom	153	187	Fixed-line and mobile phone operator	77.78	70.89
China Unicom	70	152	Mobile phone operator	69.32	61.05
First Auto Works (FAW)	136	218	Automobiles	100.00	100.00
Haier	15	30	Appliances, consumer electronics	43.60	43.54
Konka	13	12	Consumer electronics	29.06	16.68
Lenovo	23	102	Computers	46.00	65.00
PetroChina	398	1,071	Oil production and distribution	90.00	86.42
Shanghai Automotive (SAIC)	120	171	Automobiles	100.00	100.00
Sinochem	169	300	Petrochemicals, agriculture, chemical products	100.00	100.00
Sinopec	591	1,452	Oil and gas production and distribution	77.42	75.84
State Grid (SGCC)	590	1,155	Power grids	100.00	100.00
TCL	40	38	Consumer electronics	25.22	12.70
ZTE	23	44	Telecom networking equipment, handsets	44.10	35.52

* Billions of new Chinese yuan.
Source: Information compiled from each company's own Web site as well as the Shanghai and Shenzhen stock exchanges.

explains why China Mobile supports its own version of a communications protocol rather than adopting a more commonly used standard.

Huawei, the data communications gear manufacturer, is an example of a highly successful company that was once an SOE. It had a compounded rate of annual revenue growth of almost 50 percent[8] from 2004 to 2008. The company was launched in 1988, and it had close ties to the Chinese military. While many observers assume that there remains some level of government control or oversight over the privately held company, its officials insist it is 100 percent owned by the employees. While Huawei is effective in competing in global markets for base stations, the company also has a large and somewhat protected market in China.

Energy, communications, automobiles, and banking are being emphasized by the Chinese government. The government is providing subsidies as well as access to protected domestic markets to help accelerate growth in these areas.

Many of the SOEs have become large corporations. For example, Sinopec, the state-owned oil company, had revenues of $197 billion[9] in 2009.

Officials at a number of the SOE companies say that as long as the business is meeting its overall goals and is operating in a manner that is consistent with its charter, there is a low level of government involvement. If the corporation deviates from its expected strategies, then it is likely government involvement will increase. This arrangement gives government agencies extensive discretion to guide the strategic directions of the SOEs.

The top managers of the SOEs have the dual responsibilities of keeping the government happy and managing the company within its competitive industry. China is a planned economy, with strong top-down guidance. At lower levels, there is intense competition between companies. It is not possible to exercise very close government supervision at the lower levels without stifling entrepreneurship. There are, consequently, multiple levels of oversight and influence over companies.

The SOEs are major players in the advance of China's economy. They demonstrate another way the government can exert influence on segments of the local markets. The control and long-range planning are distinguishing features of the Chinese economy. While there are benefits, there are also risks to the immense power of government officials over companies—government controllers can urge bank managers to issue inappropriate loans. And bribery is not unknown as well.

Market Characteristics

Many characteristics of Chinese industry are unique to China. The country achieved its current state of development in less than 25 years, and much of the Internet-generated momentum has occurred in the last 5 years.

One of the main reasons the Chinese economy is changing rapidly is that high numbers of managers are in the 25- to 40-year age group. Many customers are also 25 to 40 years old. The Chinese market has many things that make it different. It's widely presumed that only the Chinese or people completely immersed in the culture can understand these needs, but that will change as the consumers increasingly adopt Western attitudes toward fashion and other goods.

Perseverance and Misdirection

In China, if the first wave of a product introduction is not successful, then there are succeeding waves. The succeeding waves build on the learning that was obtained from the early waves. As with the history of China's military campaigns, the persistence of Chinese companies in strengthening their competitiveness represents a key factor for long-term success.

The perseverance of individuals in China is very high. This character trait in the Chinese people is related to the turmoil in China's history, when failure to achieve a goal might result in death. Survival, even as recently as the Cultural Revolution, could require extraordinary skills. While survival is not an issue now, the success of the economy or of their company is a compelling motivation for a large number of people in China. They will commit themselves extraordinarily to achieving such goals.

While Chinese companies are seeking to compete in many markets worldwide, Chinese companies continue to be unique in their operating cultures. Foreign companies that are partners with Chinese companies need to understand the Chinese people's unique decision processes and operating culture for the partnerships to last a long time.

Many senior managers in China use concepts from *The 36 Strategies* for their negotiations. One strategy is misdirection: act as if Target A is the goal while really focusing on Target B. Using *The 36 Strategies* adds time-tested tactics to their negotiating. It also shows how the Chinese are making use of strategies developed for war in today's corporate battles.

Another characteristic of the Chinese is their willingness to wait to take advantage of opportunities. This is another of *The 36 Strategies*, and it is commonly viewed as waiting out an opponent. Indeed, Chinese managers and businesspeople in general are reluctant to be swayed by those who strike them as overly aggressive or too forceful in demanding change.

Financial Independence

While there can be support from the government for strategic industries, in most cases Chinese corporations need to achieve good financial returns so they can be self-sustaining. When the government hasn't been involved, the Chinese economy has had as many flops as home runs. A number of new companies have had strong revenue growth from their initial products, after which their revenues declined when the second generation of products did not sell well. The reason for this pattern seems to be that many companies either did not or could not make the investments necessary to develop a steady stream of winning follow-on products.

In other cases founders who achieved large financial gains from their initial products wanted to enjoy their wealth instead of reinvesting earnings to build sustainable businesses.

The failure rate among Chinese electronics companies has also been high because a number of not-promising firms nevertheless got funding through public stock offerings. This happened because in China too much investment capital is chasing too few technology start-ups. Because there have been only a small number of high-technology offerings on the Shanghai and Shenzhen stock exchanges, a number of not-worthwhile new companies received financing because they were high-tech and looked good at first glance. After they burned through their financing, they failed.

Government agencies are supporting some companies trying to become self-sustaining, but, even with all the savings in China, there is a limit to how many hands the government can hold. Its priorities are to support firms in industries such as automotive, energy generation, and pharmaceuticals.

Product Positioning and Market Control

For products to be successful long term, Chinese producers need to generate demand both domestically as well as overseas. The Chinese have achieved mastery in developing multiple price points and creating new services.

Domestic Demand

Even though the population of China is large, the buying power for high-end products is low. While there is growth potential for expensive products as the middle class becomes larger, the focus is on the large local market for low-end products, such as clothing, mobile telephones, and tiny cars.

Producers need to meet the price points of nonaffluent Chinese consumers. For example, cell phone service costs $5 to $12 per month for China Mobile. For urban residents in China in 2008, monthly per capita disposable income was $193.[10] So a cell phone service charge of $12 per month represented 6.2 percent of monthly per capita income.

That compares to $50 to $60 per month[11] for the average major carrier cell phone service in the United States. Monthly per capita personal income in the United States in 2008 was $3,313,[12] so monthly cell phone service costing $60 represented less than 2 percent of monthly personal income.

China Mobile, however, has over 500 million[13] customers.

Additional Demand for New Services

Additional demand will be created as new services are offered. With an installed base of 700 million[14] wireless handsets in China, there could be a wide range of content accessible by using wireless handsets. Mobile TV on wireless handsets is a service for which there is very strong demand in China.[15]

The content market in China has high growth potential. But the content needs to be free, which requires advertising support, or it needs to be supported with low monthly rates.

Export Capabilities

China's exports are competitive worldwide from a feature and price perspective. China is specifically developing products that meet the needs of the countries that export goods to China—for example, the Middle East (oil), Africa (raw materials), and Brazil (food). If, for example, cell phone handsets made in China would offer the features Brazilians demand for handsets, then China could exert pressure on Brazil to buy goods from China.

As the level of functionality of the products increases, Chinese corporations target developed countries such as the United States and Europe. Televisions manufactured by Chinese companies such as TCL and others are already being sold in the United States and in Europe. The handsets of ZTE and Huawei are planned to be or are already supplied on a private-label basis to some large Western carriers such as Verizon[16] (ZTE) and T-Mobile[17] (Huawei).

Demand creation can also be supported by building *brand recognition*. The China brand is being built by Lenovo (which acquired IBM's personal computer business), Haier, Hisense, and others. China is also beginning the development of brand recognition for the automobiles it is making.

A critical next phase for the Chinese industry is to *improve the quality* of its products. The image of products manufactured by Chinese companies is that of low-quality products. Poor assembly, inferior materials, inadequate quality control, and other symptoms of rapid industrialization and a focus to control costs have contributed to the perception that its products were of low quality. I'll address the quality challenge in more detail later in this chapter.

It is important to note that other Asian countries once associated with low-quality, mass–produced, and low-cost products successfully managed to change their image. Electronics and automobiles produced by Japanese companies in the 1970s and by South Korean companies in the 1990s are excellent examples.

For now the short-term emphasis is on building the capabilities that enable China to protect its domestic market. While China could be a gigantic market opportunity for outsiders, because of its protectionist barriers, many of its markets are being satisfied by Chinese companies. As Chinese companies strengthen, their branding activities will increase and become familiar to Chinese consumers. At that point products with foreign brand names but manufactured in China—for example, Head & Shoulders shampoo—will be challenged.

The buildup of the industrial base in Japan, South Korea, and Taiwan was based primarily on exports. The buildup of China's industries has been based on the combination of exports of goods that are manufactured by foreign companies in China and those products produced to meet the needs of the Chinese market. The domestic market opportunities in China are being used as bait to bring technology and management skills from outside. It is considered to be strategically important by the Chinese government agencies that Chinese corporations dominate the local market, which means that it can be difficult for foreign companies to build strong positions in the China market without a Chinese business partner.

The importance to the Chinese government of having Chinese corporations dominate the local China market has a wide range of implications for foreign companies trying to address the Chinese market. While it is possible to establish joint ventures, China may also be amenable to supporting foreign companies' selling in its domestic market some unique products that China wants to have but that its own companies cannot duplicate. The branding activities and high quality of products of foreign companies can allow effective participation in the China market. The Chinese government recognizes that the trade barriers against imports do not severely limit the competitiveness of the foreign corporations, or else they won't provide the technologies and information that the country wants and needs.

As Chinese companies achieve large revenues from the domestic market, they will have access to the financial resources required to compete in foreign markets. This crossover has been accomplished by other Asian powerhouses, such as Samsung, Toyota, Canon, and others.

To be a strong competitor in global markets requires leadership in technologies and high quality, which are areas that the Chinese companies need to strengthen. And they are certainly focused on high technology.

The Role of the Electronics Industry in the Growth of China

The electronics industry is a strategic industry in China because it offers high employment, generates exports, and satisfies the domestic market, which reduces imports. Electronics is an industry for which it has been easy for Chinese corporations to obtain foreign investors because of the large markets in China. The time from product development to high revenues for electronics products can be months, which can provide rapid returns to the investors that start new businesses. As electronic product life cycles get shorter, investors have to wait less for payback.

Government agencies in China are active in promoting the electronics industry through a range of subsidies. Their goals are to protect and satisfy the domestic market and to participate and expand with increasing power in the export market. The government-nurtured build-up of the electronics industry in China contrasts markedly with that in the United States. Companies in the United States are left on their own to create their brands and satisfy their markets worldwide.

The key products in the Chinese electronics industry include televisions, wireless handsets, computers, and MP3 players. While television has long been one of the main conduits for content, now there is also access to content on Web sites such as Baidu and other sources that can be accessed through computers or wireless handsets.

Televisions

Televisions can provide content that is not only generated in China but also elsewhere, if the government does not interfere with access to such programming.

Televisions are important to China for a variety of reasons, some of which are described below.

Televisions Yield High Unit Volumes and High Revenues

With its huge population and the potential for multiple televisions in each home, the installed base of TVs in China could exceed 1 billion units sometime between 2015 and 2020. By mandating proprietary broadcasting protocols, the government can control which corporations provide access to the technologies for the manufacturing of televisions and the supporting broadcasting infrastructure.

While it is important for consumers to get the low-cost TVs they want, it is also important to China to develop the industrial base for manufacturing the TVs that consumers demand. Chinese brands such as Hisense, TCL, Skyworth, Konka, Changhong, and Haier currently dominate segments of the Chinese TV market.

Global TV makers such as Samsung, Sony, Panasonic, and LG Electronics will be niche participants in the Chinese market unless they have local manufacturing facilities, for LCD displays, for example, to be used in TVs. Such facilities are in development.

Televisions Connect with Citizens

Television is the most important way to deliver content to consumers at home.

There is significant political power associated with the content and the way the content is delivered to consumers in many countries, including China. While television was considered a dumb platform in the past, the Chinese government has learned that the content televisions deliver can have a major impact on how people view events. Programs showing the government's efforts to save victims of the earthquake in Sichuan had a powerful and very positive impact on the Chinese people.

The Chinese government's emphasis on controlling the transmission of media and content forced Rupert Murdoch and his satellite business to withdraw from China.

TV platforms are also becoming increasingly interactive in China. In the near future, a television will become a channel through which to access the Internet.

Televisions Promote the Growth
of Expertise in Key Technologies

Making the displays for TVs is the most difficult and most expensive aspect of television manufacturing. China is expanding its display manufacturing at a rapid rate. For example, the Beijing government is allocating $4 billion[18] for a new LCD facility, which will be managed by BOE Technology. Samsung, Sharp, and LG Electronics are all establishing LCD facilities in China. In two or three years, China will be a net exporter of LCD displays.

As an interim measure, the Chinese government has provided $2 billion to buy LCD flat panels from Taiwanese companies to build up the supply base of TVs from Chinese manufacturers.

Another approach in China is to stimulate the adoption of Mobile TV, which can be accessed by the owners of the 700 million wireless handsets. China adopted a proprietary protocol for Mobile TV called CMMB. By having a proprietary protocol, China controls access to the technology. The high growth for Mobile TV to date is for the analog technology, which is low cost and has proven to operate effectively.

Until Chinese TV manufacturing reaches critical mass and domestic prices for TVs drop substantially, Mobile TV is a handy, portable way to provide access to content for the mass market. It also controls the type of content.

Domestic brands, such as TCL, Haier, Changhong, Konka, Skyworth, and Hisense, are increasing revenues from the local market and are also exporting televisions. The biggest selling point for these brands is their low price. Many of the technologies of TCL came from the United States (RCA) and Europe (Thomson). TCL entered into a joint venture with Thomson Multimedia to obtain access to television expertise (Thomson Multimedia had previously acquired the RCA television business). The level of technology obtained by TCL through the joint venture was extensive. TCL is controlling the joint venture, and it has gained market share in China and increased exports.

Gaining substantial market share in consumer products can take decades, but the Chinese are attempting to shorten the time it takes by making strategic acquisitions and entering into joint ventures.

For brands such as Olevia and VIZIO, the designs are created in Taiwan, but the manufacturing is accomplished in China. Those TVs are sold through large discount retailers. Through such initiatives, China has become a leading supplier of televisions.

The components, including the semiconductors, used in televisions, are generally designed by foreign companies. Several of the most important of these suppliers are Taiwanese companies. A number of Chinese companies are developing semiconductor products for televisions, but with technologies that are years behind those of Taiwanese companies. Both the manufacturers and the government hope that in 5 to 10 years, a high percentage of the components used in televisions manufactured for the Chinese market will be supplied by Chinese semiconductor companies.

The next phase for Chinese television companies is to increase exports, which will be done initially with components from Taiwan and elsewhere. Then the plan is to increase exports of televisions consisting of key components manufactured by Chinese companies.

The short-term goal of the Chinese government is to have Chinese corporations manufacture a high percentage of the televisions that are sold in China. The long-term goal is for Chinese corporations to gain a substantial share of the world market.

Personal Computers

Personal computer volumes in China are increasing. A December 2009 report noted that 7.2 million desktop PCs were sold in China in the third quarter of 2009, roughly 10 percent more than were sold in the United States. While the Windows operating system dominates the worldwide market, there is resistance to paying the perceived high software fees that are traditionally charged by Microsoft. To maintain high market share, Microsoft has charged low licensee fees for the Chinese market.

There is strong support for Linux in China. Many of the new netbooks use it. In addition, the Android platform of Google is being adopted by China Mobile with the OPhone platform.[19]

The availability of new, low-cost, Internet-centric netbook platforms that contain the Atom processors of Intel and the ARM processors of Qualcomm, Marvell, and others is likely to result in explosive growth of the Chinese personal computer market in the next five years. Moreover, the availability of broadband wireless connectivity in China in late 2009 will also be a catalyst for the very high growth of these mobile Internet-centric platforms.

Because of the emphasis on Internet access and the need for netbook platforms that cost under $150, it is likely that the personal computers for consumers in China will have features that are different from the personal computers considered mainstream in the United States and other Western countries. A number of companies in China are gearing up to address the Chinese netbook market. Lenovo is also targeting Internet access in this market, developing relationships with cell phone service providers China Mobile, China Telecom, and China Unicom.

Meanwhile corporations and high-end consumers will use personal computers similar to mainstream units in the developed countries. Lenovo, Acer, Dell, and HP are targeting this market.

To address the mainstream of the personal computer market, Lenovo acquired the personal computer business of IBM. With this acquisition, Lenovo obtained a management team that had a wide range of skills in managing a globally competitive computer business. It also got access to sophisticated computer design capabilities, including the capabilities for leadership notebook computers. By acquiring the IBM business, Lenovo also built up its image as a global company in the personal computer market. However, many small companies in China challenge the name brands by providing lower-cost products. The challenge for Lenovo is to have low-cost computers while maintaining technology competitiveness, something that IBM was not able to do.

Since acquiring the IBM personal computer business, Lenovo's results have been partly cloudy. The silver lining is that Lenovo is stronger with the acquisition. Without it, it wouldn't have been able to sell abroad, and it would have been restricted to its previous limited expertise in product development.

Lenovo has been having financial problems due to the weakening of the global computer market and the intense competition from companies such as Acer and ASUS from Taiwan (revenues decreased 15.7 percent[20] in the quarter ended September 2009). So Lenovo focused more on growing market share in China rather than on the export market. It has defaulted to the more risk-averse, more stereotypically Chinese approach that it's safer to gain strength in the local market before being aggressive in foreign markets.

The most important component in personal computers is the microprocessor. And Intel is the biggest vendor of them. China has attempted to develop its own microprocessor architecture, but it has failed to develop a chip that could compete against Intel's broad product line.

Since it is likely that China also will not succeed in manufacturing processors that can compete with those of Intel, AMD, or the ARM vendors, the best approach for China is to have Intel and others manufacture their products in China. Intel has assembly-and-test facilities in China and is building a chip-making plant expected to begin operations in 2010.

China's ambitions notwithstanding, a high percentage of personal computers sold worldwide are assembled in China. But most of the guts of the PCs, known as motherboards, were designed by Taiwanese companies.

Wireless Handsets

There are approximately 700 million[21] handset owners in China, including 500 million[22] China Mobile subscribers. China Telecom and China Unicom also are competing for the China market. All three participants are Chinese companies.

While voice communication has been the primary use of handsets, the growing trend is for these handsets to provide access to the Internet for music, video, and user-generated content. The ability to provide access to Internet content in China is spurring the expansion of the more advanced broadband wireless infrastructure. There are approximately 300 million Internet users in China, and the Internet's range of content is enormously valuable to them.

To support the growth of the Internet use, China is spending $59 billion[23] on broadband wireless connectivity and is adopting the following three wireless standards:

1. *A variation of one of the global standards:* China Mobile adopted this standard. Expenditures for establishing this standard in China are likely to be as much as $40 billion,[24] which is comparable to some U.S. military programs.

2. *A European standard also supported by AT&T in the United States:* China Unicom has adopted the European standard.

3. *The American standard developed by the San Diego chip company Qualcomm:* This standard is supported by Verizon in the United States. It is also the primary standard in South Korea. China Telecom adopted the Qualcomm technology.

Chinese telecommunications gear companies, such as Huawei, ZTE, and, potentially, Datang, are the primary suppliers of the building blocks of the wireless infrastructure in their country. Ericsson, Alcatel-Lucent, Nokia-Siemens, and Motorola also are supporting the buildup.

China's goal is to be world class in wireless communications by 2012 if not before. It is important to note that the Chinese Ministry of Industry and Information Technology made the decisions about which technologies were adopted by Chinese carriers, the timing of the giving of licenses, and the recipients of the licenses.

All wireless spectra in China are government owned, and, while use is granted under license, all those receiving licenses are Chinese. This shows the power of the government. China Mobile, China Unicom, and China Telecom have some public shareholders, but the technology and policy decisions are made by the government.

In addition to establishing wireless infrastructure in China, there will be an increase in the number of wireless handsets produced by Chinese companies. The number of wireless handsets[25] manufactured by Chinese companies in the 2006 to 2009 timeframe almost tripled, according to an International Business Strategies (IBS) estimate:

- 2006: 117 million
- 2007: 181 million
- 2008: 220 million
- 2009: 350 million

There are, however, high levels of volatility among Chinese handset vendors, and no single company has established a strong brand and customer loyalty. The Chinese handset vendors are strengthening, but they continue to have strong competition from Nokia, Samsung, and LG Electronics, among others.

The growth in unit volumes of the China handset vendors has been supported by buying semiconductor components from foreign companies such as MediaTek (Taiwan), TI (United States), Qualcomm (United States), Marvell (United States), Infineon (Europe), and ST Microelectronics (Europe).

With access to fully functional wireless handsets from sources outside of China, the Chinese handset vendors have only to put a case around the electronics to bring new handsets to the market within a few weeks. The role of the semiconductor companies in providing the fully functional (but without the cases) handsets is instrumental for the success of the Chinese handset vendors.

The development of features unique to the China market is being done through customized software applications. The specialty software is being provided increasingly by Chinese companies, which have a better understanding of the needs of Chinese consumers. To improve the features of the handsets, the Chinese software companies collaborate with the carriers. Meanwhile Internet-centric companies such as Tencent, Baidu, Sina, and Alibaba support this industry's progress.

Recently Baidu has outperformed Google in the search engine market in China. This shows how rapidly the technology capabilities in China are strengthening.

The convergence of the mobile handsets with the low-end netbook portable computers will represent a growth opportunity for Chinese companies, but it is likely that foreign companies, including those from Taiwan, the United States, Europe, Japan, and South Korea, will dominate the market in the near future.

The actions that China has taken and will take to promote the buildup of the local handset and netbook vendor base will bear fruit, but it will take time.

There is a wide range of activities in smart cards in China. A smart card is a bit smaller than a credit card, and it is embedded with a microprocessor. The chip enables a smart card to do many more functions than a typical credit or debit card with a magnetic strip. For example, a smart card could contain your entire medical history including what meds you're allergic to. With a smart card, any emergency medical technician or doctor assisting you would know everything he or she would need to know to identify you and treat you.

Smart cards are much more versatile than ordinary credit cards. When you present a typical debit card for payment, the merchant has to send an inquiry to your bank to verify that your account has sufficient funds for the purchase. With a smart card, such information resides in the microprocessor and memory of the card. Just swiping the card verifies that the buyer has the funds and there's no time lag for verifying elsewhere. An estimated 900 million[26] smart cards were expected to be sold in 2009.

There are already smart card technologies proprietary to China, and it is not difficult for China to set up barriers systematically to outsiders. The smart card products enable the Chinese government and companies to insulate the local market from overseas competitors for the time being.

The Internet is a powerful capability that could open up the outside world to the people of China. How much access will the Chinese authorities allow the people to have? The periodic shutting down of Facebook by Chinese authorities shows their willingness to limit access to content.

Summary of the Status of the Electronics Industry

The electronics industry has revenues of $1.4 trillion[27] worldwide, and it needs a wide range of skills, including many different types of engineers and managers. It also needs a large number of assembly workers who have great dexterity. China represents a large domestic market for electronics products such as televisions. By providing incentives and subsidies for the development of Chinese corporations, China's government is trying to reduce imports as well as generate exports.

The activities of government agencies in building the electronics industry in China have been extensive. Many of the plans are long term, and it could be 20 years before they are fulfilled.

China has selected the electronics industry as one of the pillars of its industrial growth. In the United States, the potato chip industry has a higher priority in Washington than the computer chip industry.

China: The Next Automotive Giant

China is building its manufacturing and supply base in the automobile industry. Having an automobile industry of its own provides China with a wide range of benefits. It requires China to develop skills in many technologies, including glass, electronics, and hydraulics.

The most obvious benefit is the size of the market and the exportability of the products. The worldwide automobile industry manufactures more than 70 million[28] automobiles a year, and with an average price of $20,000 per automobile, the industry's annual revenues are $1.4 trillion.

Since its faltering start in the 1950s, the Chinese automobile industry has made rapid progress. The unit volumes of automobiles and light trucks produced in China are shown in Figure 9.1. The number of cars and light trucks manufactured in China has increased from 2 million in 2000 to 7.9 million in 2008, according to the Organization of Motor Vehicle Manufacturers. With the addition of heavy-duty trucks and buses, the total number of vehicles built in China in 2008 was 8.8 million. China produced more than 11 million cars alone in 2009, with projections for 15 million cars in 2010 and 20 million in 2020.[29]

In 2007, there were 30.3 vehicles per 1,000 people in China. That compares to 844.4 in the United States.[30] So China offers the potential to sell enormous numbers of cars as its middle class becomes more numerous.

The dramatic growth of the automotive industry has been accomplished through a combination of top-level and regional planning (a number of provinces and cities want automobile factories), the commitment of large financial resources, and the extensive use of joint ventures.

China has five large automobile companies. They are First Automobile Works, Dongfeng Motor Corporation, Chang'an Motors, Chery Automobile, and Shanghai Automotive Industry Corporation (SAIC).

FIGURE 9.1

The Number of Automobiles and Light Trucks Manufactured in China

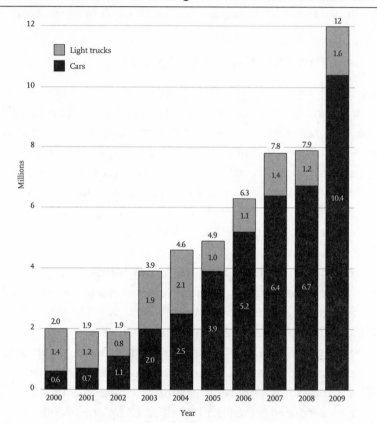

Source: International Organization of Motorvehicle Manufacturers (OICA, Paris), http://oica.net/wp-content/
uploads/all-vehicles.pdf

While the China automobile industry has been fragmented in the past, the government has encouraged the consolidation of the industry. Recently SAIC acquired the Nanjing Automobile Corporation.

The next phase, which includes a number of joint ventures with U.S., European, and Japanese companies, is to build engines and transmissions as well as automobiles in China. The late 2009 bid by the Beijing Automotive Industry Holding Company to license Saab technology and production equipment from GM is one example of this phase.[31]

Foreign companies have made large investments in the Chinese market. For example, the Volkswagen Group, which entered China in 1984, has invested more than $8.9 billion.[32]

Other companies with joint ventures in China include General Motors, Ford, Toyota, Daimler AG, Audi (independent of Volkswagen), Honda, Nissan, Volvo, Mazda, Peugeot, BMW, Fiat, Mitsubishi Motor, and Hyundai. Companies are willing to establish joint ventures in China because of the potential access to the large Chinese market. Chinese companies can have multiple strategic partners. For example, SAIC has joint ventures with GM and Volkswagen, which gives it flexibility in the automobile platforms that it can develop.

General Motors, Volkswagen, and Audi have experienced success in the China market because of the effectiveness of their partnerships and the strong promotion of their brands.

The use of joint ventures to build the automobile industry in China shows high levels of innovation in business models and China's willingness to use different approaches to build a new industry.

The initial phase of developing an automobile industry in China was through government sponsorship. In this phase, manufacturing licenses were supplied only to the government-owned companies. Because of this, China has only three independent automobile companies: Geely International Corporation, Chery Automobile Corporation, and BYD Auto. Chery has the capacity to build 450,000[33] cars per year and Geely 370,000.[34] Both companies are changing their strategies to build higher-end automobiles and to emphasize building for the export market. The initial exports are for the Middle East and South America because consumer preferences and needs in those regions are similar to those in China. China also has relatively large imports from these countries, and it is trying to balance imports with exports.

Geely, for example, acquired Volvo from Ford, which changes its global competitiveness. The acquisition provides Geely a huge opportunity in North America and Western Europe, but Geely will need to make significant investments to make Volvo financially viable. And its success depends on maintaining the historically high quality of

Volvo autos while at the same time reducing costs at the loss-ridden subsidiary.[35]

The government continues to control which companies can manufacture automobiles in China. For example, Chery had to give 20 percent[36] of its equity to SAIC to get a manufacturing license.

Auto manufacturing in China employs over 1.6 million[37] people. There are also major initiatives to build the base of suppliers. Planners hope that the employment achieved by suppliers will be three to four times the number used for auto assembly. China must also build the infrastructure of dealers and mechanics. The automobile industry in China is incredibly important for employment. By having a large and growing automobile industry, China is building a large employment base and is protecting the domestic market from foreign imports.

China is stimulating sales of new autos by offering financial incentives to the consumers. Despite the recession, China is selling more than 1 million[38] autos a month. It's ahead of its plan to build 15 million cars and light trucks in 2015.

While China is building roads for the vehicles, it also needs to improve the buying power of consumers. As the middle class expands, the demand for automobiles in China will continue to grow strongly. The automobile market in China could be double or triple the existing market in the next 10 to 20 years. China is also building additional refineries to ensure the supply of fuel for the increased numbers of cars on the road.

Chinese brands currently supply approximately 30 percent[39] of the automobile market in China, and joint venture activities of the Chinese automobile companies and their foreign partners combined provide another 50 percent. With total domestic production accounting for approximately 80 percent, it is important for demand to stay strong in order to continue to stimulate output. The result is that approximately 20 percent of the automobile purchases in China are of imports of the foreign manufacturers. There are, however, large import duties on foreign cars sold in China.

With the export of cars, trucks, and subassemblies for the U.S., European, and Japanese markets, and with the control of imports, China has a positive balance of trade for automobiles. This is a major achievement for China because of the very large value of the automobile industry. The United States has a negative balance of trade for automobiles. If the U.S. automobile companies continue to weaken, the balance of trade will become worse.

While the Chinese automobile industry is growing well, there have been attempts to consolidate the industry in Shanghai, Beijing, and Guangzhou. Nevertheless auto manufacturing continues in other cities because they don't want to relinquish such major employers.

The initiatives expected next in the automobile industry in China include the following:

- *Improving the fuel efficiency of gasoline and diesel automobiles:* There are concerns in China with not having access to enough oil or having to pay very high prices for oil in the future. Such short-term initiatives on improving fuel efficiency require access to more advanced technologies in electronics and batteries.
- *Developing new energy sources:* BYD is developing an electric vehicle, with hybrid initiatives going on at other companies in China. There are a number of companies in China that are developing new generations of lithium-ion battery technologies, with BYD claiming global leadership in this arena. It is significant that Warren Buffett has made an investment in BYD.

  If the growth in the sales of automobiles that use lithium-ion batteries is high enough, it is likely that there will not be enough lithium to satisfy global demand. As with other natural resources, it is likely that China will try to ensure access to adequate supplies of lithium.
- *Developing upscale cars that appeal to the upper middle class in China and the export market:* Upscale cars can provide competition to Japanese and European imports. To compete successfully in the upscale market requires that the quality of China's cars must win esteem in markets abroad where other brands have fine reputations. To enhance the reputation for the quality of its autos is important for the Chinese automobile industry to be competitive in the long term.

Chinese consumers have been willing to tolerate low quality in the past. What choice have they had? But as they become more sophisticated, they will demand quality that is comparable to that of imported brands.

- *Making China self-sufficient for all components used in the manufacture of automobiles:* China manages the design, manufacturing, and distribution of automobiles. It produces tires, windshields, and other nontech components. But to become fully self-sufficient, it has to make other components, including sophisticated electronics such as engine management systems. The central government and the administrators of the provinces have offered a range of financial incentives to encourage the development of technologies and manufacturing capacity for domestic production of such key components.

  New government-sponsored initiatives have been established to support the supply of semiconductor products to the automotive industry. There is the goal to have the Chinese semiconductor vendors supply a high percentage of the semiconductor products consumed in the China automotive market in the 2012 to 2015 timeframe.

  Subsidies are being provided to encourage the development and manufacturing of components and subassemblies in China by Chinese companies or through joint ventures. The subsidies are relatively large and indicate the aims of the long-range planning in China.

- *Expanding automobile exports:* By 2020, 10 percent[40] of the total number of vehicles manufactured worldwide will be Chinese exports, according to the Chinese government. With 20 million automobiles being manufactured at that time, this would be 2 million vehicles, which would provide a large positive trade balance.

China is making good progress in the development of its automobile industry. Automobiles exemplify another industry in which the strategies in China are dramatically superior to the strategies of the United States.

10

CHINA'S FUTURE LOOKS BRIGHT

MANY OF CHINA'S INFRASTRUCTURE projects and financial goals are planned to be completed by 2020. So 2020 is an important milestone in China. By 2020, most of the current top ministers will not be in power. However, the interim until 2020 is brief enough for the period to be meaningful to a high percentage of the population. The setting of ambitious goals is instrumental in focusing the use of resources and in determining how well the goals are being met.

The central government and its agencies are guiding the expansion of the industrial base that will provide employment and help China's exports succeed. The directions are clear. The key issues will be the country's efficiency in reaching the goals and how equitably the wealth is distributed.

If the smartest leaders and businesspeople are given the appropriate opportunities and if the decisions are sensible, then China will achieve its goals. If the system becomes bureaucratic, or if government officials and their families selfishly try to enrich themselves rather than create wealth for the good of society, then the system will falter. China's competitiveness worldwide will decline.

The central government needs to manage the wide differences in wealth between the elite and the common people in China. It also needs to motivate the young who are Internet savvy and can see what's going on around the world. Both generations have to feel that they are being treated fairly by their country. Both generations need to be pulling in the same direction. The government needs to help the older population provide social benefits to the younger working population, such as taking care of grandchildren, so both parents of the younger population can work. In addition, China's aging population needs to be maintained as a productive asset as opposed to being treated as a liability that is a drain on government spending.

The Chinese took great pride in the success of the Olympics. China demonstrated its ability to stage an exciting world event that was efficiently managed. The extensive coverage of the Olympics inside China combined with China's winning 100 medals[1] was a major inspiration for the population to keep working hard for the country. The Olympic games were a single event, however. The need to motivate the Chinese people will remain acute because they will have to make many sacrifices to promote the growth of the economy.

The challenges facing China are extensive, but China is using top-level planning and control actions and a wide range of growth initiatives to deal with them.

The building of the industrial base in China is being funded at the expense of social programs. The philosophy in China is that, if people work, they are paid. Because children and students will be future workers, the cost of their education is being supported. If the people do not work, they are not given money. When people do not have jobs, the burden to support them is on their family. Consumption is not supported in China unless the output of an individual is greater than his or her consumption.

The combination of the centralized planning and decentralized implementation has been successful in China. China has well-defined top-level goals for many of its industries, and employment is still growing. While the challenges are becoming more rigorous as its industries attempt to compete in markets around the world, China's management expertise is also growing.

Strategic Implications of Growth

The Eleventh Five-Year Plan, which was accepted in November 2006 (it governs from 2006 through 2010), continues to stress the importance of the growth of strategic industries.

As industries grow, China will need access to greater amounts of a wide range of raw materials. It will need the political power to ensure access to supplies as well as the financial resources to pay for them. When the leadership of countries that possess certain raw materials is unstable, China will need to have good relationships with their leaders.

China is becoming more active in the global political environment, but it keeps a low profile and uses a nonthreatening approach in most situations. There are, however, indications that China is starting to flex its political muscle, as seen, for example, in the Chinese government's rejection of the Coca-Cola company's bid to buy a Chinese fruit beverage company.[2]

Having a strong military can be advantageous in protecting supply chains for raw materials, but the most important factors are political and financial power. It is clear that China is building up its political power base.

The United States and China are the largest consumers of raw materials, but there will also be demand from Europe, Japan, India, and other regions. It's likely that future conflicts between the United States and China will result from competition for market share and access to raw materials.

While Chinese corporations do not have the same level of sophistication in managing supply chains as U.S. corporations do, the Chinese government is taking a systematic and long-term approach to ensuring its access to the required resources. One approach is to buy equity in companies that have resources.

The U.S. government is not actively promoting its access to raw materials, other than oil and natural gas. The competition eventually will be between the combination of the Chinese corporations and their government versus the corporations from the Western countries that will not be well supported by their governments.

Russia, where the government has gained effective control of raw materials, including oil and gas, exemplifies how strategic capabilities can be turned into positions of power by adroit governments. Meanwhile, the United States depends much more on China than on Russia.

It is becoming more necessary than ever to consider and understand the long-term strategic implications of the strengthening of China both economically and politically. China's large manufacturing base will promote its supplying a widening range of products to the United States, and, thus, it will exert an increasing degree of control over the supply of these products to the United States.

The manufacturing base in China will be a major source of strength because countries that do not have such low-cost manufacturing capabilities will opt to import goods from China. When China represented a small percentage of the global supply of products, the leverage of China was low. As China dominates markets, its leverage will increase.

The United States and other countries are underestimating the long-term competitive threat from China in a number of business areas. While it is inevitable that China will become stronger and will increase market share in a range of industries, including electronics and automobiles, the implications of these trends can be significant if China also controls the supply of raw materials.

China started with industries that were low technology (such as clothing and shoes). Then it progressed to heavy industries (the initial processing of raw materials). Consider what has happened in the steel and aluminum industries.

China has continued to build its steel and aluminum industries, even though there is excess capacity worldwide. China wants self-sufficiency in these vital products. To try to keep its steel and aluminum factories at or near high capacity, the government provides subsidies so the steel and aluminum companies can charge low prices for exports. This breeds increasing resentment in the United States, Japan, and Germany.

Competition from low-priced Chinese imports is crippling U.S., Japanese, and German domestic steel and aluminum companies, in some cases forcing factories to close or putting the companies out of business. In response, protective tariffs on the Chinese goods are being increased, which leads China to quickly impose or increase tariffs on imports from those countries.

The strategies being demonstrated in the steel and aluminum industries are harbingers of those that will be utilized in many industries in China in the future. If this is done systematically, industry by industry, the impact can be large over 10 to 20 years.

When China produced a small percentage of the global output of such goods, its export strategies didn't antagonize many corporations in foreign countries. Now that China is producing a high percentage of global capacity—for example, approximately 48.8 percent[3] of global capacity for steel in July 2009—the impact of the Chinese strategies on competitors in other countries can be devastating. Not surprisingly, the competitors in other countries view China's pricing as predatory. But, like it or not, the alliance of Chinese corporations with the adroit support of their government is helping Chinese exports become increasingly competitive in foreign markets and gain market share.

As we've seen, its latest initiatives are in high technology, including electronics, automobiles, and aircraft. The strategic threats from the high-technology businesses are much more concern-worthy to the United States than the leverage China had from supplying low-technology merchandise.

China will become a high-technology society that is a formidable competitor in the global market. By having the large local market and competitiveness in manufacturing, the Chinese corporations will be able to gain high market share worldwide. The large market inside China and the methods used to protect this market will result in more conflict with other countries.

Local Chinese authorities have already been targeting Japanese companies. A few years ago, Zhejiang province publicized its finding that there were many quality defects in Sony digital cameras. Sony had not been criticized for quality problems in other regions, including the United States. The result: Sony has had disappointing sales of cameras in China.[4]

When Japanese companies have competitive strengths, such as Toshiba in nuclear-powered electricity generating technologies, they can establish joint ventures in China.

As its homegrown capabilities rapidly increase, the challenge facing China is to be viewed as providing open access to outsiders while protecting China's local markets.

Many embryonic industries will require support from the government for the next decade and probably longer. However, as its industries become stronger, the amount of the government's direct involvement and support is expected to decrease, but top-level strategic direction will continue.

The growth of a large entrepreneurial business class in China is expected to result in conflicts over the control of the central government. How well the government manages that conflict will be one of the key factors that determine the success of industrialization.

The challenges facing China include pressures from competitors for worldwide markets (factors from outside China) and problems in the operations of industry and government (internal factors including government efficiency and corruption, among others).

Industry in China is strengthening rapidly. While exports account for the bulk of the revenues from many products, many exports are products of foreign companies, such as Samsung, Toyota, and HP, that are using China as a low-cost manufacturing base. The next phase of the export market development will be characterized by the inclusion of merchandise designed and developed, as well as manufactured, by Chinese companies.

Taiwanese companies are expected to succeed in the Chinese market. Certainly the common language will be an advantage. The finesse

China's government uses in managing the integration of Taiwan will affect how well its products do and how much they contribute to China's renaissance.

Consumer preferences have been secondary to the top-level industrialization goals in China, but that subordination will lessen as the middle class grows, becomes more cosmopolitan, and has money to spend.

Foreign companies are viewed as disposable if they are regarded as not very useful for the long-term economic goals and initiatives in China. This perspective applies to a range of industries. It's particularly applicable to the automotive industry.

China may view foreign governments as expendable too. In its military history China has shown a willingness to accept a large number of casualties. In 1949, during the Huai-Hai Battle, 555,000[5] people of the National Party died, and 110,000 people of the Communist Party died, figures that dwarf the horrendous battlefield casualties during the American Civil War. These large numbers of casualties show China's willingness to sacrifice people to achieve its objectives. If China is willing to sacrifice its own people, it will be far more willing to view foreign companies or foreign governments as expendable.

The United States as a market for Chinese products is important, especially because the U.S. market is wide open for so many products. So China's policymakers must balance the need for the United States as a market with its threat as a competitor for raw materials and other strategic resources.

China's leaders also have to balance the use of its resources and raw materials for exports versus domestic consumption. As long as resources and raw materials are sufficient, the balance is easy to achieve. If shortages of raw materials occur, the decision processes can become more difficult. The effect in the short term can be to increase prices somewhat for exports, but the impact over the long term is that the domestic market will be given priority.

As China has been criticized increasingly for its contribution to pollution, it is significant that it is starting to blame the countries that buy its products as being partly responsible.

As the political and financial power of China increases, China may become much more assertive and self-justifying about its conduct. The leaders of China have inherited centuries of strategic thinking. Competitive positioning and dealing from a position of strength are key parts of the history of China.

Key Challenges Affecting China's Economic Destiny

Employment and Education

Developing an economy with an employable population that offers every necessary level of skill, as well as adequate opportunities for employment and promotion, represents a major challenge in China. Compensation and room for advancement needs to increase both because employees' skills are improving and corporations are expanding.

China has not solved this issue, and it is having more trouble recently because of the recession. There were more than 6 million college and university graduates in 2009.[6] It is expected that 2 million of those graduates will not find jobs in their areas of expertise for a year or more after graduation.[7] Many will have to resort to subsistence jobs. This is happening even though the GDP is growing 8 to 10 percent a year.

If unemployment increases in China, it is likely that there could be social unrest. How disruptive the unrest will be will depend crucially on the skill of the Chinese government in managing expectations. The global recession is clearly having an impact on both the number of jobs and also the job expectations in China.

The unrest by some of the minorities in China has been dealt with decisively. The government has established a range of initiatives, including a Web-based forum by the prime minister, to temper the employment expectations of the population. A number of social programs to provide employment for new graduates have been started, and empathy is being expressed for their plight.

It is an enormous expense—a major sacrifice—for parents to educate one of their children at a university. The family can be subject to strong financial pressures if its graduate cannot find employment. That pressure now comes on top of other sacrifices the population has made in order to support the growth of the economy. Many workers have had to move away from their families and hometowns to take jobs in faraway cities. While many Chinese are becoming wealthier, this is being accomplished at great emotional and social cost.

As the population's economic expectations are increasing, it is becoming more challenging for the government to meet those expectations.

The aging of the population will be a challenge for China as well as for other countries. In China, there are 965 million[8] people (registered) aged 15 to 64. In 2020, the number is expected to reach 996 million,[9] which is the peak, and it will decline to 870 million people in 2050. At the present time, there are 10 people of working age that can support 1 elderly person. In 2030, there will be 4 people of working age to support 1 elderly person, and in 2050, the number will be reduced to 3 people of working age.

The time is short to build the employment base and to establish the infrastructure to support the aging population. As in other countries, China may raise the retirement age above 65 to manage the social costs.

Despite the lack of job opportunities facing recent graduates, China plans to expand its education systems. China has 470,000 elementary schools, 68,000 junior high schools, and 38,000 high schools. The country has between 230 and 250 million students in grade school and high school. High school enrollment is approximately 55 percent[10] of the available population, and China aims to increase this level to 75 percent in 2012.

While it is important to increase the number of university graduates, it is also important to increase the quality of the education graduates receive. A high percentage of university graduates now are not sufficiently advanced in the skills and knowledge necessary to meet the needs of the corporations. Customarily corporations need to give them more training. China needs to increase the quality of vocational training and academic education so corporations can compete effectively throughout the world.

The difficulties that recent graduates have experienced in obtaining jobs could be a sign that fundamental changes are required in the education system. It also may be evidence of the need to accelerate the growth of employment in China. A lack of job opportunities in an economy that is growing by 8 percent a year, at a minimum, is a problem brewing.

Product Quality

The quality of many products made in China is low. The country also shows disregard for health, both that of the workers and of the consumers of products. The scandals about contaminants in Chinese dairy products, including baby food, have also tainted the image of China.

While there have been attempts to address health and safety problems, it is unclear how earnest the government's commitment is to solving these problems. China's leaders are determined to present the image of being an advanced country, but at the lower levels, the emphasis is on the generation of profits and in being low cost.

Chinese consumers have not demanded high quality and have been forgiving of the companies that supply the low-quality products. American, Japanese, and European consumers expect high quality and low cost.

To compete in global markets, Chinese companies need to establish the control structures that ensure high quality. Having low-quality merchandise adds to the cost of ownership for the consumer. The cost penalties of low-quality products are not well understood in China. The country will need a change in the mindset of entrepreneurs, managers, and engineers as well as consumers to promote high quality in manufacturing.

Japan is a global leader in product quality, which it has achieved through its systematic emphasis on ensuring tight quality control over each manufacturing step. Many of the quality manufacturing concepts so effective in Japan have been adopted from U.S. experts such as W. Edwards Deming[11] and Joseph M. Juran.[12]

China will not be able to compete effectively in global markets until producing high-quality products becomes a part of the culture. Corporations in China need to establish a production ethos that will endow Chinese goods with both the reality and the image of high quality. It is also important to ensure that the health of the consumer is not harmed by using Chinese products.

Conclusion

China is managing the growth of its economy without building large deficits, and it has dollar reserves of approximately $2.4 trillion. The large dollar reserves mean that it is advantageous for China to ensure that the United States remains relatively strong in the short term. To build its employment base, China needs the United States to continue to be a large market for its products.

While the United States is weakening, it continues to be much stronger than China in a number of ways. The United States could regain leadership positions. However, the United States is focused on short-term survival. Its emphasis is on how to increase consumption through additional deficit spending—that is, how to exhaust wealth rather than build it. Its high standard of living, as well as its disposition to wallow in it, is an ever-enlarging speed bump in its economy.

Provide people with welfare payments and they can eat for a day. Building bridges creates employment, but those jobs last for only one or two years. But building thriving corporations means there can be employment for a lifetime. Also, bridges cannot generate exports, but corporations can generate exports and protect the local markets from foreign competition.

The famous John F. Kennedy quote "Ask not what your country can do for you. Ask what you can do for your country" is not being followed in the United States. The Kennedy quote would resonate very well in China. The population of China is making great sacrifices to build the country's wealth.

China is strengthening rapidly: its overall wealth is growing, and it is pushing forward numerous initiatives to continue to build the employment base and maintain a positive balance of trade. While China has many challenges, the country understands the factors involved in building wealth, and it is taking highly systematic approaches to achieving success.

The world is competitive. One country's wealth is generally built at the expense of another country's. Cooperation requires both countries to operate from positions of comparable strength. That means it is important to understand both the competitive threats from China as well as the market opportunities it offers.

The key issue with China is not whether it will grow but how rapidly. As it grows, China's emphasis will be on building up its wealth and ensuring that there are strong barriers to protect its corporate armies.

PART IV

WHAT HAPPENS
NEXT IN CHINA
AND THE
UNITED STATES

THE NEXT STEP IN CHINA's economic growth will come from the ongoing and careful courtship of Taiwan. China absorbed Hong Kong and Macao without any major economic and cultural disruptions. While there was a decline in property values in Hong Kong in the late 1990s when it was absorbed into the People's Republic of China, property values now are comparable or higher than when it was annexed.

The reunification with Taiwan has been a more delicate courtship. It is being done in many small steps, such as permitting direct flights between the two. These flights have stimulated tourism between Taiwan and mainland China.

Taiwan and China are also promoting closer relationships between their companies. The business bonding and access to the Chinese market for Taiwanese corporations is a major incentive for reunification.

China needs to progress toward the goal of reunification while ensuring that Taiwan continues to be successful in electronics and other fields. Taiwanese companies can be very strong partners for Chinese companies if the appropriate financial incentives are in place.

The Chinese government has allocated $19 billion[1] to encourage Taiwanese companies to establish manufacturing facilities and set up businesses in China. A number of Taiwanese companies, such as Acer in laptops and the Taiwan Semiconductor Manufacturing Company (TSMC), have already developed successful operations in China. In addition, the Taiwanese contract manufacturers such as Hon Hai have already established large manufacturing facilities in China, with Hon Hai alone employing over half a million people. The contract manufacturers have the ability to compete in global markets. This initiative can provide China with access to technologies and management expertise from Taiwan as well as strengthening the economic ties between the two countries. As the Chinese electronics market grows, Taiwanese companies will be well positioned to take advantage of these growth opportunities.

The process poses some risks, however. If China does not continue to make progress with reunification, then the leadership in China will be viewed as weak and it will lose face. Yet a too-hasty takeover of Taiwan could cause China to lose momentum in its own industrialization, especially in the electronics industry.

There is strong resistance to reunification by a large number of people in Taiwan, and it is unlikely that this resistance will be completely placated. There would be a loss of face for China if the reunification were postponed indefinitely. On the other hand, China can't be too aggressive if it wants its working relationship with Taiwan to progress. The reunification will require finesse and adroit financial incentives to be smooth and seamless. As I explain in Chapter 11, the reunification will test the diplomatic skill of China's top leadership.

But the task of China's reunifying with Taiwan is relatively easy compared to the challenges faced by the political and business leaders in the United States. In Chapter 12, I describe a restructuring plan for the United States. Like most business restructuring plans, the recommended changes aren't easy to implement. The key ingredients include a recognition that there is a major problem—itself politically unpalatable to elected officials who want to remain in office—and a list of specific actions that need to be taken.

While many of the recommendations have been discussed for years in the United States, a lack of political will and leadership has prevented substantive action. As we've already seen, the rise of the Chinese economy and manufacturing engine considered in light of the almost simultaneous decline in U.S. competitiveness should shift the restructuring discussion to the top of the United States' agenda.

11

TAIWAN AND ITS SYNERGY WITH CHINA

TAIWAN IS AN ISLAND with a population of almost 23 million[1] people and scant resources, but it has become an economic powerhouse.

Taiwan has established a strong industrial base over approximately 20 years. Taiwan's achievement was brought about through the joint efforts of a group of ambitious entrepreneurial business leaders and a group of high-level government leaders who contributed guidance and support.

The growth of Taiwan's gross domestic product (GDP) is shown in Figure 11.1. The GDP of Taiwan was $450 billion in 2000 and $698 billion in 2009[2]—more than 50 percent growth in less than a decade. On a per capita basis, the GDP almost tripled from 1980 to 2009, from almost $11,000 per person in 1980, based on a population of almost 18 million,[3] to almost $30,000.

While the GDP decreased in 2009 compared to 2008, it's expected to resume growing in 2010. Taiwan has a positive balance of trade and an efficient stock market. So entrepreneurs have access to substantial funding for ventures.

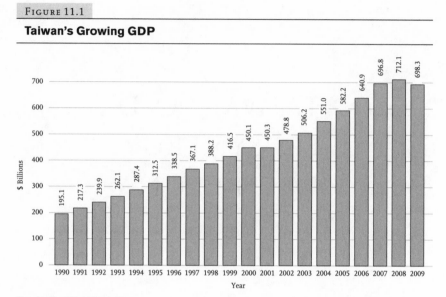

FIGURE 11.1

Taiwan's Growing GDP

Source: The World Bank Group

Taiwan is heavily dependent on exports. While the United States has been its major export destination, China will be the biggest customer for its exports during the next several years.

Taiwan controls which of its factories can be located in China. It won't send its crown jewels—its most advanced liquid crystal display (LCD) and its semiconductor wafer fabrication facilities—to China.

However, more open trade and greater cooperation between Taiwan and China in the near future are expected to benefit companies in both countries. Taiwan has the more advanced industrial base. China has a far larger market and vast resources of labor. They share a common language and heritage. The synergy is clear. The only ingredient remaining to be invested in the partnership is intelligent implementation.

Taiwan's economic development has been noteworthy. Some of its hallmarks are described below.

The primary emphasis of Taiwan's industrialization has been electronics. It's a world-class producer of semiconductors; completely assembled integrated circuits (ICs); flat-panel displays for televisions, desktop personal computer monitors, and laptop computers; wireless handsets; and other products.

Taiwan has evolved from assembling high-value components supplied by others to making finished electronics products with components all made in Taiwan. One of Taiwan's standout examples is Acer, the second-largest computer vendor in the world. VIZIO, a U.S.-Taiwanese partnership, is positioned to be the third-largest television vendor in the next two to three years.

The growth in demand for electronics products that Taiwan can expect to get from China could be an enormous boost to its prosperity. Taiwan does not have a large population and cannot be a source of low-cost labor or robust, near-at-hand demand. The natural solution is to establish manufacturing facilities in China, while technology development is pursued in Taiwan. The cultural barriers are low, and Taiwanese managers are highly effective in running factories in China.

Taiwan historically focused on manufacturing many of the key building blocks used in the electronics industry. More recently it has been building the finished products, with control over the supply chains.

The combination of supplying the key building blocks with the strength of Taiwanese finished-product facilities, along with its extensive contract manufacturing facilities, has made Taiwanese companies indispensable suppliers for companies with global brands, such as Apple, Dell, and Sony.

The availability of venture capital in Taiwan makes it a favorable place for start-up companies as well as for established large corporations looking to expand. There is plenty of liquidity for founders of companies since financiers have earned good financial returns from their investments. The ample supply of capital also helps provide high compensation for employees by means of stock options, which encourages them to be part of start-up companies.

Taiwan's track record is one of a willingness to establish new businesses. Many founders of companies have become very wealthy.

Taiwanese leaders of new businesses have been willing to work long hours to make their companies successful.

Great emphasis is placed on engineering and technology in the universities in Taiwan because of the many growth opportunities in the electronics industry. Electronics is a glamour industry in Taiwan that can provide a path to being wealthy.

The Industrial Technology Research Institute (ITRI) was established in Taiwan to be a bridge between the research and business environments. A number of start-up companies emerged from ITRI. For example, Taiwan Semiconductor Manufacturing Company Ltd. (TSMC), the world's largest independent maker of semiconductors, had its roots in ITRI.

While the universities in Taiwan are improving in academic excellence, many of the top graduates obtain masters and doctorate degrees outside of Taiwan (primarily in the United States). In the past, a high percentage of Taiwanese graduate students stayed in the United States. However, because the United States restricts the number of work visas for overseas nationals, many highly trained Taiwanese engineers and researchers are forced to return to Taiwan. This shift back to Taiwan greatly enriches its pool of highly skilled labor.

Taiwan's government focuses on building electronics corporations that can export either finished products made entirely in Taiwan or the important components to be incorporated in products finished elsewhere. Since Taiwan is too small to support really large corporations, especially businesses that require large capital expenditures, it needs to focus on exports to operate its factories at or near full capacity.

And it has been very successful in developing the large, export-oriented industries. Taiwan's share of the market for manufacturing certain electronics equipment is shown in Figure 11.2.[4]

The global market share of Taiwanese corporations in a number of important product areas has become very high because of its technology, business savvy, innovation, and cost competitiveness. Furthermore, Taiwanese corporations have benefited from the establishment of low-cost, highly efficient manufacturing facilities in China. It is im-

FIGURE 11.2

The Market Share of Taiwanese Companies in Manufacturing Selected Products in 2009

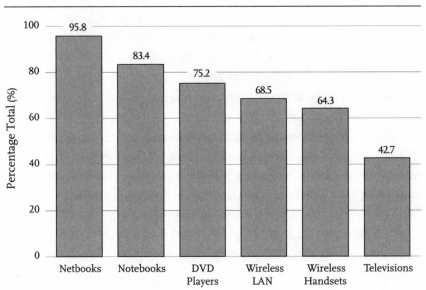

Source: International Business Strategies (IBS)

portant to note that they have kept the higher-value design work in Taiwan.

If Chinese corporations successfully adapt many of the business models from Taiwan, the growth of Chinese corporations will be spurred. China, however, has its own strategies in industries such as automobiles. Taiwanese corporations have not emphasized automobile design and assembly.

Taiwanese companies could reap enormous benefits from the growth of the middle class in China. However, there will be increased competition between the local Chinese electronics vendors and the Taiwanese electronics vendors. How divisive the competition will be will depend on both the political and the business environments. If there is conflict, the synergies will be low. If there is cooperation, the benefits will be large.

A number of Taiwanese electronics equipment vendors believe that China offers the largest growth opportunities over the next five years. While many in Taiwan are concerned about the reunification with China, the countries have grown much closer in a number of business areas. The business closeness is much greater than the political closeness.

Because of the vast difference in their populations, Taiwan is the pilot light to the enormous water heater that is China. Alone, Taiwan is an influential force in many market segments. By working closely with China, Taiwan's potency will be extraordinary.

China's gains from an alliance with Taiwan are very useful and can shorten the time for China to become a global powerhouse in the electronics industry. It is important to understand the capabilities that have been developed in Taiwan and the value of these capabilities to Chinese corporations and to the Chinese economy.

The global recession was serious for a number of Taiwanese companies, including TSMC, MiTAC, and Quanta. These and other companies showed substantial revenue declines from 2008 to 2009. However, these and other Taiwanese leaders rebounded due to a combination of their advanced and compelling technologies and strong end user markets. Quanta, for example, is the world's largest assembler of notebook computers.

The Taiwanese government has helped Taiwanese companies very much by providing support focused on building employment and expanding exports. More generally, the government has helped in the creation of research institutes and in establishing an environment in which technology is considered important. The government has also facilitated the provision of plenty of electricity, water, and other resources. That has been a big challenge for an island with limited resources.

The growth of wealth in Taiwan has been based on building a strong industrial base in electronics. While Taiwan has encouraged its businesspeople to strive for wealth, for years the government felt it might have to defend itself against an invasion from China. So another of the motives for strengthening its economy was to have the money (and the alliance with the United States) to buy military equipment.

Things have been changing gradually for the better, and China has become an increasingly important commercial partner of Taiwan. But China still poses a threat to Taiwan in that China may try to annex Taiwan on terms that Taiwan would consider unacceptable. This threat puts Taiwan in a delicate position. It knows that China has plans to absorb it, and the clock is ticking, even if no Chinese leader conspicuously looks at his or her watch in front of the Taiwanese. If China does not annex Taiwan, China's top politicians will lose face. Yet, if China rushes reunification, or seeks to do it in a way that antagonizes the Taiwanese, the consequences for Taiwan and the United States could be serious. Without access to electronics components and manufacturing support from Taiwan, the U.S. electronics industry would be plagued with supply issues.

It's probably a blessing that the way China annexes Taiwan will depend increasingly on business interests that could be mutual and are so evident to both Taiwan and China. Courtships usually have happier endings than abductions, especially, as in this case, where the bride has so much to offer if she is willing. It helps also that the annexation of Taiwan will happen after the fairly smooth annexation of Hong Kong. That precedent should assuage some of the concerns of many Taiwanese.

Taiwan's Competitiveness in Global Markets

Taiwan has established large, world-class manufacturing capabilities in capital-intensive and design-intensive industries. That's a tribute to the close cooperation between industry and Taiwan's financial institutions.

For example, Taiwan has established global leadership in the fabrication of semiconductor wafers, which are the disks imprinted with integrated circuits that serve as the brains of computers, cell phones, music players, and other devices. Large companies such as Intel and Samsung make their own wafers. Companies such as TI, Qualcomm, and Broadcom buy wafers fabricated by vendors. The wafers obtained from semiconductor vendors, whose factories are called *foundries* or *fabs*, can typically represent between 25 and 40 percent[5] of the selling prices of semiconductor products. Semiconductor prices, in turn, can represent

10 to 30 percent of the selling prices of the devices in which they are installed. If the makers of electronic devices can control the supply of semiconductors from a foundry or can negotiate extremely advantageous prices from their semiconductor vendors, that will greatly improve the profit margins from the sales of the devices.

Taiwan is semiconductor world headquarters. It supplies 80 percent[6] of the total global market for wafers from independent foundries. The largest semiconductor foundry operator is TSMC, which has annual revenues of approximately $10 billion[7] and a market capitalization of almost $50 billion.[8] Intel is the only other semiconductor vendor with higher market capitalization. TSMC has 48 percent of the global wafer market and an even higher percentage of the global market for advanced technologies. The market share for the most advanced TSMC wafers in 2011 and thereafter will depend to some extent on the strategies of Globalfoundries, the new competitor formed jointly by Abu Dhabi and the Advanced Micro Devices (AMD) company.

The second-largest semiconductor foundry vendor is the United Microelectronics Corporation (UMC), which is also Taiwanese. Another large vendor in Taiwan is Vanguard, which is 37 percent[9] owned by TSMC. Other prominent wafer fab vendors are Samsung, which is in South Korea, and SMIC, which is in China.

The concentration of foundry suppliers in Taiwan and Asia is due in part to the willingness of corporations in those geographic regions to make big investments in capital-intensive industries. Taiwanese vendors have also been fortunate because engineers and managers trained and employed in the United States have returned to Taiwan. This migration of technology experts to Taiwan has also helped Taiwan gain access to advanced technologies.

In addition to making integrated circuits (ICs), the brainy building blocks within electronics, Taiwan also makes over 80 percent[10] of the motherboards. These are the printed circuit boards on which the most important components (such as ICs) for personal computers are attached. Motherboards are crucial for computers, and Taiwan is crucial for their manufacture. Taiwan is a world leader in the manufacturing and design of printed circuit boards in general. This expertise has been used to design and manufacture not only computer motherboards but also boards for other products such as wireless handsets and televisions. The technology expertise in manufacturing in Taiwanese companies is extraordinarily high. It would be very difficult to displace Taiwanese companies in the high-volume, price-sensitive segments of the markets for electronic components.

The long-range vision for Taiwan-China synergy is for Taiwan to design the motherboards and have them made in China in facilities of the Taiwanese contract manufacturers. This will allow Taiwan to do the engineering-intensive tasks and China to do the labor-intensive tasks. In addition to the manufacturing expertise established by Taiwanese companies, they also can arrange and supervise the supply chain for many of the vital components from other Taiwanese companies. A hierarchy of capabilities has been built by Taiwanese companies, and this represents a fortress that would be difficult to conquer by corporations from other countries, including the United States. Or think of it this way: Taiwan is strengthening its corporate armies. The pressing issue is whether there will be alliances or conflict with Chinese corporations.

In addition to the wafer foundry and printed circuit businesses, Taiwanese companies have gained 35 percent of the market for large-format, liquid crystal displays (LCDs). These displays are for high-definition televisions, computer monitors, wireless handsets, global positioning system (GPS) platforms, and other applications. The revenues of the two leading Taiwanese LCD vendors, AU Optronics and Chi Mei Optoelectronics, were $12.9 billion[11] and $9.6 billion,[12] respectively, in 2008.

The LCD industry is capital intensive. A new facility can cost $3 billion or more. There is a high level of technology required for the manufacturing of flat-panel displays.

Other leading participants in the LCD market are Samsung and LG Display from South Korea. These two companies had approximately 40 percent[13] of the global market. A high percentage of the remaining 25 percent of the LCD market is supplied by Japanese vendors, including

Sharp and Panasonic. Note that they are increasing their LCD production capacity.

Meanwhile, LCD production is ramping up in China. China is five years behind Taiwan in LCDs, a big lag in electronics manufacturing. However, huge investments by China will shrink the gap. There have been $12 billion[14] in LCD factory commitments in China.

Taiwanese companies have not participated in the high growth potential of the LCD market in China because of concerns about technology transfer. Taiwanese companies are reluctant to expose their crown jewel intellectual property at this time. Over time, though, the knowledge will transfer.

There are no large-panel LCD production facilities in the United States or Europe, which means that other vendors will import the components and the finished products, such as televisions, that have the displays.

Taiwanese companies are able to set up new generations of LCD factories because of the willingness of Taiwanese venture capitalists and financial institutions to invest in their homegrown capital-intensive industries.

Because of this forward-looking opportunism, Taiwan is also advancing in the development of new display technologies, including organic light-emitting diodes (OLEDs). OLEDs aren't in wide commercial use, but they have a number of advantages compared to LCDs. OLEDs are thinner (they could be thinner than a sheet of paper) and lighter, and they use less power. They also are brighter, show more colors, have better contrast, and have a wider viewing angle. Because they can be made on flexible media, OLEDs can be embedded in fabrics, clothing, or paper. While the leading developers of OLED technologies are in Japan (Sony) and South Korea (Samsung), Taiwan is developing the skills for high-volume manufacturing of this promising technology. The country's greatest asset may be its strong optimism about future opportunities.

Taiwan's Semiconductor Industry Strategy

Taiwan emphasizes its semiconductor industry for two reasons. First, the semiconductor market is gigantic: over $260 billion in 2009, according to a report by KPMG. Second, semiconductors represent the building blocks within electronics systems. While U.S. semiconductor companies such as Intel dominate product areas such as microprocessors, there is a wide range of semiconductor products in computers, cell phones, televisions, video game consoles, and other systems.

The early approaches of the Taiwanese companies were to design and manufacture the printed circuit boards that the semiconductors were used in. The present approach is to also design and manufacture the semiconductor products. They successfully expanded their skills to be given responsibility for an increased percentage of system value.

The pioneering Taiwanese semiconductor vendors, such as VIA and SiS, tried to get into the personal computer integrated-circuit business in competition with Intel. But the Taiwanese vendors were unable to develop leadership products compared to those of Intel, and these vendors therefore experienced large losses. These semiconductor companies have survived, but they have not had much success over the past 10 years as global chip suppliers.

The second wave of the Taiwanese semiconductor vendors focused on the customers in Taiwan and China, where there is proximity and cultural similarity to the organizations that are designing the equipment. There was also some emphasis on customers in South Korea.

The focus of the Taiwanese semiconductor companies now is on the consumer, computer peripherals, and wireless handset markets. These markets are high volume and price sensitive. These segments are the ones being focused on in the top-level strategies of the Taiwanese government for long-term growth. The result? The revenues of the top 10 Taiwanese semiconductor companies quadrupled from $2.5 billion[15] in 2000 to approximately $10 billion in 2009. During this time, the integrated-circuit market had grown by 27 percent,[16] which means that the Taiwanese companies have been gaining market share.

MediaTek is the largest integrated-circuit vendor in Taiwan, with revenues of over $3.5 billion[17] in 2009; the revenues of MediaTek were $399 million[18] in 2000. The company has become the third-largest fabless IC company globally after Qualcomm and Broadcom.

MediaTek became the global market share leader for semiconductors for digital televisions. Its customers include Samsung, Sony, and Sharp. MediaTek also supplies over 70 percent[19] of the integrated-circuit products for the Chinese wireless handset market, and it has earned high profits from the Chinese market.

MediaTek offers complete application solutions for the mobile handset market. A handset maker with a small number of engineers can bring a new handset to the market in three months or less by using one of the MediaTek designs as well as its components. This approach is useful in China, India, and other developing-country markets, where many of the local customers do not have strong engineering teams.

MediaTek achieved high market share in the Chinese wireless handset market against global leaders because MediaTek understood the real needs of the customers—a complete solution including the design as well as all of the components. Speaking the same language is also a competitive advantage for MediaTek with customers in China.

Intel, which is the largest semiconductor company in the world, originated the concept of providing a full application solution (along with Microsoft) to the personal computer market. MediaTek applied that approach to makers of consumer applications, such as the wireless handset business.

The ability to gain a high market share against global competitors in a high-profile and highly competitive market segment such as wireless handsets demonstrates the effectiveness of Taiwanese competitors in the China market. As the China market grows, there will be more opportunities for the Taiwanese semiconductor vendors to increase their revenues and build their market share positions provided that there are no political barriers.

A number of other semiconductor vendors that don't have factories of their own (the companies are called "fabless") in Taiwan are gaining market share in areas such as display electronics and television chip sets. (*Chip* sets are a bunch of support circuits on a motherboard; they control how other components interact with the computer's central processing unit.) In addition to focusing on the market in Taiwan, these fabless vendors are also trying to gain market share in other Far East regions.

Japan has been self-sufficient in semiconductors in the past, but due to modest investments, its global competitiveness has weakened. Other Asian countries, including Taiwan, China, and South Korea, will become self-sufficient in the future. By some estimates, the China market will represent almost 50 percent[20] of the global market for semiconductors in 2015 compared to less than 20 percent in 2000. That would offer very high growth potential for companies.

The vertical supply chain that is being established in Taiwan—semiconductor makers who have factories, fabless semiconductor vendors, display vendors, and printed circuit board design and assembly vendors—encourages the development of local supplies of a range of products. The proximity and the engagement of these firms with each other has been and will continue to be extremely important for creating a sustainable base of capabilities in Taiwan. That homegrown synergy will amount to a strong competitive advantage within the China market.

The strengthening of the semiconductor product base in Taiwan has been rapid. It has fostered a variety of innovative business models, which have led to growing revenues and profits. More recently Taiwanese firms have been expanding from providing the functional hardware alone to also providing support software for their semiconductor products.

Software could have high growth potential for Taiwanese companies, but it is likely that they will collaborate with Indian companies that are advanced in this area. It is also likely that many of the engineers needed for software development will be in China.

Many of the business models adopted by Chinese semiconductor vendors will be based on those used by Taiwanese companies. If that happens, it's likely that the electronic components and subsystems that will be manufactured in China and Taiwan will grow in complexity and value. Over the years the Taiwan-China partnership will move higher up the value chain, increasingly focused on the finished products. This should enable them to retain the United States and Europe as large markets.

Market opportunities will decline for U.S., European, and Japanese semiconductor companies. Also, the level of content imported from Taiwan and China of the electronics products that are manufactured by U.S. companies, such as Apple, HP, and Cisco, and are bought by U.S. consumers will increase.

The capabilities base in semiconductors in Taiwan has grown rapidly over the past 10 years. How short that period has been for the Taiwanese may suggest how quickly the Chinese can become established competitors in the same industries. The revenues of the Taiwanese semiconductor vendors are derived primarily from exports. Chinese companies will have their own domestic market as well as the export market.

Taiwan has been endowed with dynamic entrepreneurs, venturesome financiers, and top-level government support that have enabled it to build a strong semiconductor and electronics business. While Taiwan itself is not a major threat to the United States, the combination of Taiwan and China has great promise for dominating segments of the electronics industry and the supporting semiconductor supply chain.

How Taiwan's Contract Manufacturers Have Helped Build the Electronics Industry

Contract manufacturers assemble equipment for brand-name electronics companies such as Cisco, Dell, and Motorola. The revenues of some large contract manufacturers [also called *electronic manufacturing services* (EMS) *companies*] are shown in Figure 11.3. In 2009 the revenues of the top 10 EMS companies were over $111 billion. Foxconn had revenues of over $56 billion. The large revenues of the contract manufacturers and the rapid growth of several of them from 2004 suggest the crucial importance of these companies.

Companies such as Apple, Nokia, and HP could not bring products to market as fast or offer the breadth of products they do without the support of companies such as Foxconn. For example, Apple's iPhone is manufactured by Foxconn in China.[21]

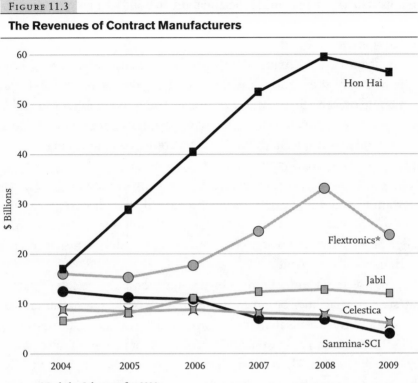

FIGURE 11.3

The Revenues of Contract Manufacturers

* Includes Solectron after 2006

Source: IBS, Inc.

Most of the contract manufacturers have a strong presence in or some advantageous connection with Taiwan, and most have manufacturing facilities in China. For example, Flextronics is headquartered in Singapore, but most of its manufacturing facilities are in China.

The facilities of the contract manufacturers in Taiwan have contributed to their high market share. They have been supported by the work ethic in Taiwan, the availability of funding, and the country's willingness to make large expenditures for very large and state-of-the-art manufacturing facilities. Taiwan also provides EMS companies with a base from which to manage high-volume factories in China.

Contract manufacturers initially assembled low-cost, low-complexity components. Over the years their capabilities improved, and brand-name manufacturers increasingly relied on them to build highly complex components, subassemblies, or finished products as well as to design electronics equipment.

Outsourcing the manufacturing of laptop computers, GPS devices, iPhones, and other sophisticated electronics provides many benefits to the brand owner, other than lower-cost assembly. It essentially provides cost parity for companies in high-cost geographic regions. Outsourcing the manufacturing enables the U.S. electronics companies to focus on product design, marketing, and distribution—that is, the core competencies that provide a relatively high return on investment. Also, it is important to note that design, marketing, and distribution require relatively small staffs to accomplish, so the U.S. brand companies can avoid large head counts by outsourcing. Outsourcing reduces the short-term cash needs of companies.

Also, as the factories become increasingly complex, the cost of setting up such new facilities becomes very high. Effectively, Taiwanese companies' huge investments in manufacturing and the infrastructure created a huge barrier to entry—it would be very difficult for new entrants to participate in the market. Then too, the Taiwanese have already trained their labor force and established quality control procedures. Taiwan is building exports as well as generating high profits from its manufacturing facilities.

The services of contract manufacturers are complemented by those of *original design manufacturing* (ODM) *companies,* which provide design services as well as manufacturing. The differences between contract manufacturers and original design manufacturers are becoming less pronounced. Foxconn and Flextronics have been strengthening their capabilities in design since 2006. All of the top 10 ODMs are headquartered in Taiwan, while their manufacturing facilities are in China, Taiwan, and elsewhere. The top 10 ODMs collectively had over $106 billion in revenue in 2009. The revenues of the top 5 ODM companies from 2004 to 2009 are shown in Figure 11.4.

The revenue growth of the ODMs has slowed for two reasons: the global recession and the increased competition from contract manufacturers. The EMS companies are increasingly offering design services.

FIGURE 11.4

ODM Revenues

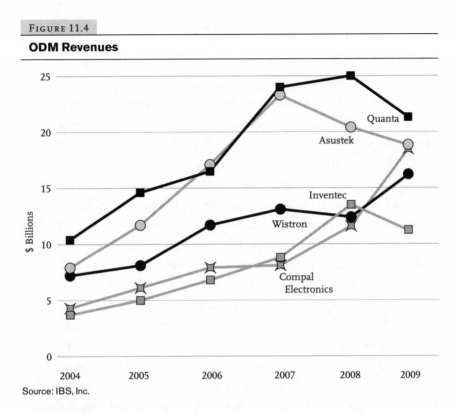

Source: IBS, Inc.

The goal of the ODM companies is to take on a higher percentage of equipment design and also to become increasingly influential in determining the components that are used in the systems of their customers. This trend will result in preference being given to the local Taiwanese companies. The ODMs have enlisted and developed a large pool of highly trained employees, which is a competitive advantage that will be difficult to duplicate by an original equipment manufacturer.

The ODM companies initially produced notebook computers for companies such as Dell, Compaq, and HP. While previously a large amount of the equipment design was done by the U.S. and Japanese computer companies, now their systems are designed primarily by the ODM companies.

ODM companies are also designing televisions, DVD players, game consoles, MP3 players, digital cameras, and camcorders. They are also building expertise in the design of wireless handsets.

The ODM business model involves having highly efficient manufacturing, low overhead, and low R&D costs. By using engineers in China as well as Taiwan, ODM companies have much lower costs than competitors or customers in developed countries.

One effect of the ODM model is that the Western consumer electronics industry has migrated to the Far East. For example, Philips moved most of its consumer business to China. It is using ODMs to manufacture its products in factories that are in China.

As the contract manufacturers from Taiwan and other parts of Asia take over increasing portions of the design function, they can account for an increasing amount of system value (which ups their fees). They are also well positioned to support the new system companies in China. This frees the Chinese companies to focus on distribution channels in China and to supply them with goods similar in features to the more established companies already in the country.

There is an ecosystem developing around the contract manufacturing and the original design manufacturing companies in Taiwan, and the symbiosis within that ecosystem is strengthening. Brand-name electronics companies have increasingly bought components from Taiwan and China, and the system design as well as system manufacturing have increasingly been managed by or accomplished in Taiwan with the help of their Chinese facilities.

This synergy between Taiwan and China will increase, and it will strengthen the financial performance of corporations in both countries. Meanwhile the United States, Europe, and Japan will become increasingly dependent on companies in Taiwan and China for the supply of many products.

Taiwan's Impact on China's Electronics Industry

The Taiwanese have demonstrated a willingness to make large investments in developing leadership technologies and in establishing the facilities to make high volumes of products. Many of the most capital-intensive facilities, such as those required to make silicon wafers and flat-panel displays, are located in Taiwan. The high-volume assembly facilities are located in China. Taiwan has the technology, and China has the large pool of low-cost labor.

With their common language, it is very easy for the Taiwanese to communicate with the workers in China. The common language represents a major competitive advantage for the Taiwanese companies compared to Western countries that set up manufacturing facilities in China and have to rely on translators. China is also a large market for the products manufactured by Taiwanese companies, and as the middle class in China grows, the synergies between the two geographic regions can strengthen.

A range of restrictions have reduced the ability of Taiwanese companies to provide their most advanced technologies to China. It's been a thorny issue for the Taiwanese corporations: how much of their high-level intellectual property (IP) to share with China. While Taiwanese companies consider access to low-cost Chinese labor to be important, they're worried about losing important technologies to Chinese companies. TSMC and SMIC have waged bitter lawsuits against the Chinese for, they allege, copying their intellectual property.

The Taiwanese government has imposed restrictions on which technologies can be transferred to China. For example, the most advanced wafer manufacturing technology from 1995 is still not allowed to be shared with Chinese companies, even though it is outdated. However, many of the restrictions have been relaxed by the Taiwanese government. The government of Taiwan realizes that China needs to be viewed as an opportunity.

Note that the United States has had no compunctions about sharing 2004-era technology with China's SMIC. This level of wafer technology that the U.S. government has allowed to be shared with China is essentially state-of-the-art technology.

However, the United States and other nations with leadership intellectual property might have great reluctance to share their crown jewel technologies with Taiwan if they consider it to be nothing but a conduit to and accomplice for Chinese IP theft. So getting closer to China—technologically—could damage Taiwan's relationships with other countries to whom it sells a lot.

China is a high-reward but potentially high-risk market for the Taiwanese corporations. China offers Taiwan the chance to duplicate the island nation's present success on an absolutely vast scale. Or China could use the IP to further expand its own success and rob Taiwan of a huge opportunity. The most likely outcome is a combination of the two scenarios—some Taiwanese intellectual property will be used by the Chinese to advance their own industries, while Taiwan will have a huge opportunity to sell additional goods in China.

With the technology capabilities in Taiwan strengthening rapidly, the importance of technology from the United States, Europe, and Japan will decline in the future in a range of market segments. Indeed, China will need far fewer of the technologies from the West as its relationship with Taiwan deepens.

If China effectively adopts many of the business concepts that have been successful in Taiwan, the growth of many industries in China can be rapid.

Taiwan is an example of how a small but driven country can experience dramatic growth in 20 years or less. The rapid growth of the electronics industry in Taiwan shows the effectiveness of the combination of entrepreneurialism and top-level government support.

12

A RESTRUCTURING PLAN FOR THE UNITED STATES

To AVOID FURTHER DECLINE in the economic and political fortunes of the United States, the government and its corporations have to rethink how they operate and how they view each other and their roles in society. It will require a restructuring of their relationship if America is to regain its competitive strength and establish the ChinAmerica partnership. The growing trade and fiscal deficits will lead to calamity if radical changes aren't made immediately. The role of the United States in global affairs, its standing as a partner of China, and the standard of living of American citizens is at risk.

Three wealth-generating goals should drive the U.S. restructure:

1. Achieving a positive trade balance by reducing imports and increasing exports

2. Reducing large government deficits

3. Increasing employment in wealth-producing industries, such as service- and manufacturing-based industries, with an export component

Meeting eight prerequisites will achieve those goals. These are the policies and behaviors the U.S. government and industry need to adopt to help the country collectively dig itself out of the deep economic hole it is in and achieve the wealth-generating goals.

Table 12.1 summarizes the prerequisites, and the rest of this chapter provides more details on the specific tasks that need to be accomplished to achieve the prerequisites. Each of the eight prerequisites needs to be established and implemented so that the United States can regain its global leadership position.

The old Yankee culture of thrift and hard work needs to be reborn. That means reversing the entitlement mentality in the United States. Oblivious consumption must be reversed, so that the people in the United States produce more than they consume.

The mentality that people can become rich without real effort, as occurred with the housing boom and decades of overindulgence, needs to be changed. The United States needs to focus on providing the foundation to help the children of the next several generations achieve wealth. A spirit of sacrifice for the next generation, commonly found in China, needs to be established in the United States.

China is adopting many of the concepts that made the United States successful in the past. It is using those concepts and its energy and enormous population to not just emulate our success but surpass it. Unfortunately, China's route to surpassing American success will come at a high cost to the United States.

That means the wealth war is real. The United States needs to understand that unless there are changes, we are in a downward spiral as China advances.

There is the need to establish the battle plans and develop the strategies required to win the global war and ensure that we are strong enough to overcome the external competitive pressures.

And the first step is improved leadership.

TABLE 12.1

Eight Prerequisites to Building Wealth

Prerequisite	Comments
1. Leadership with vision, control, and management	Government needs leaders who create an environment that stimulates corporations to grow, focused on contributions that help achieve a positive trade balance.
	Government leaders also need to take control of costs and real benefits. Performance metrics need to be applied to governments.
2. Strong corporations that are active in multiple markets	Corporations need to be active in many industries, where aggregate sales levels provide positive trade balances.
	The focus of businesses needs to be consistent with the social environment.
3. Creativity in products and business concepts	New product concepts need to be developed, and new industries need to be built to expand the economy.
	Creativity needs to be recognized and rewarded.
4. Access to the required raw materials	Corporations need access to the raw materials and resources required to gain a high market share of global markets.
5. Access to the required funding and an efficient banking system	The financial system needs to provide liquidity at a low cost.
	Financial institutions and businesses need to collaborate closely.
6. Distribution of wealth so that society becomes wealthy	While it is important for entrepreneurs and risk takers to obtain high financial rewards, there is also need for workers to be well compensated.
	Wealth needs to be efficiently distributed.
7. Cohesive society with a low level of infighting	Society needs to have well-defined goals, and the levels of social conflict need to be low.
	The enemy is outside, not inside.
8. Efficient infrastructures, which include transportation systems	People, goods, and data need to be able to move efficiently and at a low cost.
	High commute times are a tax on the time of people.

Leadership, Control, and Management

A critical need for the creation of wealth is strong and visionary government leadership. Government leaders must be able to imagine and articulate a goal for the future, and be able to articulate that vision to the voters, especially taxpaying voters. Leaders who cling to the past and wish for the good old days do not help the country in the long term, though it may appeal to nostalgic voters in the short term.

Recognizing reality is a crucial part of leadership. Jack Welch, formerly the highly regarded CEO of General Electric, was famous for insisting that his managers face facts about markets, products, and competitors.[1] The United States needs leaders who understand the current competitive environment.

Savvy government leadership founded this country, composing the U.S. Constitution based on their vision. Many of their basic concepts are still valid 200 years later. Rewarding creativity (the patent system), supporting business (protection of the general welfare), regulating business (the Interstate Commerce Clause), and providing a national defense are as appropriate now as they were when James Madison, Benjamin Franklin, Thomas Jefferson, and George Washington signed the document in 1787.

Many of the principles established by the founding fathers continue to be powerful, but now they must be reimplemented as part of the global economic environment. The United States is no longer a freed colony that has to strive to exist. Today it is the military and political leader of the free world.

As we have seen, savvy government leadership is found in China. Modern-day China started from a communistic vision, but radical changes were initiated by Deng Xiaoping in 1979. He encouraged entrepreneurship as the way out of poverty, rejecting many of the policies of the past to achieve his vision of the future. Many of the business concepts of modern-day China occurred because of the strategy developed by Deng Xiaoping to build a strong industrial base. Another visionary Asian leader who has had a strong influence on China's Industrial Revolution has been the prime minister of Singapore, Lee Hsien Loong. He has been a strong advocate of private enterprise on the island nation.

While China is building a large and diversified industrial base, there continues to be strong central control by the government. The top-down directions combined with an environment that supports entrepreneurship are key attributes of the building of wealth in China. The United States needs its leaders to take the same approach, within the rules of the U.S. Constitution, of course, but by establishing new industries.

It is critical that U.S. government leaders be driven by the goal of supporting the generation of wealth in the country. They should be leaders who understand the vital role corporations play in creating national wealth. Government leaders need to support the development of the new technologies that can form the basis of the future corporate armies. To do this, government leaders need to formulate 5- and 10-year plans to establish the new industries. The entrepreneurs in the United States have the drive and the competence to build new industries, if their government clearly shows its commitment to long-term support.

In addition, these leaders need to have a firm grasp of the economics and psychology of production and consumption. Since the government has a low level of control of production in the short term, there is, consequently, the need for the government to have control over consumption. A critical factor in the generation of wealth is the need to ensure that consumption based on borrowing does not become the approach to keep the population happy and apathetic.

Mastering Performance Management

Successful business leaders in the twenty-first century have mastered the science of performance management. They identify and use metrics to measure performance. Metrics vary from industry to industry, but they include returns on investment, costs of capital, labor productivity, sales growth, customer satisfaction, and other key performance indicators. Similar sets of metrics need to apply to federal, state, and local governments.

Leaders properly applying metrics can better manage the cost of government. At a time when a substantial number of investments are being made by government—TARP, the stimulus package, and other programs—it is crucial for government leaders to develop suitable metrics. Taxpayers will demand to know the return on their investments. Developing suitable metrics for government operations will not be easy. While corporations such as IBM can measure themselves against competitors such as Fujitsu, to date, there are no accurate models that can be used for governments. Also, a new generation of leaders will have to face a challenge from the entrenched bureaucracy, which will not want to be measured because inefficiencies will become obvious.

The United States should take the lead in developing models to determine the efficiency of its government agencies. A key issue is who will lead this effort—it will not be led by the U.S. government.

Government processes in the United States are highly inefficient and becoming high cost. The U.S. government process at the present time is clearly not the same process that made the United States successful in the past. The right set of metrics, and the right leadership, can fix this.

Today the leadership and the role of the government in China are much stronger than in the United States when it comes to the building of the industrial base and of wealth. It is true that, in China, the industrial base is being built at the expense of social programs. It is also true that the leaders are controlling consumption in the short term to build the structures that can provide the basis for building wealth in the long term. This is an attitude seen in the past in the United States usually by waves of immigrants beginning at the dawn of the twentieth century. That attitude needs to prevail again.

With global competitiveness for the generation of wealth, governments need to provide leadership and structural support for corporations in the same ways governments supported their conquering armies in the past.

Building Strong Corporations in Multiple Industries

To build wealth, there is the need to support the building of corporations that have high shares of local markets as well as global markets.

The key baseline capability in the building of wealth is that corporations can provide products and services for both the export and local markets. The corporations must be profitable so that they can provide good returns to the investors and also allow new products to be developed and promoted in the marketplace.

A large amount of the profit generation and employment base of the corporations needs to be local. The ability of corporations to export can generate a positive balance of trade, which is essential for increasing wealth in the long term. Without a positive balance of trade, the U.S. dollar will continue to depreciate. It will take more dollars to buy raw materials, such as oil.

An example of a company that has obtained a high market share of a global market is Nokia in wireless handsets. Nokia is generating large revenues, which benefit the shareholders and employees and also the economy of Finland. Nokia's growing cellular handset sales increase domestic employment and generate positive exports for Finland.

There is a similar situation with Samsung and LG Electronics in South Korea. They are exporting a range of consumer-centric products, including televisions and wireless handsets. Samsung and LG Electronics are increasing employment at home plus boosting exports from South Korea.

A key characteristic of Nokia, Samsung, and LG Electronics is their need to have high market share in global markets because their local markets are small. Without being global market share leaders, Nokia, Samsung, and LG Electronics would be small companies and would not provide major benefits to their respective countries.

Nokia, Samsung, and LG Electronics have emerged as major global companies in the last 10 to 15 years. Consequently, it is likely that Chinese companies other than Huawei will emerge as major factors in global markets in the next 10 to 15 years. The time pressures on the United States are increasing, which means that it is critical to start taking actions immediately. A key problem, however, is that the U.S. government appears to be oblivious to the seriousness of the situation, and it has been trying to get China to revalue its currency rather than attacking the problems within the United States.

It is naive and pointless for the U.S. government to try to have China stimulate internal consumption because China is controlling its internal consumption to ensure that it does not build up deficits.

The key requirement for the U.S. 5- and 10-year plans to build wealth is the need to determine which industries the United States should focus on. Internet-based consumer electronics, advanced data and voice communications equipment, and new software concepts and content search are all high-growth, high-potential industries.

In the United States, individual companies such as Cisco, Apple, IBM, Google, Microsoft, and HP are highly innovative and have high market share in these industries around the world. A number of these companies are also creating new market opportunities. It is, consequently, important to regard these companies as a part of the solution for building wealth. But they are not enough. Additional corporations in other markets need to be stimulated so that in the aggregate they create a positive trade balance.

Many market opportunities will emerge in the future—there is no shortage of areas of potential business growth. The combination of the Internet, mobile broadband access, need for better medical care, and the need for more efficient automobiles and transportation systems will create a range of new business opportunities. But U.S. government and industry leaders must be careful which ones they select for the five-year plans. Employment and export growth should determine which industries should be focused on.

The new and existing corporations need open access to global markets. However, access to many segments of the Chinese markets is managed by the Chinese government, to allow local companies to strengthen. The goal of the Chinese government is to ensure that foreign companies do not dominate markets in China. The invasion by foreign armies that pillaged and raped China a century ago will not be repeated by foreign corporations.

The United States either needs to have its corporations outperform the Chinese corporations in terms of product features, quality, and price, or the United States should adopt many of the same concepts used in China. If either nation resorts to tariff barriers, those decisions will lead only to increased global tensions and possibly another economic meltdown. Not a good selection of choices.

China adopted many of the approaches used by the United States in the past to build its corporate armies and wealth. The United States now needs to adopt many of the concepts that are being effectively used in China.

The strategies for building wealth require an understanding of the competitors' strategies and effective countermeasures to those strategies. Many of the approaches advocated in *The 36 Strategies* are being used by the Chinese government to strengthen the competitiveness of their corporations. The Chinese government clearly understands the global competitive environment, and it is using ideas more than 3,000 years old to build the wealth of China.

The time for the United States to pressure a competitor such as China to open its markets is when that competitor is weak. In our dealings with China, that time is almost gone. As China builds the financial, technical, and business strengths of its corporations, it will become increasingly difficult to apply political pressure against it.

Consequently, while the China market has very large potential, the ability of the United States to obtain high market share and obtain good financial returns from the China market will involve the combination of activities by the U.S. government as well as by the U.S. corporations.

The Role of Creativity

The role of creativity is important in the building of wealth. Creativity includes the development of new products and concepts. It also includes effectively promoting the products to obtain high revenue growth.

An example is Apple under Steve Jobs. They developed very creative products, such as the iPhone, with highly effective marketing activities. Together the products and the marketing efforts generated substantial revenues and momentum for the rest of the Apple product line. Apple developed creative business models with carriers such as AT&T. Apple obtains a part of the service revenue streams, unlike other handset providers that receive only hardware revenues from the carriers. Apple has also established structures for generating revenues from content, through iTunes.

Apple has taken mature products such as MP3 players and telephones and changed them from being passive products to products that support interactivity. The key attributes of Apple are those of having product and revenue stream creativity.

The Silicon Valley in California, the home of Apple and thousands of other high-tech companies, provides an environment that is highly conducive to creativity. The combination of strong competition and high rewards (social as well as financial) for the successful entrepreneurs coax the best out of people. A creative environment such as the fertile academic, social, and business climate of the Silicon Valley is a prerequisite for new product and service success.

New networking product concepts that involved high levels of creativity have been developed by another Silicon Valley stalwart, Cisco. The initial technology concepts of Cisco were developed at Stanford University.

Another highly successful company that emerged out of Stanford is Google. While Google has highly effective technology (its search engine capability), the company also has established business models that provide good financial returns.

The role of universities is important in the creation of innovation, but there need to be vehicles for the commercialization of the concepts. That requires venture capital funding for new concepts.

Businesses need to operate in an environment where they can obtain funds to implement new products and ideas, based on the expectation that the funds will generate good financial returns and obtain liquidity for the investors.

Creative Leaders

Perhaps more important than the Silicon Valley's warm weather or close proximity to Stanford has been a cadre of extraordinary business leaders. Business creativity was one of the key characteristics that made GE under the leadership of Jack Welch highly successful. While GE was not always the leader in technologies, many of the business concepts of the company in the 1980s and thereafter, which involved gaining high market shares and gross profit targets and metrics, were highly effective and original.

Consider the performance of a Silicon Valley company with legendary leadership. Intel has been highly creative in not only having leading microprocessors but also in having business models that generated high profits based on controlling the architecture of the end system. Intel established the prices for its microprocessors based on the value of its products in the end systems. The business models of Intel were developed by Andy Grove, who was highly innovative in shaping business concepts as well as technologies.

The United States historically has had highly creative leaders, business concepts, and technologies, and these strengths need to be utilized effectively. There is, however, the need to have an environment where the creativity can be commercialized. The worst situation is one in which governments place many restrictions and impose high costs on new businesses and place high taxes on the people who create new ideas and build wealth.

There also has to be a plan as to which industries to support in the next 5 to 10 years. While the support by the U.S. government in new battery technologies can provide benefits, the level of investment is much too small to have a major impact on the U.S. economy in the next 10 to 20 years.

To build long-term wealth, the United States needs to support the growth of new industries, where creativity is rewarded. A key part of the growth of wealth will come from the development of new industries as well as innovation in existing industries.

The United States is starting from a strong position in innovation and creativity, but its momentum in building new industries is weakening, demonstrated by the decline in venture capital activities. China is starting from a weak position, but it is strengthening rapidly. The entrepreneurial environment in China, as evidenced by the number of its small shops and new businesses, should not be underestimated. China is promoting an environment where start-up companies are actively supported with a range of subsidies, where innovation and creativity are encouraged. In China, there is the philosophy that it is good for the country to create new industries that create employment. While the level of technical creativity in China is not close to that of the United States, the level of business creativity is very high. The result is that the environment in China is very attractive for starting new companies— indeed, tens of thousands of new companies are formed every year.

Access to Raw Materials

Countries such as Saudi Arabia have large amounts of natural resources, but most countries need to import a wide range of raw materials. The United States is an example of a country that imports many types of resources, with oil having the highest cost.

When there is plentiful supply of resources and all countries have access, the critical need is to have the funds to be able to pay for resources. In the cases of shortages, it will be the countries with the largest financial resources and political power that will have access to the required raw materials. That time is coming sooner than most people in the United States realize.

To build the broad base of what are now legacy industries, a range of materials was required—iron ore, copper, coal, lithium, and other materials, in addition to petroleum. Also, the electronics industries need silicon wafers and flat-panel displays. Many of these raw materials are in countries that have modest internal needs. They can export the excess to be able to buy finished products from other countries.

Historically the U.S. corporations were very active in buying companies that had raw materials in multiple countries. Barrick Gold, Newmont Mining, and other gold and metals mining organizations bought full or partial ownership in companies in Tanzania, the Dominican Republic, and other geographic regions. The U.S. corporations, however, have become more cautious about buying assets in foreign countries. They fear the political risks, and they have also become more cautious about spending money on hard assets.

Russia, Venezuela, and other countries regard their natural resources within their geographic boundaries as key assets. They exert government power to establish and control the relationships with foreign corporations. It is estimated that approximately 80 percent of the world's oil reserves are controlled by governments.[2] In the future, there will be more government control over strategic minerals and other raw materials, which will mean more government-to-government negotiations. The U.S. government must be ready and willing to negotiate intelligently with other countries over access to raw materials for its corporations. Some U.S. corporations continue to try to strengthen their access to resources, but the U.S. government is passive in supporting the activities of these companies, unless they are in the oil industry.

There are also activities in the United States to find alternate approaches to ensuring an oil supply, such as developing ethanol and electric cars, but many of the activities are based on the lobbying of special interest groups rather than the systematic structuring of priorities. The U.S. government does not place priorities on long-term access to raw materials. This has to change because the competition is focused on it.

China, for example, has a number of initiatives, including the following:

- *Accumulating gold reserves:* Allows protection of the currency as well as ensuring access to a strategic asset.
- *Increasing copper and other metal reserves:* China has been buying metals when their prices were low.
- *Buying raw material mining rights in different geographic locations, including South America, Africa, Australia, and Canada:* Chinalco tried to invest $19.5 billion into Rio Tinto,[3] for stakes in aluminum, bauxite, copper, and iron ore projects. As part of the agreement, $5.15 billion was to be spent to obtain 15 percent of Hamersley Iron,[4]

$3.39 billion for 15 percent of Escondida (copper), and 30 percent[5] of Weipa (bauxite). Chinalco would have also owned 25 percent of Kennecott Utah Copper through this deal.

The Australian government rejected the Chinalco offer, which caused strong resentment in China. It is, however, likely that Chinese companies will continue to acquire a wide range of mineral resources.

- *Engaging in a full-court press to obtain access to oil and gas:* An example is China's support for CNPC to buy a portion of Suncor Energy/ Petro-Canada. CNPC also bought PetroKazakhstan (PK) for $4.18 billion[6] in cash in 2005, which accounts for 16 percent of the oil output of Kazakhstan. CNPC is also trying to buy oil assets in Libya and elsewhere.

China has its own oil exploration activities, but it is likely that China is protecting many of these reserves for the future. The short-term approach is to obtain oil and oil rights from sources outside of China.

- *Building up its expertise in specialty chemicals through investments and joint ventures:* China National Chemical Corporation (ChemChina), which is a state-owned enterprise, purchased ownership of the Adisseo Group (France). ChemChina also purchased Qenos of Australia, and Qenos is the largest manufacturer of polyethylene.

The activities of the Chinese companies in gaining access to raw materials and the supply chains for the raw materials is being accomplished through top-level guidance. There has been an acceleration of activities when prices are relatively low.

China is using its supply of foreign currencies and reserves to increase access to raw materials. These activities show the long-term planning by China in strengthening the factors that will provide success in the future in continuing to build its industrial base and therefore its wealth.

Armies need food and ammunition. Corporations need access to raw materials and financing sources. China is planning ahead. The United States is consuming.

The United States needs to establish strategies for gaining access to its required raw materials and for having ways to pay for them. Again, the need for long-range planning is paramount. A series of 5- and 10-year industrial plans would incorporate a global raw materials strategy in addition to new business development. The 5- and 10-year plans would need to be bipartisan and based on national goals as is currently the case with the U.S. military.

After having the appropriate government operating structures and plans and the building of corporations, ensuring access to the required raw materials should be an area of high priority for the United States.

Access to Required Funding

Corporations need access to funds to grow, and the cost of borrowing those funds needs to be low. Businesses also need efficient access to the funds. Funding is required for new companies to be established and for existing companies to grow. Having the required liquidity and credit facilities is a critical factor for the building of wealth.

And for all this wealth building to happen, the returns for the investors need to be positive so that there are incentives to invest.

There are multiple entities that provide investment vehicles. They range from the early-stage investors, such as the venture capitalists, to the large banks that generally enter the scene at a later stage. Typically, banks focus their investments on large corporations.

The U.S. banking system was considered to be the best in the world until it effectively collapsed in 2008 because of excessive leverage and greed. The U.S. banking system is recovering, and a key issue as it does so will be that of the level of government control. How much lending will be available to businesses to create new products or services or expand their existing operations? It is not clear what kind of support for corporations will be forthcoming from the traditional banking industry.

The banking system in China has effectively managed the impact of the global financial crisis. It maintained an adequate supply of funds for consumers to purchase housing and for industries to grow. The leverage in China, however, has been much lower than in the United States, and, consequently, the costs to maintain growth have been much lower. China clearly has access to a large amount of funds, and growth will not be limited by liquidity.

With the recovery from the global financial meltdown, there will be adequate liquidity to support future growth of industry around the world. However, there will be competition for access to the funds. The key challenge for the United States will be to keep interest rates low, to limit interest on the deficits. Low interest rates, however, will put pressure on the dollar, which makes investments in businesses that are linked to the dollar potentially high risk.

Concern over inflation in the United States, and in other countries deploying massive amounts of stimulus capital, will remain high for years. At some point, it is likely that the United States will go into a high-inflation phase. No one knows when, or how serious the inflation spiral may be. If it occurs, the U.S. government will be challenged to maintain business growth while containing inflation.

I am confident the United States will remain highly skilled in financial management. Access to the required financial resources will not be a limitation for U.S. corporations, as long as the government takes a supportive role.

Distribution of Wealth

Successful societies depend on a fair distribution of wealth. The uneven distribution of wealth creates an environment where the very wealthy gain excessive power and the people without wealth are very dissatisfied. Remember the French Revolution? The end of czarist Russia?

In the twenty-first century in the United States, wealth should be distributed through equitable compensation. Employees who contribute to success should share in the growth of corporations by receiving stock options, bonuses, and other rewards. Shareholders also need to obtain good financial returns. It is, however, critical to be cost competitive. Taiwanese companies, such as TSMC and MediaTek, use stock options and bonuses to provide high compensation to their employees while also being cost competitive. Similar compensation approaches are also being taken in China. Many of the stock compensation and other incentive concepts used in many countries were developed in the United States.

More equitable rewards for employees will become politicized if U.S. corporate leaders don't recognize the wave of dissatisfaction and respond to it. The late 2009 news that Goldman Sachs planned to award $19 billion in bonuses and other rewards in early 2010 triggered a firestorm of criticism, especially since the Wall Street investment firm had used U.S. government money to stay afloat just 12 months before.[7] While Goldman Sachs later changed the bonus structure to long-term stock options instead of cash for its most senior employees, the issue of executive compensation remains a red hot issue.

It is important for CEOs on Wall Street and elsewhere and government leaders to remember that excess concentration of wealth becomes a demotivator over the longer term. Of course, the leadership of corporations need to be well rewarded, especially if compensation is tied to performance. CEOs on Wall Street and Main Street, and U.S. government leaders, must determine the appropriate balance—unchecked greed harms us all.

In addition to compensation, successful societies provide upward mobility so that the high achievers have successful careers and are well compensated independent of their starting positions. Promotions as well as raises, bonuses, and stock options should be based on performance, not merely on seniority.

The approach of corporations in Japan to give promotions and associated compensation based on seniority, and not performance, is clearly not effective. It has created a highly stratified work environment. The result is a low-risk approach to decision making in Japan because a large mistake can result in a reassignment to a lower-status position. As companies become more stratified, the level of innovation declines due to the modest rewards and substantial punishments for failed risk taking.

A key strength of the United States in the past was that while there was a wealthy class, new wealth could be obtained within a few years through the building of successful companies. There were many areas of growth, with opportunities for many entrepreneurs. Many billionaires emerged though they were poor at birth. Also, each decade brought major new opportunities for building wealth.

Beginning in 2000, though, there has been abuse of the opportunities in the United States by some individuals. A large amount of wealth was taken from corporations without significant contribution into these corporations. This type of abuse is not good for the building of the overall wealth of a country. There is, consequently, the need to restrict the activities of exploiters while rewarding the activities of the achievers.

In addition to the wealth of the high-achieving managers and executives, the workers also need to share a part of the wealth. It is important for wealth to be distributed. However, the cost of management and workers needs to be competitive on a global basis. If direct and indirect compensation is too high, there will be low profits and poor returns for the investors.

The distribution of wealth requires a balance among several dimensions: rewards for excellent achievement, the ability of the population to live comfortably, and being cost competitive in global markets. The level of comfort required by the population is based on the expectations as well as the needs of the consumers. The Scandinavian countries are an example of where compensation levels have been sensibly managed.

The United States is entering a phase in which taxes on the high earners will be increased, which has risks of suppressing entrepreneurship. A problem for the United States, however, is that there are not enough high-wage earners to pay for the government's deficits so that even with the additional tax revenues, the deficits will continue to be large.

In the past, the United Kingdom has raised the tax rates on its high earners, which has suppressed entrepreneurship. The result has been that the industrial base in the United Kingdom has become very weak. The United States is adopting many of the concepts used in the United Kingdom, at its peril. The United States is abandoning its past principles of rewarding energy and ingenuity.

A key strength in the past of the United States was its ability to manage wealth distribution effectively and to give high rewards to high achievers. It is important for the United States not to lose this strength through the excessive taxation, controls, and increased power of the government.

While the present government in Washington is committed to the redistribution of wealth, it is critical that entrepreneurship is not stifled. The indications, however, are not positive for the U.S. businesspeople.

China is also going through a phase in which many high-wealth individuals are being created through the building of successful corporations. The high visibility being given to these individuals, where many are under 40, is encouraging others to start new businesses.

A key problem in China, however, is that government officials and their relatives are also building wealth rapidly through their positions of power. Politicians and their relatives who use the system to build their personal wealth represent a hidden tax on society and can demotivate the high achievers. A low level of visibility into the activities of government agencies and state-owned enterprises encourages corruption, which will ultimately weaken the country.

For example, the hiring of government officials' offspring for lucrative positions in the government agencies and in the state-owned enterprises, ahead of high-achieving graduates, is a potential problem in China. While outright bribery is being more vigilantly prosecuted in China, it remains a problem, especially outside of the major metropolitan areas.

As long as the average compensation in China increases, the level of dissatisfaction by society can be controlled. If the growth of the economy slows, there can be the building of disillusionment of the political system. That could lead to increased unrest in China.

The advantage of a democracy is that, if it is efficiently managed, there is the ability to monitor the distribution of wealth provided the electorate is well informed. A democracy where there is the use of a high percentage of taxes to allow the low achievers to consume without contribution is, however, not effective distribution of wealth.

If the majority of voters do not pay the appropriate levels of taxes and support increases in taxes for additional consumption, democracy loses its benefits.

Distribution of wealth is a relatively minor problem in the United States compared to the other problem areas. A key problem that will emerge in the United States is that of not enough wealth to distribute.

A Cohesive Society

A cohesive society is one in which the population is committed to a common goal and in which the commitment leads to achievement of the goal. Society should be harmonious and cohesive, avoiding a high level of internal conflict. Internal disputes distract from achieving the common goals.

A key quality of the United States in the past was its ability to remain a cohesive country while absorbing millions of immigrants. Indeed, part of the reason for the success of the United States was the immigrants' contribution to the generation of wealth within a short time. Working together and achieving success, based on nationwide acceptance of ethical behavioral standards, led to pride in the United States. An external enemy was usually the rallying point to encourage Americans to focus on a task and achieve it. America had King George III of Great Britain, the Germans of World War I, Hitler of World War II, and the Soviet menace in the Cold War of the 1950s. They were all examples of how the American people rallied around a call to defeat a common enemy. This focus extended to politics and economics as well as the military.

Since the collapse of the Soviet Union, though, America hasn't had a clearly defined external enemy to focus on. Yes, the Vietcong of the Vietnam War and Al Qaeda after 9/11 were identified as the common enemies, but much of the general population either refused to accept the notion (the antiwar protests during the Vietnam War era) or refused to make any sacrifices to defeat an elusive enemy (Osama bin Laden).

The United States has also become less cohesive. The goal of increasing a secure wealth for the country has been replaced by the goal of achieving wealth for individuals. The culture of the country has changed for the majority to optimizing consumption rather than optimizing production.

Indeed, the United States is starting to become more polarized, with the hardening of the positions of the far left and far right. A divided country is extremely vulnerable to a focused and united external threat.

Interestingly, there is a lack of cohesiveness under the surface of China. On the outside China appears very cohesive, but inside there are high levels of internal competitiveness. The internal competitiveness in China can be an asset if it is channeled effectively, but it can also slow the growth of China if it is divisive.

However, the approach of divide and conquer of the internal hierarchy continues to be widely used within China. This is potentially an area of major weakness in competing in global markets. The "fighting at home" approach can lead to top-down control to maintain order, but it weakens competitiveness against external competitors.

To succeed, China needs its central government to provide strong leadership, but not to the point that the population feels oppressed. If there is a weakening in the control of the central government, China can go into a phase in which there will be extensive internal conflict. That will weaken the growth of the economy. The risks to China of not having a cohesive society are relatively high, but the central government has a clear understanding of the political threats.

Efficient Infrastructures

Efficient infrastructures are a prerequisite for building national wealth. Extensive and well-maintained highways and secondary roads, railroads, airports, and clean and plentiful water and energy generation are vital for the production and the distribution of goods for domestic consumption as well as for exports. The better the infrastructure is, the more efficient the society. And the more efficient the society, the more national wealth it can build.

A current example of a prescient approach to energy infrastructure development is the commitment of France to nuclear power. France has been highly effective in ensuring adequate supply of low-cost (on a relative basis) electricity.

The United States is increasing its emphasis on attaining self-sufficiency in energy production, but it still does not have clear long-range plans. A key requirement in the United States is to build the energy generation technologies that provide low-cost power throughout a highly efficient distribution system. The "smart grid" concepts promoted by the U.S. government and many companies promise to save energy by more precisely managing the distribution of power.[8] The concepts are innovative, but the system will be very difficult to manage over the long term because it requires retrofitting tens of millions of electric meters and appliances around the country.

The U.S. transportation systems also need to become more efficient, including large increases in energy efficiencies. If the United States can develop and manufacture aircraft that are the best in the world, the United States should be able to develop leadership automobiles, trucks, buses, and trains that are the best in the world. Japan, France, and Germany have established industries to manufacture transportation vehicles that are competitive globally, but the United States has not shown the same level of initiative.

The U.S. government has proposed building a high-speed rail system throughout the nation. However, it is unlikely that this will be built because of the power of local communities—they will object to high-speed railroads passing through their neighborhoods. As we have seen, the performance of U.S. corporations in the automobile industry has been disastrous, so there is no leadership growing to promote alternate transportation systems such as highly efficient rail systems.

In fact, the United States has clearly neglected its highway, bridge, and rail infrastructures for decades. There is the need for long-term planning for the management of the infrastructures. In addition, the United States needs the commitment of the appropriate financial resources to ensure adequate access to electricity, water, and other services.

China is making large expenditures to build its railroad and road infrastructures. It will take 10 to 20 years for China to have an efficient transportation system, but it will be built. This infrastructure is an important requirement for a country with 1.3 to 1.5 billion people who are becoming increasingly mobile.

A key challenge for China is that of ensuring adequate water to the northern areas. Rainfall is not nearly enough for the water usage in China. To rectify the gap, either large numbers of people will need to be moved, or new water distribution systems will need to be developed.

China has the resources to build its infrastructures, but it is starting with a weak base. The United States is neglecting the building and strengthening of its infrastructure and instead supporting short-term consumption.

Strategies for Building Wealth

When armies attempt to conquer foreign countries, there is the need to have well-planned strategies for the battles. When armies protect a country, there is also the need to understand the capabilities of the aggressors and develop the appropriate defensive strategies. A similar type of strategic planning needs to exist for corporations in the drive to build wealth. Top-level concepts are developed by the government, and they are implemented by the corporations.

The actions in China involve strong government support for the building of companies that include the development of strategies on how to win market share. The Chinese government continues to be active in managing companies, with many of its business concepts being similar to the approaches used in Singapore. It is, however, not considered appropriate for governments to manage companies over the long term because of the conflicts of interest that are likely to emerge as the organizations stratify.

While there is a migration of some of the management functions from the government to entrepreneurial leaders in China, this transfer is being made cautiously within a number of the state-owned enterprises in China. A problem for China in making this transfer is that many of the legacy power structures continue to be maintained, which reduces the competitiveness of these companies. In short, many are overstaffed and bureaucratic.

It is the competitiveness of corporations operating in growth market segments that generate wealth, provide employment, and provide buying power for natural resources. That combination becomes the beginning of a virtuous cycle of wealth building. The importance of corporations is well understood in China—it adopted the best business models and strategies from many countries, not just the United States.

Many of the wealth-building philosophies and strategies of Singapore's Lee Kuan Yew were adopted by Deng Xiaoping, and they have become a baseline operating philosophy for building industries in China. Singapore stressed the development of manufacturing facilities with government support. Similar types of approaches have also been established in China for the building of manufacturing facilities, but the scale of investment and growth of the industrial base in China is dramatically greater than practical in Singapore.

A number of the strategies established and effectively used in Taiwan are also being adopted in China. An example is that of the emphasis on capital-intensive areas of the electronics industry. First in Taiwan and now in China, government and industry are working together to assemble a complete array of support companies for their chip makers. They are following the strategies of Toyota, GM, and Ford—each encouraged a broad array of component manufacturers to establish their operations around the automakers' assembly plants.

The key baseline capabilities in China for the growth of industry and wealth are very similar to the approaches taken by the United States in the past. A major difference, however, is that China is achieving in 10 years what it took the United States 50 years to achieve.

The government actions that have helped the growth of corporations in Taiwan, South Korea, and even Japan are not fully appreciated in the United States. The support from these foreign governments included subsidies, favorable tax treatments, and protection of local markets. It is important for the United States to understand the strategies of the competing countries and corporations and to take the appropriate competitive actions.

The global competitive environment also keeps on changing, and new competitors are constantly emerging. While the United States has been able to compete effectively with Japan in computers and data communications, Japan won most of the markets for the consumer products, such as televisions. The competitive environment has, however, changed, and South Korean, Taiwanese, and Chinese companies are currently destroying the Japanese consumer electronics industry. With the change from analog to digital televisions and to LCD technology, Japan has lost one of the key pillars of its industries, and this has occurred over a five-year timeframe.

It is, consequently, important for the strategies that are established in the United States to be flexible and allow corporations to respond quickly to changes in the competitive environment.

The strategies to build successful corporations are well understood by management in the United States. The problem for the United States is that while individual corporations are strong, the aggregate of the contribution of the corporations results in large trade imbalances.

Most of the individual corporations in China are not as strong as those in the United States, but the strategic leadership in China is stronger. As a result, the aggregate activities in China are building momentum rapidly against the United States.

Why China Will Strengthen and the United States Will Weaken

As the economy of China strengthens, the political power of China will also increase. It is likely that in the next 10 to 20 years, there will be two superpowers—the United States and China. In 20 to 50 years, it could be one superpower unless the United States takes the required actions.

The Chinese government's well-defined five-year plans to build its economy have already yielded significant successes. In 2000, Chinese automobile companies built 2 million cars, trucks, and buses, but it more than sextupled[9] that amount in 2009, despite a highly competitive market.

A key part of their plan for the Chinese automotive market was protectionism. In China's automobile market, 80 percent of the sales are cars made by Chinese companies, primarily via joint ventures. The foreign companies fight for the remaining 20 percent.

Another key part of the Chinese five-year plans is the building of transportation infrastructures in China. A $24 billion high-speed rail link between Beijing, Shanghai, and Guangzhou is under construction. Also, $22 billion[10] is being spent on freight railroad lines in the Shanxi Province, and $17.6 billion is being spent on passenger lines in northern China. In total, China spent $88 billion on railroad construction in 2009—double the amount spent the year before and seven times the total invested in 2004.

The railroad programs are now part of the $585 billion[11] that China has committed to the stimulus package in 2009 and 2010. While there are, however, funding constraints for the stimulus programs—the budgets of the central government and provinces need to be balanced—most of the major infrastructure projects are being implemented.

Meanwhile, U.S. government investment in its decrepit railroad system is pathetic. The initial appropriation was $2.5 billion for 2011, which was on top of the $8 billion in the stimulus package. The Chinese are spending eight times more on railroads than is the United States, and most of the Chinese spending is for new, high-speed services. Most of the United States' spending is earmarked just to maintain the current dilapidated system. The United States has established an efficient military infrastructure system, and a similar approach needs to be taken to the transportation system. The U.S. government needs to establish the appropriate transportation infrastructure and allow it to be run by private industry. The U.S. government should not run any of the transportation businesses, but it should monitor them to make sure they help, rather than hinder, America's global competitiveness.

Another area that the United States should improve is its communications infrastructure systems. The Chinese are way ahead of us in that vital aspect as well. The $59 billion[12] being spent on an advanced wireless communications infrastructure in China will give it technological parity with other geographic regions. It is expected that 50 to 60 percent of the orders for the infrastructure equipment will be given to Chinese companies—Huawei and ZTE will be the key beneficiaries. The next phase will be to expand the installed base of mobile platforms that use the infrastructure, and it is likely that a relatively high percentage of these platforms will be provided by Chinese companies too.

The carriers for the broadband wireless infrastructures are China Mobile, China Telecom, and China Unicom—all Chinese companies with large government ownership.

In the future, wireless communications capabilities in the United States will be significantly weaker than they are in China. As already noted, Europe, South Korea, Japan, and other countries have much better wireless communications technologies than the United States. And it won't be too long before China's wireless broadband infrastructure is superior to that in the United States.

China is willing to make large financial commitments to improve its infrastructure as well as its industrial base because of the positive impact on the efficiency of corporations and the ability to provide mobility to the population. There is also large employment from the building of infrastructures. While the United States is also increasing expenditures on infrastructures, the levels are 10 percent of what is being spent in China. Also, most of the expenditures in the United States are for repaving existing roads rather than building new roads. And the expenditures in the United States are being funded through deficits, so future generations will have to pay the debt so that we have better roads now.

The Widening Unemployment Gap

Expenditures on education are being increased in China, with ambitious goals to increase the number of university graduates. The need for those graduates to find jobs will drive another wave of industrialization in China. Don't forget that a high percentage of the current pool of graduates is having difficulties in finding appropriate jobs, in part due to the global economic slowdown.

The pressures in China to expand employment for the higher-level workers will, consequently, increase over the next decade. In 2015 to 2020, there will be the need for China to employ close to 1 billion workers, or roughly seven times the entire workforce of the United States in 2009. Imagine how much China's industries will have to grow to provide jobs for even half of that workforce.

Not only will China expand the number and type of industries it develops to employ all of those workers but it will also have to create jobs and industries higher up the value ladder. Assembling a lot more children's toys and strollers won't cut it. Instead, it will need to create advanced technology companies like its data communications gear maker Huawei. And it will need to do so on an almost weekly basis to absorb the trained workforce. That climb up the value ladder will increase the intensity of the competitive climate vis-à-vis corporations.

The increased competition within many market segments will benefit consumers and other buyers in the United States and around the world through lower prices in the short term. But in the long term, the dependence of the United States on China will increase. As the dependence on China increases and the financial position of the United States weakens, the leverage that can be obtained by China over the United States will increase.

At the same time, the tension over the control of natural resources will increase as well. As consumption in China and other developing countries such as India increases, there will be increased demand for natural resources. Prices of many natural resources will increase, which will negatively impact the trade balance of developed countries while providing a boom for Africa and South America. The countries that have a positive trade balance, such as China, will be able to absorb the impact of the price increases. The countries that have a negative trade balance, such as the United States, will face larger trade deficits. The countries that cannot build their exports to counter the increase in imports will experience a decline in wealth.

China's large positive balance of trade can be used both as an offensive as well as a defensive capability. The approaches of the Chinese government to buying companies that have access to raw materials are part of an offensive strategy. While the Japanese bought golf courses and tall buildings in the United States, it is likely that the Chinese will buy farmland and companies with strategic assets.

What the United States Should Do

The United States needs to take the following actions to develop a successful partnership with China:

1. Accept the fact that countries rise and fall based on their ability to compete in global markets. And they successfully compete in global markets by having an efficient and low-cost government. U.S. corporations need to be competing on a level playing field in global as well as in the home markets.

2. The United States needs to develop 5- and 10-year plans to establish forward-looking industrial policies, based on the type of strategy development and implementation used by the military.

   The military has offensive and defensive strategies for fighting wars. Corporations need to have both approaches for protecting local markets (their defensive strategies) and approaches for gaining high market share in foreign markets (the offensive strategies).

3. Metrics need to be established that determine the national value of corporations, specifically focused on the following:
   - *Providing employment in the United States and the level of employee compensation, both of which impact consumption and taxation levels.*
   - *Gaining value from exporting products.*
   - *Gaining value from having high shares of local markets, which limits imports.* The values for exports and for the local

markets need to be based on net local contribution rather than total sales. What this means is that if the assembly operations for a product of a U.S. corporation is accomplished in China and it accounts for 20 percent of the selling price, then only 80 percent can be included in local supply. This is a new concept, but it is important to have metrics that truly reflect our wealth-building efforts. By having metrics, the value of corporations as the wealth armies can be measured, and the aggregate benefits from their activities can be quantified. The quantification allows for prediction, which can be the basis for the planning process, and actual results can be determined by the balance-of-trade data.

4. The United States needs to allocate funding to build the next generation of corporations and also to propel the growth of the existing corporations.

   The amount of funding will be determined by the potential value of specific industries such as medical electronics, automobiles, solar energy, and windmills in contributing to the growth of wealth.

   The funding levels in the United States will need to be driven by individual business plans that are aggregated at the national level.

   This is a new concept in the United States, but it is essential for it to develop the metrics to determine competitiveness in the long term.

5. The United States needs to prioritize the conflicting funding demands of social and industrial programs. There is the clear need for the politicians to both understand the competitive threats and also to take the necessary actions required to build wealth in the long term. Within the present political structure, it will be very difficult to achieve access to the required funding support without the expansion of the

government's deficits, which are already very large and growing rapidly. Social program spending will need to be cut in the short term to fund the industrial investments. This will be a difficult and painful action for politicians and voters, but the United States has reached a point where it can't pretend that it can have it all.

6. The United States needs to provide more financial incentives to corporations to increase exports. While exports need to be increased generally, it will be important to focus on countries where their surpluses vis-à-vis those of the United States are large—China, Japan, and Germany. Agreements with these countries will be needed to support the buying of U.S. goods to offset the current and future trade deficits. China is already taking this approach with some of its supplier partners, such as Brazil and the oil-supplying countries.

   There will be a need for high levels of skill in negotiating the trade agreements with the respective countries. However, this type of agreement is similar to military agreements. There will also be a need to stimulate the U.S. corporations so that they are able to support the export opportunities.

7. The United States will need to build up new industries, such as new generations of medical electronics, ultra-high-efficiency vehicles, and products based on nanotechnologies, as well as products related to energy generation. The necessary subsidies, tax incentives, and other supports will need to be incorporated into the overall operating structure of the U.S. economy.

8. High-efficiency manufacturing facilities will need to be built to achieve low unit costs, similar to what Canon has built in Japan and China. If these facilities are not built, products developed in the United States will continue to be manufactured in China. And the benefits to the United States

will be lower than if the products are manufactured in the United States.

Manufacturing costs in the United States will need to be competitive, which requires automation and the development of products that can be manufactured economically in the United States. Also, the trade unions will need to cooperate in supporting low-cost manufacturing with reasonable pay. In exchange, the government and industries will provide high levels of training for U.S. workers.

Intellectual property (IP) protection will need to be tight. New technologies for ensuring IP protection will need to be developed.

These steps will need to be taken by the United States to strengthen its competitiveness. Time is the enemy.

There is still time for the United States to make the required changes, but the time window is getting shorter. Without the appropriate changes, the employment base in the industrial segments of the United States will continue to decline, and wealth of the population will also decline rapidly.

By 2015, the actions that will need to be taken to reverse the decline will be much more draconian than they were when this book was written in late 2009. If nothing is done now, in five years China will be much more powerful and the United States will be far weaker. While the United States is descending, China is ascending.

ENDNOTES

Part I

1. http://bbs.chinadaily.com.cn/redirect.php?gid=2&fid=33&tid=637756&goto=nextoldset

Chapter 1

1. http://www.bloomberg.com/apps/news?pid=20601087&sid=alZgI4B1lt3s
2. http://www.nytimes.com/2009/11/16/opinion/16ferguson.html?_r=1&sq=schularick&st=cse&adxnnl=1&scp=1&adxnnlx=1258473896-0bkm1teB12NXGF6n6xHP7g&pagewanted=all
3. http://www.ft.com/cms/s/0/76a47408-3f3a-11de-ae4f-00144feabdc0.html
4. http://online.wsj.com/article/SB126047365539485893.html
5. http://www.census.gov/foreign-trade/statistics/highlights/annual.html
6. http://krugman.blogs.nytimes.com/2009/08/27/a-note-on-the-bush-fiscal-legacy/
7. http://money.cnn.com/2009/10/16/news/economy/treasury_deficit/index.htm?postversion=2009101615
8. http://money.cnn.com/2009/11/16/news/economy/bad_business.fortune/index.htm

Chapter 2

1. http://www.nokia.com/careers/graduates/nokia-graduate-program
2. http://www.mpaa.org/researchstatistics.asp
3. http://www.itri.org.tw/eng/about/article.asp?RootNodeId=010&NodeId=0103
4. Source: International Business Strategies (IBS).

5. Ibid.
6. http://www.shanghaidaily.com/sp/article/2009/200902/20090204/article_389762.htm
7. http://www.exim.gov/pressrelease.cfm/434FDA5F-B2D8-AE78-D3632FFE08174C2A/
8. http://globalfoundries.com/newsroom/2009/20090724.aspx
9. http://www.nytimes.com/2008/04/26/washington/26farm.html?_r=1&ref=us&oref=slogin

Part II

1. http://www.bea.gov/national/nipaweb/TableView.asp?SelectedTable=1&ViewSeries=NO&Java=no&Request3Place=N&3Place=N&FromView=YES&Freq=Year&FirstYear=1998&LastYear=2008&3Place=N&Update=Update&JavaBox=no#PtrFriend
2. http://www.cars.gov/faq
3. http://taxvox.taxpolicycenter.org/blog/_archives/2009/7/8/4243062.html
4. http://www.census.gov/Press-Release/www/releases/archives/income_wealth/014227.html
5. http://money.cnn.com/2009/10/21/autos/auto_bailout_rattner.fortune/index.htm
6. http://www.freep.com/article/20091207/BUSINESS01/91207051/1320/Marchionne-says-he-will-have-to-split-his-jobs
7. http://online.wsj.com/article/SB124385428627671889.html
8. http://www.uaw.org/gm/gm01.cfm
9. http://money.cnn.com/2009/10/21/autos/auto_bailout_rattner.fortune/index.htm
10. https://www.cia.gov/library/publications/the-world-factbook/geos/country template_ja.html
11. https://www.cia.gov/library/publications/the-world-factbook/geos/country template_us.html

Chapter 3

1. http://www.nytimes.com/2009/04/28/business/28auto.html?_r=1
2. http://oica.net/wp-content/uploads/world-ranking-2007.pdf
3. http://www.reuters.com/article/GCA-Autos/idUSTRE5A15KT20091102
4. http://wheels.blogs.nytimes.com/2010/02/23/spyker-completes-deal-for-saab/?scp=2&sq=Saab&st=cse
5. http://www.ford.com/about-ford/news-announcements/press-releases/press-releases-detail/pr-ford-posts-third-quarter-2009-net-31244
6. http://www.nytimes.com/2009/04/09/business/09ford.html?_r=1&n=Top/Reference/Times%20Topics/People/M/Mulally,%20Alan%20R

7. http://oica.net/wp-content/uploads/world-ranking-2008.pdf
8. http://online.wsj.com/article/SB10001424052748703808904574527480072025844.html
9. http://www.11alive.com/rss/rss_story.aspx?storyid=136834
10. http://www.census.gov/foreign-trade/Press-Release/current_press_release/exh7.txt
11. http://www.census.gov/foreign-trade/Press-Release/current_press_release/exh8.txt
12. http://money.cnn.com/1998/05/07/deals/benz/
13. http://www.daimler.com/dccom/0-5-7145-1-858191-1-0-0-0-0-0-11979-0-0-0-0-0-0-0-0.html
14. http://www.gao.gov/products/GAO-10-151
15. http://articles.latimes.com/2009/jun/24/business/fi-autos-loans24
16. http://oica.net/category/production-statistics/
17. http://oica.net/category/production-statistics/2000-statistics/
18. http://www.caam.org.cn/zhengche/20100111/1705034322.html&prev=_t&rurl=translate.google.com&twu=1&usg=ALkJrhjKlqRHCwb1RzObt7OqELOwpvdPBQ
19. http://www.thetruthaboutcars.com/15m-or-more-cars-in-china-how-it-affects-peak-oil-and-global-wrming/
20. http://chinaonmeta.com/news?nid=3192
21. http://phx.corporate-ir.net/External.File?item=UGFyZW50SUQ9MjA3ODl8Q2hpbGRJRD0tMXxUeXBlPTM=&t=1
22. http://www.gmchina.com/english/corporate_info2/company_overview.jsp
23. http://oica.net/wp-content/uploads/fiat1.pdf
24. http://www.cnn.com/2006/AUTOS/01/23/american_cars/
25. http://www.businessweek.com/magazine/content/10_12/b4171032583967.htm
26. http://gm-volt.com/chevy-volt-faqs/
27. http://www.inc.com/news/articles/2009/06/tesla.html
28. http://www.teslamotors.com/media/press_room.php?id=1356
29. http://www.daimler.com/dccom/0-5-7153-1-1222301-1-0-0-0-0-0-9293-7145-0-0-0-0-0-0-0.html
30. http://www.thetruthaboutcars.com/abu-dhabi-drops-green-into-tesla/
31. http://www.worldsteel.org/?action=storypages&id=330
32. Ibid.
33. http://www.chinadaily.com.cn/cndy/2009-12/09/content_9143262.htm

Chapter 4

1. http://www-03.ibm.com/press/us/en/pressrelease/28842.wss
2. http://www.computerworld.com/s/article/9139380/Acer_passes_Dell_as_second_largest_PC_vendor

3. http://www.acer-group.com/public/The_Brands/index.htm
4. http://www.moeaidb.gov.tw/external/ctlr?PRO=filepath.DownloadFile&f=publication&t=f&id=372
5. http://news.cnet.com/8301-1001_3-10157403-92.html
6. http://www.chinadaily.com.cn/china/2009-03/11/content_7569950.htm
7. http://www.nokiausa.com/find-products/mini-laptops/nokia-booklet-3g
8. http://www.businessweek.com/bwdaily/dnflash/content/mar2009/db20090325_626883.htm?chan=rss_topStories_ssi_5
9. ftp://ftp.software.ibm.com/annualreport/2008/2008_ibm_annual.pdf
10. http://www.edn.com/blog/1750000175/post/200019020.html
11. http://www.ibm.com/news/in/en/2008/01/23/v141107r67598o89.html
12. http://blogs.wsj.com/digits/2010/01/07/ces-value-outweighs-price-amtran-says/
13. http://www.tradingmarkets.com/.site/news/Stock%20News/2700682/
14. http://newsroom.cisco.com/dlls/2009/corp_031909.html
15. http://online.wsj.com/article/SB10001424052748704402404574529580903832644.html
16. Source: International Business Strategies (IBS).
17. http://www.mercurynews.com/bay-area-news/ci_14664576?source=rss&nclick_check=1
18. http://speedtest.net/global.php
19. http://www.bloomberg.com/apps/news?pid=20601087&sid=an7JsKUJYAFg
20. Source: IBS.
21. http://investor.ti.com/releasedetail.cfm?ReleaseID=416547
22. Source: IBS.
23. http://www.boeing.com/history/chronology/chron16.html
24. http://www.gctl8.com/getStory.php?GUID=G5D66VXHNL1QFSK8HFLE

Chapter 5

1. http://www.aigcorporate.com/GIinAIG/owedtoUS_gov_new.html
2. http://www.washingtonpost.com/wp-dyn/content/article/2010/03/04/AR2010030405063.html
3. http://www.treas.gov/press/releases/hp1207.htm; http://www.federalreserve.gov/bankinforeg/tarpinfo.htm
4. http://www.recovery.gov/About/Pages/The_Act.aspx
5. http://www.startribune.com/local/south/41833082.html?elr=KArksi8D3PE7_8yc+D3aiUo8D3PE7_eyc+D3aiUeyc+D3aUU
6. http://europa.eu/rapid/pressReleasesAction.do?reference=MEMO/09/235&format=HTML&aged=0&language=EN&guiLanguage=en
7. http://www.samsung.com/global/business/semiconductor/newsView.do?news_id=827
8. http://news.xinhuanet.com/english/2009-08/31/content_11973065.htm

9. http://online.wsj.com/article/SB123932068946706913.html
10. http://machinedesign.com/article/engineering-in-germany-1107
11. Ken Auletta, *Googled: The End of the World as We Know It*, Penguin Press, New York, 2009.
12. http://www.forbes.com/lists/2006/12/XC25.html

Part III

1. http://www.economywatch.com/world_economy/china/population.html
2. https://www.cia.gov/library/publications/the-world-factbook/geos/us.html
3. http://www.uschina.org/statistics/economy.html
4. http://www.uschina.org/statistics/tradetable.html
5. http://www.uschina.org/statistics/tradetable.html

Chapter 6

1. http://www.economywatch.com/world_economy/china/population.html
2. http://www.economywatch.com/economic-statistics/country/China/year-1980/
3. http://www.uschina.org/statistics/economy.html
4. http://www.chinability.com/GDP.htm
5. http://www.bloomberg.com/apps/news?pid=20601087&sid=a2v.AWwaVpj8
6. http://news.xinhuanet.com/english2010/china/2010-02/22/c_13183728.htm
7. http://www.nytimes.com/2009/04/11/business/global/11chinatrade.html
8. http://www.nytimes.com/2009/12/10/business/economy/10consume.html?_r=1&ref=business
9. James Surowiecki, "The Frugal Republic" *New Yorker*, December 7, 2009, p. 35.
10. Ibid.
11. Ibid.
12. Ibid.
13. https://www.cia.gov/library/publications/the-world-factbook/geos/ch.html
14. https://www.cia.gov/library/publications/the-world-factbook/geos/us.html
15. Surowiecki, "The Frugal Republic."
16. http://www.pbc.gov.cn/english//detail.asp?col=6400&ID=1459
17. http://www.bloomberg.com/apps/news?pid=20601089&sid=azu2GgdtzJqQ
18. http://www.stats.gov.cn/ndsj/information/nj97/D011A.END
19. Source: U.S. Central Intelligence Agency (CIA), *The World Factbook 2008*.
20. http://news.bbc.co.uk/2/hi/asia-pacific/7802561.stm
21. http://www.autonews.com/article/20091014/RETAIL/310149955/1131
22. http://www.un.org/esa/population/publications/wup2001/WUP2001_CH2.pdf

23. http://www.economywatch.com/world_economy/china/population.html
24. http://www.npfpc.gov.cn/en/detail.aspx?articleid=090805150529500469
25. http://www.economywatch.com/world_economy/china/population.html
26. http://en.shac.gov.cn/nyxw/200409/t20040910_109318.htm

Chapter 7

1. http://www.nsf.gov/statistics/nsf08321/pdf/tab1.pdf
2. https://www.cia.gov/library/publications/the-world-factbook/geos/ch.html
3. http://chinadatacenter.org/chinageography/chaptersectionview.asp?cid=6&sid=3.9

Chapter 8

1. http://www.chinese-outpost.com/chinapedia/economy/foreign-aid-and-foreign-investment.asp
2. http://www.google.com/hostednews/ap/article/ALeqM5g1sok8y6wSItAhFYBJFCJZvHBRNAD9C9B6P02
3. http://population.mongabay.com/population/china
4. SMIC Investor Fact Sheet: www.smics.com.
5. http://www.britannica.com/EBchecked/topic/241131/Grand-Canal
6. http://www.cleanairnet.org/caiasia/1412/article-70348.html
7. http://online.wsj.com/article/SB124104805235170859.html
8. http://www.fhwa.dot.gov/interstate/faq.htm#question11
9. http://www.bloomberg.com/apps/news?pid=20601209&sid=aIyClpqVb4O4&refer=transportation
10. http://english.peopledaily.com.cn/90001/90778/90857/6551019.html
11. http://www.railway-technology.com/projects/beijing/ and http://www.chinadaily.com.cn/china/2010-03/15/content_9588140.htm

Chapter 9

1. http://www.history.navy.mil/faqs/faq86-1.htm
2. http://www.customs.gov.cn/publish/portal0/tab2453/module72494/info207788.htm translated with Google translate
3. http://www.huawei.com/corporate_information/annual_report/annual_report_2008/fve_year_summary.do
4. http://www.businessweek.com/print/globalbiz/content/jul2006/gb20060725_294763.htm
5. http://www.commodity-trading-today.com/crude-oil-consumption.html
6. http://www.china.org.cn/health/2009-07/29/content_18227606.htm
7. http://www.fas.org/sgp/crs/row/RL34106.pdf
8. http://www.huawei.com/corporate_information/annual_report/annual_report_2008/fve_year_summary.do

9. http://english.sinopec.com/investor_center/presentation/20090330/down load/pre090330en.ppt

10. http://www.uschina.org/statistics/economy.html

11. http://news.cnet.com/8301-1035_3-10307726-94.html

12. U.S. Department of Commerce, Bureau of Economic Analysis.

13. http://www.chinamobileltd.com/ir.php?menu=11

14. http://www.economist.com/specialreports/displaystory.cfm?story_id=1448 3896

15. http://www.cellular-news.com/story/30839.php

16. http://www.fiercewireless.com/story/zte-releasing-android-phone-2010/ 2009-11-18

17. http://www.pcmag.com/article2/0,2817,2356999,00.asp

18. Ibid.

19. http://androidcommunity.com/lenovo-ophone-android-smartphone-for-china-mobile-20081212/

20. http://www.lenovo.com/ww/lenovo/pdf/report/E_099220091125.pdf

21. http://www.economist.com/specialreports/displaystory.cfm?story_id=1448 3896

22. http://www.chinamobileltd.com/ir.php?menu=11

23. http://online.wsj.com/article/SB123932068946706913.html

24. Source: International Business Strategies (IBS).

25. Source: IBS.

26. Source: IBS.

27. Source: IBS.

28. International Organization of Motorvehicle Manufacturers (OICA, Paris), http://oica.net/wp-content/uploads/all-vehicles.pdf

29. Ibid.

30. http://www1.eere.energy.gov/vehiclesandfuels/facts/2009_fotw577.html; http://www-cta.ornl.gov/data/tedb28/Edition28_Chapter03.pdf

31. http://online.wsj.com/article/SB1000142405274870486930457459532123 1 566810.html

32. http://vwcorp.ogilvy.com.cn/cds/?menu_uid=553#Search1

33. http://www.chinadaily.com.cn/bizchina/2009-11/02/content_8900271.htm

34. http://www.reuters.com/article/privateEquityConsumerGoodsAndRetail/ idUSSHA5505320090921

35. http://www.reuters.com/article/idUSHKG13086720091201

36. http://www.reuters.com/article/rbssAutoTruckManufacturers/idUSSHA2 5423220090603

37. http://www.ilo.org/wow/Articles/lang—en/WCMS_115469/index.htm

38. http://online.wsj.com/article/SB1000142405274870380890457452542057 7 987440.html?mod=googlenews_wsj

39. http://www.businessweek.com/print/globalbiz/content/may2009/gb20090 518_095449.htm

40. http://english.people.com.cn/90001/90778/90861/6819601.html

Chapter 10

1. http://sports.espn.go.com/oly/summer08/medals
2. http://news.xinhuanet.com/english/2009-03/19/content_11032929.htm
3. http://www.worldsteel.org/?action=newsdetail&id=273
4. http://news.xinhuanet.com/english/2005-12/16/content_3927788.htm
5. http://www.marxists.org/reference/archive/mao/selected-works/volume-4/mswv4_43.htm
6. http://www.atimes.com/atimes/China_Business/KJ22Cb03.html
7. http://www.universityworldnews.com/article.php?story=20090409203634912
8. https://www.cia.gov/library/publications/the-world-factbook/geos/ch.html
9. http://data.un.org/Data.aspx?d=PopDiv&f=variableID%3A88
10. http://www.moe.gov.cn/edoas/en/level3.jsp?tablename=1256021701783630&infoid=1256174538360293
11. http://www.asq.org/about-asq/who-we-are/bio_deming.html
12. http://www.asq.org/about-asq/who-we-are/bio_juran.html

Part IV

1. http://edition.cnn.com/2008/WORLD/asiapcf/12/22/china.taiwan/index.html

Chapter 11

1. https://www.cia.gov/library/publications/the-world-factbook/geos/tw.html
2. The World Bank Group.
3. http://twgeog.geo.ntnu.edu.tw/english/population_geog/population_geog.htm
4. Source: International Business Strategies (IBS).
5. Ibid.
6. Ibid.
7. http://www.tsmc.com/uploadfile/ir/quarterly/2009/3s5bH/E/3Q09FS.pdf
8. http://www.tsmc.com/english/e_investor/e01_financials/e0101_fundamentals.htm
9. http://www.vis.com.tw/annualreport/2008/english/pdf/vis08ar_en.pdf
10. http://www.chinaconnections.com.au/May-/-June-2008/Crossing-the-Strait.html
11. http://auo.com/auoDEV/download.php?path=information&file=Form_20-F_2008.pdf
12. http://www.cmo.com.tw/opencms/cmo/Investor_relations/ir_news/index.html?news_no=13&year=null&_locale=en

13. Source: IBS.
14. Ibid.
15. Ibid.
16. Ibid.
17. http://www.mediatek.com/en/ir/
18. http://www.mediatek.com/upload/files/ac1487c6bac5a9cb7bd40ad5c13f84 fa.xls
19. http://www.masterlink.com.tw/DownloadFile.aspx?filename=2009110508 3794.pdf&tableName=ResearchRpt12&serialNo=427
20. Source: IBS.
21. http://www.appleinsider.com/articles/09/12/10/foxconn_reportedly_tapped _to_manufacture_next_gen_iphone.html

Chapter 12

1. http://www.businessweek.com/1996/44/b34991.htm
2. http://tonto.eia.doe.gov/energy_in_brief/world_oil_market.cfm
3. http://www.riotinto.com/shareholders/Chinalco.asp
4. http://www.asx.com.au/asxpdf/20090226/pdf/31g8vkjc8v84ms.pdf
5. http://www.riotinto.com/documents/Media/PR716g_Rio_Tinto_announces _pioneering_strategic_partnership_with_Chinalco.pdf
6. http://www.chinadaily.com.cn/bizchina/2009-03/02/content_7525448.htm
7. http://www.guardian.co.uk/business/2009/dec/06/goldman-bankers-bonus-recovery
8. http://www.oe.energy.gov/smartgrid.htm
9. http://www.bloomberg.com/apps/news?pid=20601068&sid=aE.x_r_l9NZE
10. http://www.nytimes.com/2009/01/23/business/worldbusiness/23yuan .html?_r=1&pagewanted=print
11. Ibid.
12. http://online.wsj.com/article/SB123932068946706913.html

INDEX

ABOUT THE AUTHOR

Handel Jones has more than 35 years of experience as a strategic business consultant for large multinational companies. He is the founder, chairman, and CEO of International Business Strategies, Inc. of Los Gatos, California, which for more than 21 years has provided highly detailed and rigorously researched information about competitive positioning and key market trends of the electronics, computer, and consumer products industries.

Handel Jones has developed a deep understanding of the global business environment through the providing of strategic support to corporate giants in multiple geographic regions over the past 30 years. Jones has developed a deep understanding of the factors that impact future competitive positioning of countries and corporations through his international experiences.

The corporate environment is highly results-oriented, which forces rigorous analysis in order to maintain credibility over an extended timeframe. These disciplines combined with a strict mathematics education at an early age have been the basis for the thorough analysis process in *ChinAmerica*.

As founder, chairman, and CEO of International Business Strategies, Inc., Jones has had a consistent record of providing highly detailed and methodical information to international clients within the electronics industry.

Clientele has included IBM, GE, Samsung, LG Electronics, Sony, Toshiba, Nokia, Philips, Motorola, Intel, Fujitsu,

Microsoft, TSMC, China Resources, and others. In addition, Jones has also provided consulting support to financial institutions, including Blackstone, Carlyle, Bank of America, Citi, JP Morgan Chase, and others. Support has also been provided to Ex-Im Bank of Washington, D.C. The analysis of the changing global business environment and the impact on the competitiveness of the United States and the growth of China stimulated the writing of *ChinAmerica*.